STAYING AT
THE TOP

The Life of a CEO

STAYING AT THE TOP

The Life of a CEO

Sonny Kleinfield

NAL BOOKS

NEW AMERICAN LIBRARY

NEW YORK AND SCARBOROUGH, ONTARIO

ACKNOWLEDGMENTS

I am indebted to Ed Klein, editor of *The New York Times Magazine*, whose idea this was, and to Ken Emerson and Margarett Loke, for their editorial assistance and encouragement.

For information address New American Library

Published simultaneously in Canada by The New American Library of Canada Limited

NAL BOOKS TRADEMARK REG. U.S. PAT. OFF. AND FOREIGN COUNTRIES
REGISTERED TRADEMARK—MARCA REGISTRADA
HECHO EN HARRISONBURG, VA., U.S.A.

SIGNET, SIGNET CLASSIC, MENTOR, ONYX, PLUME, MERIDIAN and NAL BOOKS are published *in the United States* by New American Library, 1633 Broadway, New York, New York 10019, *in Canada* by The New American Library of Canada Limited, 81 Mack Avenue, Scarborough, Ontario M1L 1M8

Library of Congress Cataloging-in-Publication Data

Kleinfield, Sonny.
  Staying at the top.

  1. Avon Products, inc. 2. Waldron, Hicks. 3. Directors of corporations—United States—Biography. 4. Executives—United States—Biography. I. Title.
HD9970.5.C674A95   1986   338.7'6685'0924 [B]   86-8657
ISBN 0-453-00521-7

Designed by Marilyn Ackerman

First Printing, September, 1986

1 2 3 4 5 6 7 8 9

PRINTED IN THE UNITED STATES OF AMERICA

CONTENTS

1 □ THE SUN KING

Standing around a broad oblong table in a partially darkened room are seven men. They seem slightly anxious, as though they are guests waiting for a dinner party to begin. The room could belong to a palace. It has burnished wood paneling, tactful carpeting, and beautifully upholstered chairs, enough to feed the dreams of any starry-eyed businessman. All of the congregants are costumed in the appropriate uniforms of business—white shirts, sober suits, decidedly unraffish ties.

Now a door opens and in walks a pensive-looking man. Everything goes very quiet. The man is running slightly behind schedule and he gives his Tiffany watch a sidewise look. Just in the way he moves and talks, he seems to embody assertion. He calls out greetings. Courteous phrases of welcome come back.

"Hello, Hicks."

"Hello, chief."

Looking at the oblong table, he sees that all the central seats have papers before them.

"I've got no place to sit," Hicks Waldron makes a show of protesting.

"Now you do," Peter Thauer, the assistant secretary, says, and he expeditiously shoves his papers aside to afford Waldron the center spot.

It is a drizzly, bone-chilling afternoon in late February 1985. This is the boardroom of Avon Products, Incorporated, the world's biggest beauty products company. Hicks Waldron, its chairman and chief executive officer, is the person who runs it. The meeting being held is the first plenary session of the group ultimately responsible for the annual stockholders meeting, that corporate May ritual at which the actual owners of the corporation, down to the ninety-two-year-old lady from Tulsa who holds three mighty shares, get their whacks at the boss.

Meetings abound in the corporate world. This is a meeting whose sole purpose is to plan for another meeting. On occasion, there are meetings to prepare for meetings to prepare for meetings.

Once Waldron arranges his frame in his chair, the group settles down to business. Waldron, though an old and experienced hand at running companies, is fairly new to Avon. He came a little over a year ago from R. J. Reynolds Industries, the tobacco conglomerate, having been wooed to try to rejuvenate an ailing empire. Avon grew to glory by following a formula that was simplicity itself. It would hire unemployed women, who were mostly sitting at home in bathrobes watching soap operas, to go out and ring doorbells and pitch beauty preparations to other jobless housewives. Each year, it would round up more "ding-dong-Avon-calling women" and therefore sell more cold cream and make more money. By the mid-1970's, however, strong breezes were blowing of the storm that had come to be known as the "women's movement." Women wanted good jobs, full-time jobs that included offices and benefits, and they demanded them and got them. So not only did the pool of women available for Avon to recruit from dry up, but the doorbells

began to ring in empty households. For the first
time in its history, Avon was having harrowing dif-
ficulty. Both its sales force and its sales were shrinking inexorably.

Waldron, though, has no time to be distracted by
all that right this minute, for his immediate attention is riveted on the upcoming meeting of shareholders, people whose investments had caved in
because of the beauty business's slide. Avon shares
had traded as high as $140 in the early 1970's, and,
on this February day, they were worth only about
$22. These shareowners were losers of a new porch
for their house or part of a future nest egg, and they
were not a happy bunch. Waldron has to fret about
appearing cool and confident to these people as he
reinvents Avon in an alien era.

Pressing questions—pressing at least to the assembled group—have to be addressed. The first is
what to do from an aesthetic point of view to tickle
the fancy of the attending shareholders. Peter
Thauer hands Waldron a sheaf of color photographs
showing the pylons in the lobby of the Plaza Hotel
adorned with huge pictures of Avon products.
These were mounted at the shareholders meeting
at the hotel last year. Discussion begins on what to
do this year.

Waldron looks disconcerted. "Wait a minute," he
says. "Where are these?"

Thauer says, "They've been destroyed. That's
the first thing I asked because these are pretty expensive."

Waldron says, "Well, they sure as hell are. Why
did we destroy them?"

Thauer squirms a little, mashes a handkerchief in
his hand. "They made the circuit of the subsidiaries," he says, "and then they got destroyed."

A public relations functionary says, "Well, it

seemed that there were some problems with the photos and making them adhere to the pylons, and so by the time they made the circuit they were in pretty bad shape. Also, the products have become dated."

Waldron asks if there is some sort of less expensive display that can be substituted, especially if whatever is used gets decimated each year. Why not, he suggests, put the actual products on display?

Thauer says, "I checked on that and the price was about the same."

Waldron says, "How many people really looked at this?"

Someone says: "There were quite a few wandering around."

Then Waldron says, "How many shareholders did we have—a hundred or so?"

Thauer says, "Maybe a hundred or two hundred."

Waldron says, "I do believe they'd rather have the dividend."

John Cox, the public relations chief, says, "I don't think there would be a great many complaints if there were not elaborate displays."

Waldron says, "Well, I understand we got several because we didn't serve coffee two years ago."

Then Waldron says, "How much does this cost?"

Thauer says, "About twenty-five thousand dollars."

Waldron looks heavenward and says, "Ugh!"

Waldron suggests, as an alternative, that the company pass out gifts to attending stockholders. It is agreed that something in the neighborhood of ten dollars per shareholder would suffice.

Thauer says, "Now, for the setup inside the meeting room, it's been suggested that just you and Tom [W. Thomas Knight, the legal counsel and secretary] would be up on the podium, rather than all the division managers, since they'd have little to do."

Waldron says, "I think it's awful myself."

Thauer nods. "It gets kind of lonely up there."

Cox says, "There might be questions that you'd want the division managers to be available to field."

Waldron examines his fingernails and says, "Maybe the four division managers below on one tier and then me and Tom on another."

He thinks that over for a moment, then quickly adds, "No, that's too much like a king and his court. How about three on one side and three on the other?"

Everyone accedes to the suggestion.

Thauer now shows Waldron a sample of the type of name tag used for the Avon executives last year —it is a plain, rectangular tag—and asks if that will be all right this year.

Waldron says, "Fine."

Thauer trots out a couple of old programs and asks if this year he wants a bifolded program or a single-sheet program.

Waldron glances at them, turns them over in his hands, and decrees, "Let's just have a card. High-quality and class."

Thauer says, "Do you want coffee?"

Waldron looks pained. "Oh, God, I want to get out of that decision."

Everybody rocks with laughter.

Waldron says, "Let's have Brim. I want everybody to fall asleep."

Thauer says, "Okay, no coffee."

Then Thauer asks, "The office tour? Do you want to do that again?"

Waldron rakes his fingers through his hair, then says, "Boy, I find it hard to believe we need that."

Thauer says, "Well, some people like to come over and look around."

Waldron shrugs and says, "Okay, we'll have the office tour."

Thauer then directs Waldron's attention to a tailor's dummy at the far end of the room and says, "These are the hostess jewelry and uniforms."

Waldron says, "I can't see anything but the jacket. I presume there's something underneath it?"

One of the functionaries gets up and collects the uniform and shows it to Waldron. It includes a lace blouse and a cream suit. The jewelry is a gold necklace. All Avon products.

Waldron glances flickeringly at the getup and says, "Very nice. Lovely."

With that, Waldron pushes his chair away from the table and gets up. He steps across the hall to his office, stopping to inquire of his secretary, "What's the next meeting?" In his highly scheduled, hurly-burly routine, he is never sure where he should be at what time for what purpose.

His secretary, Maureen Ivory, gives him a quick briefing.

"This for me?" he says, picking up a fat wad of money lying on her desk. He had asked her to fetch him some spending money from the bank.

"Yes, that's yours."

"I get paid by the day now," Waldron says. He gives a short, rumbling laugh.

□ □ □

IT'S A WORLD that seems like a paradise. There's the Croesian salary. The art-filled office. The sleek limousines. The jets. The power. The prestige. Musing about the glittery trappings, a former inhabitant once remarked, "They sort of handle you like a precious egg."

The world of the chief executive officer is a mysterious one, rarely penetrated by anyone but those who live in it. The chief executive fills a range of roles: coach, politician, diplomat, Sun King, and Roman god. Thousands of people, dozens of divisions, hundreds of products orbit around him and respond to his pronouncements, his whims, his vision.

In ascending to that position, one inherits a broad range of powers and responsibilities. A CEO is many things, most conspicuously the person who is ultimately responsible for the performance and behavior of his company. He sets its vision and direction and then, like a coach, must motivate his underlings to carry them out. He is the flag-bearer and the chief spokesman for the corporation. He must present and preserve its image to both the internal and external world, and so he spends a good amount of time journeying to subsidiaries and representing the company to multiple constituencies—from employees to Wall Street to charitable organizations to legislators to the visiting Brownie troops from Topeka. Frenetic schedules inevitably characterize the lives of CEOs.

Something like ten thousand CEOs are employed by the country's publicly owned companies and by its substantial-sized private enterprises. The odds against anybody who goes into business becoming a CEO are enormous, and the chances of becoming the boss at a billion-dollar company are very small. A study by the executive search firm of Korn/Ferry International gives a thumbnail sketch of who the people are who do make it: Average age fifty-one, white, male, Protestant, generally boasts an undergraduate degree from a state college, picked up an

M.B.A. or some other advanced degree from Harvard or Columbia, politically conservative and a registered Republican, married with three children, works fifty-six hours a week, takes only fourteen vacation days, is on the road ten weeks a year, is obsessed with putting profits on the bottom line. Certain lamentable omissions persist. At the five hundred biggest industrial companies, there is only one female CEO, Katherine Graham of the Washington Post Company. There are no blacks.

Until fairly recently, the most glaring trait of CEOs has been their relentless dullness. But an evolving breed of CEOs has sprouted up who have stepped out from behind the mahogany desk and become public figures. They eschew the old tired ways of managing and have brought new excitement to rusty companies. Rather than closet themselves in heavily barricaded palaces, these CEOs hop into the corporate jet and confront the troops themselves, slapping backs and inspiring through the force of their own charisma and speech-giving skills. They speak their minds, crack jokes, tell anecdotes, star in commercials for their products.

Business, indeed, has become a bigger and sexier story for the nation's media, and going into business has intrigued a rising number of people. Megabuck takeovers are reported almost daily on the front pages of newspapers, everybody seeming to be swallowing everybody else, and CEOs turn up on the evening news trying to justify them.

Iacocca: An Autobiography is one of the most successful books in American publishing history, and both Lee Iacocca and T. Boone Pickens have recently graced the cover of *Time*. The public now seems to view the members of this once routinely vilified breed as heroes in gray flannel. It can't hear enough about what makes them tick. Not since the days of the great industrialists and robber barons at the turn of the century have the reputations of so many chief executives taken on such Protean proportions.

Along with all the sparkle, the job comes with almost unending stress. As corporations have grown awesomely large, more far-flung, subject to more complex forces, students of management have wondered whether any mortal can effectively manage them. How does the CEO stay on top of how the ballpoint pen division is doing in Germany at the same time that he must follow mop sales in the Midwest and the chain-saw business in Latin America? Many venerable corporations have passed through stormy times recently, and some household names have teetered on the edge of and even fallen into bankruptcy. Long-term profit performance and efforts at innovation have been disappointing. The vicissitudes of the big companies have thus led many to question the prowess of those who run them.

Many CEOs, of course, fend all this off without any more ill effect than an occasional sleepless night. For others, though, the pressure can turn paradise into a bottomless hell. What is life like, then, for those who scale the corporate pyramid? How do they cope when the footing gets treacherous? Do they confuse themselves with gods? What dreams do they dream?

I wanted to spend a lengthy amount of time with a chief executive of a major corporation who would grant me entry into the corporate suite. Rare, however, is the CEO who would let a reporter very deeply into his domain; most of them take an intensely proprietary view of what they do, and they are typically cautious about baring their private lives. A willing party, though, was eventually found in Hicks Waldron of Avon Products. He seemed to typify the new strain of gutsy, media-conscious CEO. More than that, he seemed interesting because he was confronted with one of a CEO's greatest predicaments: reversing the fortunes of a company in the face of a monumental sociological movement.

During a ten-month period after Waldron's acceptance, I watched him conduct his meetings, formulate strategies, promote his company to the various constituencies, handle the constant demands on his time, keep up his personal life, and cope with both crises and appalling trivia. There were some ground rules. Certain meetings, such as one-on-one strategy sessions with one of the division heads, were made off-limits to me. In others, I agreed to refrain from divulging certain proprietary information. But for the most part I had free rein. No one at Avon had any chance to review anything that I wrote. It was a novel and unprecedented opportunity to obtain an unvarnished and rounded picture of a world that has remained enigmatic.

2 □ THE TREADMILL

EACH MORNING, Hicks Waldron snaps off the alarm clock at six o'clock, stretches, and swings his legs out of bed. Waldron, at sixty-two, is a large, well-set-up man with dark hair that he keeps well-flattened, and penetrating eyes. There is a whiff of the outdoors about him—the closely clipped fairways of a golf course, the freshly packed snow of a ski slope. There is also an air of flinty command that would probably be there even if he were a functionary rather than a CEO. Waldron laughs easily and naturally and has a penchant for brief, tension-shattering jokes. Sometimes he has an aura of saintliness and innocence. Sometimes he is cagey, often positively friendly. He can be impatient and demanding, also warm and sensitive. He has the sort of intoxicating personality and knack for persuasion that make people forget to think when they are advised to roll downhill in a barrel imbedded with spikes. More than a few people I spoke with volunteered that Waldron was the sort of person you would bust through walls for.

His apartment, which he bought in 1983 for $2.2 million, is a six-room angular edifice on the penthouse floor of Manhattan's Trump Plaza, the superluxury coop located on East Sixty-first Street, a block from Bloomingdale's. Waldron's next-door neighbor, and a good friend, is Chuck Barris, a

game-show producer who has had considerable
success with ideas like *The Gong Show* and *The
Newlywed Game*. They became friends because
their wives became friends when their respective
apartments were being built and they found themselves weeping a lot together. As Barris puts it,
"You watch a man tighten a lightswitch and watch
him crack your whole wall of glass because he tight-
ened it too tight, and then you have weird odors
come up from your ventilator, and it seems to bring
on tears." Barris is absolutely bowled over by Waldron. "He's sort of my hero," he told me. "He's three
hundred and sixty degrees different from me. He's
a conservative, WASP, chairman of the board or
whatever. But I find him to be one of the warmest
people. And I think he's a real character. He's able
to make a spoon stick on the end of his nose at a
family gathering and have a picture taken of it and
not be afraid to have it shown. I pattern things after
him. He came back from a sales conference once
and told me about a guy who really impressed him
who said that whenever something goes wrong to
remember, it's only an inconvenience. So I had a
needlepoint made up and framed for him that says,
'It's only an inconvenience.' And I had one made
up for me, and I use that phrase a lot." Dick Clark
and his wife live on Waldron's floor too, but they're
not around that much. The occupant of the building who seems to attract the most attention, when
she happens to be there, is the tennis star Martina
Navratilova.

Waldron's L-shaped living room is comfortably
furnished: overstuffed sofas and chairs, antiques, a
baby grand piano, a fireplace, a telescope. The
three bedrooms are downstairs. There are two bathrooms ranging off the master bedroom. Evelyn,
Waldron's second wife, is too sloppy for Waldron's

taste, so he refuses to use her bathroom or dressing area. When the apartment was built, therefore, the master bedroom was laid out with dual bathrooms.

The Waldrons share the apartment with a black German shepherd dog named Yogi, who has a penchant for naughtiness in the presence of company. When I dropped over for drinks one evening, Yogi saw fit to finish off the hors d'oeuvres while the rest of us were taking a tour of the place. Yogi's bed is arranged on the floor in the Waldrons' bedroom. To keep Yogi fit, they employ a "dog walker" service, one of those inimitable New York enterprises that makes a mint out of the mundane. Two partners operate it; each walks a dozen dogs at a time, taking them for about an eight-mile jaunt.

For Waldron, the hour or so after waking follows a set routine. He pads out into the hallway and enters the second guest bedroom. He unfolds a thin exercise mat, lays it out on the floor, plops down on it, and, his fingers interlaced behind his head, engages in twenty minutes of calisthenics. Then he mounts a stationary bicycle and pedals for six or seven minutes. Refreshed, he goes to the kitchen and makes himself the same parsimonious breakfast every day: cornflakes, orange juice, a piece of toast, and decaffeinated coffee. On many fronts, he is a man of intransigent habits. While he eats, he flicks on either Cable News Network or the ABC Morning News.

Done eating, Waldron deposits the dishes in the sink, and between seven-thirty and seven-forty he leaves the apartment and strolls over to the office.

Along Fifty-seventh Street, between Fifth and Sixth Avenues, there is a Rizzoli bookstore, the Stuart Gallery, Vitamin Quota, the Building for Brotherhood, Asuman Gowns, Tony Rossi Hair Cutting Salon, and Bolton's. Just past Rizzoli is a weird, sloping building. It is just about all glass, and it curves inward and upward, like a children's slide. The address is hard to miss. Standing right outside on the sidewalk is a tremendous red numeral nine. Avon's corporate world headquarters consists of twenty-six of the floors in this glass-sheathed office tower. Throughout the floors, objets d'art represent the more than thirty countries where Avon facilities exist. Pictures of Avon women through the hundred years of the company decorate the walls.

The elevator to thirty-six, the executive floor, opens onto a hallway. At the end is a reception desk, and beyond that is a seating area framed by wall-to-wall windows. The eye is drawn to the view, a seductive panorama of Central Park. The sky presses in on the windows. A lithe receptionist with a cloud of dark hair sits behind a marble desk. She is usually on the phone. When she isn't, her nose is often buried in a current best-selling paperback novel.

If you make a right at the receptionist's desk, stroll a hundred feet or so and then make a hard left, you come to the office of the chairman and chief executive.

People have a feeling of force when they enter Hicks Waldron's office. I have seen company minions who don't visit it often visibly goggle and show unmistakable signs of unease when they are in it. There are others, ambitious young lions, who stare at his chair with a glint in their eye that seems to say, "No question about it. That's going to be mine one day."

A chief executive is entitled at most corporations to an office that suits his own style and taste. Waldron's philosophy is that an office should be as aesthetically pleasing as one's home. "If you think of

the number of hours people are awake," he says,
"you spend well over fifty percent of those hours in
your office. So it should be as comfortable as your
home. Someone shouldn't feel as they leave their
home that they are taking a huge step down when
they go to work." When David Mitchell, Waldron's
predecessor left, Waldron had his office entirely re-
done. Unlike some CEOs, Waldron doesn't believe
in getting too extravagant with offices—putting in
oak paneling, perhaps a bar in the corner, a display
of valuable antiques—but he likes a high-quality
look. When he saw Mitchell's office, Waldron felt it
was awfully dark. And so he hired a decorator to
liven it up.

The room is spacious but not excessively large or
posh by CEO standards (I have seen CEO offices
the size of a supermarket). In the left-hand corner,
there's a private bathroom. A mahogany table
serves as a desk; it has a few narrow drawers and
relatively few papers stacked on it. Clutter is said
by decorators who specialize in office design to un-
dermine authority, and so the desks of many executives have no drawers and often virtually nothing
on them. On the credenza behind the table is the
phone, with a receiver of simulated gold. Inside
one of the credenza drawers is a picture of Waldron's first wife, taken four months before she died
of cancer. Every time he looks at it, he gets misty-
eyed. "I just like everything to be right," he told
me once when he had it out. "I don't like it when it
isn't." Perched on the far right-hand side of the credenza is a framed color photograph of Evelyn.

Against the side wall is an unassuming sofa and a
pair of brocade-covered easy chairs. A stack of Avon
catalogues is ranged on one side of the chrome-and-
glass coffee table. On the other side is a pile of
coffee-table books: *The Great Dessert Book, Inside*

the Personal Computer, Shooting for the Gold, Discovering Italian Wines. The floor is covered with ocean-blue carpeting that is kept immaculately vacuumed.

He sits on an amply padded brown chair slightly larger and higher off the ground than the visitor seating. I had been told by people who seemed to know what they were talking about that it is a common practice among chief executives to adjust their chairs so that they look down on visitors, the intention being to radiate authority. I was also informed that a visitor is not to sit closer than seven feet from him, the minimum to maintain formal social distance. (Fulfilling whims is important. Sanford Weill, the former chairman of Shearson/American Express, thought it would be nice to have a working fireplace in his office on the hundred-sixth floor of the World Trade Center. He got it.)

Waldron usually arrives at his office by eight. Jimmy Smoak, the shoeshine man, saunters by and buffs Waldron's shoes, while he scans *The New York Times* and *The Wall Street Journal.* At eight-thirty, it's generally time for the first of the daily succession of meetings.

Waldron, relaxing in his office, tells a little about what he does: "Some people think the CEO sits there and says, Yes. Yes. No. No. Yes. Yes. No. No. I would put decision making fairly low down on the list of things of how I spend my day. It's a teaching, coaching, leadership, directing job on the one hand, and on the other hand a selection, multiple-choice job. You are continually okaying someone else's decision, or else you're selecting from multiple possibilities almost as if you were taking an exam in school. If you think about it, this would be similar to a top military job—say on a ship. The captain doesn't plot the course of the ship. He carries out what someone else has plotted."

Now it is ten and he has a meeting to set the agenda for the next board of directors meeting. Seven people cluster around the boardroom table. Though he is ostensibly beholden to his board of directors, the CEO usually holds office long enough to have hand-picked many of the members of the board. So long as the numbers are good, his power will be safe.

The matter of granting more stock options to reward up-and-coming managers is briefly analyzed, and then Waldron decides to request from the board the approval of five million shares worth of additional options.

Waldron says that it will be announced at the meeting that one of the company managers will be promoted to vice-president of marketing research. "We want to convey to the troops that we are a consumer marketing company. We'll do it with this."

He is reminded that he is to wish happy birthday to Charlie Locke. Any director celebrating a birthday the month of a meeting is bid well by Waldron. Corporate ritual. Little ministrations done by big people have long been considered valuable management tools in motivating workers. Hence, every new employee is presented with a framed copy of the homey principles that Avon's founder laid down to guide the company (for example, "To serve families throughout the world with products of the highest quality backed by a guarantee of satisfaction"), autographed by Waldron. He also sends out five thousand Thanksgiving Day cards to Avon employees. But these little things don't always work so perfectly. One employee lambasted Waldron for sending him a card four weeks before he was laid off.

Waldron says, "We've got a wedding to take care of, too."

It is mentioned that David Mitchell, Waldron's predecessor as chief executive officer and still a board member, got married over the weekend. Waldron asks if a gift was sent. He is told that, yes, a lovely crystal vase from Tiffany was sent with a telegram from Waldron.

Peter Thauer continues reading the agenda. Everything is accorded specific amounts of time. He gets to "approve proxies for annual meetings of subsidiaries—five minutes."

"What the hell is this?" Waldron asks.

"All the subsidiaries have annual meetings and we need to approve their proxies," Thauer says. "Strictly routine."

"Okay," Waldron shrugs. "That will be the shortest five minutes in history."

A distraction now intrudes, in the form of a starring role in a film. Junior Achievement, an organization devoted to spreading the gospel of business and free enterprise to young people, is preparing a promotional film to sing its own praises. Waldron, a long-time supporter of the organization, has been asked to sit still for a short bit to be inserted somewhere in the pitch.

The film crew has occupied the small conference room that is just down the hall from Waldron's office. The Write People, a film firm, has been hired to make the movie, and a bearded man named Gordon Auchincloss is here from the organization to do the interrogation. IBM is picking up the tab for the film, so an IBM public relations man, Robert Slack, is on hand to function as director of the shoot.

Waldron saunters in, wearing a dark blue hair-line-pin-striped suit, a light blue shirt, and a maroon tie.

(Some comments on Waldron's attire: He is no slouch on dress. Very much in keeping with approved high-corporate-officer look. Dark suits: gray, navy blue, charcoal, the only variety an occasional pin-stripe. Shirts: white (probably 99 percent of the time) or some light shade of blue. The chief executive hates to shop. Twice a year, he goes to Allen Collins in West Hartford and buys three or four Southwick suits off the rack (size 44 regular), a sport jacket, "and maybe a pair of socks." As a rule, he pays between two hundred and three hundred dollars for a suit. Waldron had this to say about corporate dress: "I would like every man and woman to look like he or she manages the world's best beauty company. I had two women give a seminar to the corporate management committee on how to dress and pick colors and on shape categories. I haven't noticed anyone who looks any better, though. But I think people take their cue from the leader. If the leader dresses rather formally, then you won't see many blue blazers around. I dress fairly formally, so most people here dress fairly formally. I'm in shirt-sleeves during the day, so most people are in shirt-sleeves. I am also a stickler for informality. I don't want the place to be like a locker room of a high school, but I don't want it to be as stiff as a funeral parlor. There should be a decorum to project that you're a pretty serious business organization. That doesn't mean everyone rolling around in jackets and turtleneck sweaters and golf shirts. Having said that, I think the people at Avon are way up on the rating scale. Sometimes I think some of our women could be better advertisements of our cosmetics business. A lot of women just don't use the makeup. I think a lot of them think they're being very smart and trendy by coming to work with no makeup. We're not running a steel mill or a bank. We're running a beauty company. I think it's unacceptable not to be a living example of your company's products. In Louisville, when I was vice-president of GE's refrigeration division, to show you I'm a bit of a square, my secretary came to work in a pants suit. It was nice, attractive, and I sent her home to put a dress on. Boy, did I catch hell in the office. She didn't like it, but she went home and put a dress on.")

"We need to put a microphone on you," one of the technicians says.

"Wire me," Waldron says. "Hit me."

The technician proceeds to attach a microphone with masking tape underneath Waldron's tie.

"Can we check the sound?" somebody says.

"Sure," Waldron says. "I can talk about Junior Achievement for three hundred minutes straight or not at all, as the case may be."

"That's fine," a technician says.

"Jacket and tie all right?" Waldron asks.

Auchincloss says, "The tie could be a little higher."

"It was all right before they taped me up," Waldron says.

Then Waldron says, "A little trivia question. Do you know what is the largest blueberry-producing state in the country?"

Auchincloss says, "No, Mr. Waldron. What is the largest blueberry-producing state in the country?"

"Are you excited?" Waldron says. "New Jersey!"

The filming commences.

Auchincloss says, "Now can you give us a statement that Junior Achievement has kept up with the times or to that effect, and then say that Junior

Achievement has changed a lot since you were growing up in Amsterdam or whatever."

Waldron, staring into the camera, begins, "Well, of course, Junior Achievement has been around a long time. I can remember when Junior Achievement meant pounding nails in wood or making bird feeders in high school at night with some supervision. I guess I would characterize Junior Achievement today as being in the middle of a renaissance . . ."

Auchincloss interrupts. "Oh, I'd like to break it up a little. You had a very good opening statement with the renaissance. Then I'd like you to say what it was and then what it is today."

Take 2.

Waldron: "Junior Achievement is really going through a change, going through a renaissance. I can remember growing up in Amster . . ."

Auchincloss: "Just a minute. After you say the renaissance, could you then say what Junior Achievement is today?"

Take 3.

Waldron: "Junior Achievement is today . . ."

Auchincloss: "No, start with the renaissance."

Take 8.

Auchincloss: "That's great. That's just fine. I'm happy as the day is long."

The IBM man, however, says now that he thinks Waldron should say something about Junior Achievement and the free enterprise system.

Take 9.

Waldron: "For us in business this means a lot of people go into business who would not have gone into business . . . And they're better people."

Auchincloss: "Very good."

Slack: "I'm happy."

Auchincloss: "And that's a wrap."

A still-photographer importunes Waldron for some shots that Junior Achievement could use for publicity purposes. Waldron consents and is herded into the reception area. Once he gets out there, it's apparent that two chairs had been moved slightly into new positions. Waldron spies several not overly offensive scraps of litter on the carpet that had previously been concealed by one of the chairs. He seems flustered and alarmed, as if there were several dead rats supine on the floor.

Turning briskly to the receptionist, he says coolly, "Get someone up here with a vacuum cleaner. This shouldn't be."

The cheerfulness bleeds from the receptionist's face. She simply nods.

The photographer crouches down on one knee and begins busily shooting, tripping off click after click. Seemingly hundreds of pictures are snapped. Waldron is visibly getting testy. Finally, after perhaps the one-thousandth shot, he announces, "Done," and abruptly stands up and thanks the photographer.

After Waldron bustles back to his office, a small impromptu powwow is held by Avon functionaries to decide whether a vacuum does need to be rushed to the thirty-sixth floor to capture the offending lint. Debate. Decision. The chair will be shoved back to its original position, thus once again obscuring the litter.

3 □ THE RISE
AND FALL OF THE
AVON LADIES

THE KINGDOM that Hicks Waldron presides over ranks one hundred and twenty-seventh on the Fortune 500 list of the world's largest industrial companies, just behind Warner-Lambert and just ahead of the Whirlpool Corporation. In the beauty products industry, it ranks an indisputable number 1. Avon's sales in 1984 amounted to more than $3 billion. Its profits were $160 million, not the rosiest they have been; the record was nearly $244 million in 1979. The company employs more than thirty-eight thousand people. But that doesn't include the bountiful army of 1.3 million representatives, the fabled "ding-dong-Avon-calling" women (actually five thousand are Avon-calling men) who peddle Avon beauty products door to door. According to Avon's reckoning, one in six women has at some point sold its cosmetics. It boasts some 650 products, give or take a dozen: Slick Tint Lipstick, Ultra Touch Hot Oil Nail Treatment, AMM Perfecting Loose Face Powder, Nutura Creamy Wash-off Cleanser, Night Support Skin Revitalizing Formula, Vivage Perfume, Golden Dreams Porcelain Music Box, Embossed Hummingbird Notecards, Avon Soft Rose Floating Candles. They are sold in more than thirty countries.

Avon came about through the diligence of a former door-to-door book salesman of pluck and vision named David H. McConnell. In 1886, looking to get into a business revolving around a product that consumers quickly used and replaced, he mixed a batch of perfumes in a cramped pantry on Chambers Street in lower Manhattan. He liked what he smelled. The first product line, known as the Little Dot Perfume Set, consisted of three bottles of perfume and an atomizer. His five initial fragrances were Violet, White Rose, Heliotrope, Lily-of-the-Valley, and Hyacinth. To build up acceptance, he started out selling the product for half of what the ingredients cost him.

Drawing on his book days, McConnell elected to use "canvassing agents" to sell the perfume by ringing on doorbells. He called his company, oddly enough, the California Perfume Company (changed to Avon Products in 1939) because of the profusion of flowers that grew in California. The fragrances were soon joined by almond balm, shampoo, tooth tablets, and witch-hazel cream. (The first products to carry the Avon name came out in 1920 and were a toothbrush, a cleanser, and a vanity set.) To run the business while he busied himself in the pantry mixing exotic-smelling concoctions, McConnell hired a stern-looking woman named Mrs. P.F.E. Albee of Winchester, New Hampshire, the very first Avon lady. Within a dozen years, she had recruited and trained a field force of some five thousand high-button-shoed representatives.

Avon rode the crest of a century-long wave, happily selling its rouges and lipsticks to the housewives of America. For decades, it never wavered from its basic strategy, which was to stock the products that the door-to-door salespeople liked best, run a fortnightly campaign from a catalogue, then process the orders quickly and have the representatives deliver the goods to the customers while taking the next order. Growth came strictly from adding more and more representatives, whose numbers grew to 401,000 in the United States by 1979.

Then it hit some shoals. Gloria Steinam and Betty Friedan had begun to issue their calls for women to get out from behind the ironing board. "Women's lib" had entered the lexicon, and the housewifery of America had risen up against the male chauvinist pigs. In one of the most fundamental shifts in modern history, women began leaving the home and joining the work force in ever-increasing numbers, and they weren't interested in wandering through neighborhoods hawking beauty preparations, either. And so Avon found itself no longer able to meet its voracious need for women to ring doorbells. The world had passed the company by. Management, lacking savvy in modern marketing techniques, didn't know what to do and basically did nothing. It made forecasts and then had to eat them. Profits slid downhill. Waldron likes to say, "I compared the problem to the mechanic who opens up his toolbox and there's only one tool there—add more women."

When Waldron arrived on the scene in August 1983 by way of General Electric, Heublein, and finally R. J. Reynolds, he got going devising a curative plan. He quickly hired Robert Pratt, a pioneer of planning who had worked at GE and Heublein, and set into motion exercises in strategic planning that would forge totally new directions for Avon. Pratt likes to refer to planning as "organized common sense." "The heart of planning," he explains, "is what the hell is the situation, where do I want to get and how am I going to get there and how am I going to monitor the situation so I know I'm getting there."

Avon had by this point diversified and split up

into four divisions. The backbone of the company was the Avon beauty division. In 1982, for $712 million, the corporation bought Mallinckrodt Chemicals, a maker of specialty chemicals, drugs, and medical diagnostic equipment, which accounted for about 15 percent of corporate sales. One of its products is acetaminophen, the active ingredient in Tylenol and other nonaspirin pain relievers. Avon, though, was having trouble fitting the chemical company into the family. Foster Medical, a home-health-care company, was bought in 1984 for $220 million. It was fitting in quite nicely and represented the fastest-growing family member. The fourth division was Direct Response, consisting of Avon Fashions, women's apparel sold through the mail, James River Traders, which sells men's fashions, and Brights Creek, a children's clothing direct mail catalogue. In 1979, Avon bought the ritzy Fifth Avenue jewelry store Tiffany & Company for $104 million, and then sold it, at Waldron's insistence, in 1984 for $135 million when it couldn't keep its profits from declining.

The plans that Waldron asked for took a while to develop, and weren't perfected until the summer of 1984. Waldron had to review them and balance them against each other, for if every division got all the things it wanted, Avon would be broke. As Pratt would say, "Waldron would make trade-offs. If Avon beauty wants to go into ten new countries, okay, then Avon fashions won't be able to add thirty new James River Traders ties." In doing his heavy thinking about Avon, Waldron sliced the corporation into thirty-two separate chunks and put them under a microscope to find out which were the winners and which were the dogs. The conclusion was that most of the future growth lay in seven of the chunks: the domestic beauty business, Foster, Mallinckrodt's critical-care business (a small piece of big Mallinckrodt), Avon Fashions, Avon Japan, Avon Mexico, and Avon United Kingdom. The decision was made to funnel most of the corporate resources into those seven. All the others, unless they showed new promise, would be potential candidates for divestiture. Around the Avon watercoolers, the elite group came to be known as the "Magnificent Seven."

Waldron's overall goal for the corporation was to prop up the stock price. Specifically, he wanted the stock to more than double by 1988. That was a quite ambitious target, but one of Waldron's favorite sayings was, "Think the unthinkable."

Key to achieving the unthinkable was the revival of the domestic beauty business. The division, with Waldron's help, had recast itself with a bold new plan. The division had gotten into trouble, and it had done so because it had badly misjudged the ramifications of the working-woman movement. Jim Preston, the division's head, would admit, "There is no question this company was late in recognizing what impact the working-woman phenomenon would have on our ability to run this business as we had. For a time, we thought we could run counter to the trend. We thought we had the size and the franchise to beat the trend. But we were wrong."

The division, which had about 400,000 representatives, had been expecting to reach a level of 650,000 by 1986 or 1987. It was decided that that was a false hope. Instead, the decision was made to live with a force of about 400,000 and to focus instead on getting higher productivity from each salesperson, in part by training each in influence and motivational techniques. It was decided to rely less on the tastes of the representatives and instead to study the socioeconomic trends in the market-

place, such as the increase in working wives, the
shrinking size of households, soaring inner-city
crime rates, increased brand competition, and
changing distribution trends. The company would
learn to tailor products to specific markets, like
black women, and to specific regions. It had been
selling sunscreen, for example, only in the summer,
even though Floridians rub it on all year. Pretty
elementary stuff for a Procter & Gamble, say, but
Waldron was finding that Avon was in the Dark
Ages of marketing. Furthermore, it was decided
that to reach the forty to fifty million women not
called on by its smaller field force, it would expand
into new channels. It would sell at offices. It would
sell by direct mail. It would try electronic kiosks in
shopping centers.

Wars flared between the merchandising managers and the brand managers. If the brand managers set the price for a product at, say, $3.59, the
merchandising managers, who were in charge of
the catalogues of Avon offerings, would then knock
it down to a $2.99 special, because they liked pro-
motional specials that would excite the representatives. Waldron decided to invest the power for
product and pricing in the brand managers.

He went to work on the catalogue, which was an
unpredictable grab bag of beauty products, acces-
sories, novelty items, candy, personal-care items,
and cheap knickknacks. There were frequent special discounts. There was inconsistency. Items appeared and disappeared from the catalogue without
warning. There was a flow of some 250 new products a year, and so an equal number of old ones had
to be junked, often products that were maturing and
reaching their most profitable phase. The company
had neither the best image nor the lowest prices,
neither the best quality nor the best values. It was

looked on as a low-quality, bargain-basement line. Considering all the things it seemed to be doing wrong, it was amazing that Avon remained the champ of beauty products, with 12 percent of the America market.

Avon had never gotten to know very much about its customers and what they wanted. It just gave them what it thought they wanted. Not staying close to your customer is always a surefire way to bankruptcy court. So Waldron commissioned a mammoth and costly consumer research study designed to reveal for the first time accurate profiles of the Avon customer. The result was a three-foot-high stack of bound printouts.

Attention was given to improving the compensation for representatives, in order to deal with the fact that the turnover rate of representatives was a staggering 140 percent a year. Though the high-producing Avon lady can earn about eight dollars an hour, and full-timers can gross between thirty thousand and forty thousand dollars a year, there are plenty who just want to get out of the house and have tea with friends or earn some spending money before Christmas. The goal now was to build a more stable core staff.

While these plans were being mapped out, the beauty business sank further. So Waldron's hope was to halt the erosion in 1985 and stabilize the force at about 400,000, while at the same time improving productivity and testing the new channels for the future. As Waldron put it, "It was kind of like with a patient. You've got to keep that patient from getting worse and then you can give it the transfusion or the surgery or whatever the hell the remedy is." To keep the patient from worsening, some radical moves had to be made at the end of 1984.

One of the first things that had to be done was to downsize the management structure that had been put into place to manage the chimerical field force of 650,000. Waldron, in addition, wanted to grant greater authority to the field managers and not have New York call all the shots. It was decided to do it in one swoop. As Jim Preston put it, "We wanted to conduct the operation and start the healing process as soon as possible." So, in the final months of 1984, 400 district sales managers were fired. The title of group sales leader (a sort of glorified representative) was eliminated. The Kansas City distribution center was shut down, putting another 400 people out of work.

While this was happening, Avon had begun talking about how it was going to test new ways to sell its beauty preparations. It would experiment with direct mail and kiosks, and the word "retail" even crept into the conversation. So insecurity was rampant. "Are they getting out of the direct selling business?" was a question on a lot of minds.

The plan of the division was that all this dislocation would cause the number of representatives to dip another 12 percent or so in the first three or four months of 1985, then begin to build back to a level equal to 1984 by the end of the year. Then, next year, some of the new channels would come into being and business would start to grow. And so, in the early months of 1985, the field force did indeed shrink. Skepticism was muffled. After all, it was in the plan. And Preston said fine. And Waldron said fine. Because he believed that, if he stuck to the course that he had okayed, then the force would come back and by 1987 he would witness that final phase of "Hallelujah, brother, we've done it and it's up, up, and away."

4 □ DELEGATION, DELEGATION

ANOTHER WORKDAY. Maureen Ivory comes into Waldron's office and announces that his next appointment is waiting.

"Send them in," he says. Through the door come Donald Moss, vice-president of human resources and administration (he would later leave the company), Bruno Vassel III, director of training and management development, and Nancy Reardon, a manager in the corporate personnel department. Some time ago, they had been asked to come up with a management evaluation system, and they are here to present their ideas.

Avon, surprisingly, had had no performance review system for officers of the corporation, only for those in the beauty products group. The chess game of putting people on different squares to see who will be the next leaders is a rather important chore that is neglected by many chief executives. (Some, it is said, can't stomach the thought of their mortality and thus don't want to even think about succession planning.) Waldron wants executives to think constantly about succession. If something happens to someone, then the company can consult the forms.

The group gathers around Waldron's couch. He sits on the sofa, one foot propped up on the coffee table. No one else, of course, dares to put his or her

31

feet on the table. Bruno Vassel III starts off the meeting, pointing out that the review system that they have patched together followed study of the methods at some other "excellent companies, including GE, Exxon, IBM, and AMF." Then he says that what they plan to use is a "terraced approach."

"Terraced?" Waldron interrupts. "What the hell is that? A new buzzword?"

Vassel says, "We start lower in the organization and look at the people and the organization and then we move up to the next level and do it again and on up."

"We used to call that bottom-up," Waldron says. "Now it's terraced, huh?"

Vassel now gives the floor to Nancy Reardon, who is a new recruit from General Electric. When she walked in, Waldron commented that she seemed to "have that GE glow." As is true in most meetings, an agenda and some charts have been prepared and mimeographed and are now passed out to the participants. Entire forests must be leveled for the paper that gets consumed by big corporations for duplicate reports.

Nancy Reardon plunges into a long, zestful recitation, as the others follow the printed copy, which is replete with corporate jargon and in places incredibly simpleminded and boring.

Reardon, frequently smiling, zips along. Waldron listens with an unfocussed stare, pointing with his right forefinger to things that confuse him or dissatisfy him. Frequently, he interrupts Reardon to pose questions. He is constantly ahead of her. She keeps answering his queries with, "We'll get to that." At one point, he tells her prefatory to a question, "Now I know you're going to get to this, so don't tell me, you'll get to this."

At the same time, he also spurs her on with one-word platitudes.

"Good."

"Excellent."

The blueprint, as it is mapped out by her, is a rather complicated one, with numbers and colors to signify how someone is doing and whether a position is likely to be open and when. Among other things, the plan encompasses room to single out high-potential employees. She notes that "although no target percentage is mandated, many companies recommend that no more than twenty percent of employees should be identified as high-potential."

Waldron, referring to the part of the plan dealing with high-potential employees, says, "Can we change the wording here to 'level' rather than 'layer.' Maybe it's me. Everytime I hear the word 'layer,' I think of the people at the annual meeting who say you have too many layers of expenses."

Reardon now shows Waldron a proposed memorandum on the new evaluation system, to go out to managers under Waldron's name. He skims it quickly.

Then he says, "One suggestion I would make is to change the tone more to evolution from revolution, for two reasons. Because that's what it is, and we've already had enough revolution around here to last for decades."

Everyone, Reardon in particular, jots down dutiful notes on what Waldron has said.

Some discussion goes on now about affirmative action. Waldron says, "This high-potential category doesn't quite do it. This needs more urgency or currency. There should be someone challenging me on the board. 'When are you going to get a black on your corporate management committee?' Not, 'How many people are high-potential in this category?' "

Vassel says, "So you want to know when, not just figures?"

"When and why not sooner," Waldron says, "because the answer is always going to be too late. And who."

Lots of note scribbling.

Then Waldron says, "I want to have some sort of continuity sense. Not the sense that every year there's some goddamn new thing dumped in my lap. So let's think of the word 'continuity.' If you think you have it here, fine."

Then Waldron brings up the subject of succession planning. Is there anything in the evaluation system about that?

Reardon says, "Yes. Best person for the job."

Waldron says, "And is that the best person no matter where he's at?"

"Yes," Reardon says. "Wherever. Inside or outside the company."

Waldron says, "Last year, we didn't do too well. We had like three people recommended from outside the company."

Reardon says, "I know. I was talking to one person and they said, 'Well, if you're going to recommend somebody for another job, do you need their manager's permission?' No-o-o-o."

Waldron says, "Christ, you'd ruin all the fun."

Then, summing up, Waldron says, "I'm very impressed. I think this is terrific. Anything else?"

"That's it," Vassel says.

Reardon says, "That's it."

□ □ □

AFTER THE THREE LEAVE, Waldron sits down behind his desk and says to me, "I have to be so many places that, really, I come in here in the morning with ten phone calls I should make before I start the day. I often leave here without hardly saying hello to my secretary.

"The CEO job has become much more complex," he goes on. "It's almost totally due to outside constituencies. The only internal one that's changed is the working-woman phenomenon. The fishbowl that the CEO is in at all times is just incredible. It adds costs to doing business. There are time issues. It used to be that you worried about prices, costs, customers, and shareholders. Just those four areas. Today we're worried about what's going on in Washington, to say nothing of state governments. Because so much of the gross national product is public money—like Medicaid and Medicare—that affects us. There's OSHA, ESO, SEC, EPA, FDA— all the other alphabet soups. Then of course you have the nonstructural influences—the various pressure groups working outside the company. Twenty years ago, nobody ever heard of a takeover. Nobody ever taught that in business school. Now there's this takeover mania. You have far more complex financing instruments today. Before, you either sold stock or borrowed from the bank. Then you have the area of technology that has added a level of complexity and a level of sophistication to the business. There's the surge and importance of pension money as a major economic force in this country. The future pensioners own American industry. I heard an interesting idea recently—that people who will be getting the pension money should vote the proxies at shareholder meetings. Also, pressure groups for minorities and women and gays and animal rights and the handicapped.

You just can't hardly move without finding someone out there with a picket sign."

Waldron's view of the purpose of business is: "To
provide the working mechanism for the country.
What is the purpose of the heart—to pump blood to
make the body work. I don't know if people will be
happy comparing the corporation to the heart of the
country. It's maybe the lungs or the pancreas or
something else. But it's something that's important
to what makes this country work."

Though some CEOs believe that they have only
one central master to serve—namely, shareholders
—Waldron's conviction is that there are multiple
"stakeholders." "I think to say a corporation exists
to serve shareholders is a gross oversimplification
and wrong," he says. "The shareholder plays an
important role in the business scene, but not a
preemptive role. Example: I buy a hundred dollars
worth of a mutual fund and that mutual fund invests
a hundred million or three hundred million in
stocks. Say a hundred dollars ends up in a share in
company A. The question of how much company
A's dedication should be to that mutual fund is the
big question. I think we are coming to the end of
the era where the shareholder is the only constituency. I'll probably be struck dead for heresy before
you finish writing that. But, as the CEO of this company, I have almost as much responsibility to the
one-and-a-half million women selling Avon products around the world as to the shareholders. The
reason is, any time of the day or night that one of
my shareholders is unhappy with his investment,
he can divest that stock in five minutes with a telephone call and he can buy part of somebody else's
company. That's called freedom. And when anyone
buys or sells a stock, he or she makes or loses
money. And it's generally not bread-buying money.

But when I'm out messing with these one-and-a-half million women, they can't do that. They can't sell their job or easily get another one. That money they make is not pin money. It's often all the money they have. Another important constituency is the employees of the company. The forty thousand employees. They have cast their lot with this corporation. And I can go on with similar metaphors about customers and suppliers and the communities in which we work, some of which have given us tax breaks so we can be there, some of which have put in streets to allow us to get to our parking lot. It's a narrow view when one thinks that the owner of a share of Avon stock has any more influence over what a corporation does than these other stakeholders."

In a company that employs thirty-eight thousand people in thirty countries, Waldron's power is considerable. He can, without asking anyone else, wipe an Avon product off the face of the earth. If one morning in the shower he becomes unshakably convinced that a mauve nail polish for German shepherds is a surefire winner, he can have Avon put it on the market. He can fire anyone he wants to. He could, if he so desired, eliminate an entire division, close down a plant.

The official Avon Delegation of Authorities statement spells out certain of the key items that the board must approve and those which Waldron must approve. (He himself, as I found out once when I asked him, doesn't remember the particulars.) The board's responsibilities include, among other things, any guarantee of Avon debt, any incurrence of Avon debt, any pledge of Avon assets over $5 million, any sale or purchase of Avon stock, the salary for all corporate officers, approval of the annual budget of charitable contributions. Waldron's list of particulars includes mergers, acquisitions, and divestitures up to a value of $5 million; capital expenditures of up to $5 million; the initial lease of a fleet of cars for use by Avon managers; any change in an employee benefit plan (other than the U.S. employee retirement plan), with an incremental annual cost to Avon of up to $1 million; supplemental payments to retirees, with a total annual cost of $500,000; investments in a new subsidiary up to $250,000; and establishment of a base salary level, increases, and new employee salary to a total compensation level of up to $150,000 (with the exception of corporate officers).

W. Thomas Knight explained to me, "A little like the Constitution, everything that hasn't been reserved for the shareholders to do and for the board to do is allocated to Mr. Waldron. And in a small company—the local hardware store—that's where it stops. But in a complex, multinational corporation, you have to delegate authority. So Mr. Waldron can, and does, divest the responsibility for things. But he can't delegate the accountability."

The more I saw of Waldron, the more I wondered how he kept on top of everything. Corporations today are almost inconceivably big. How is it possible to keep an eye on everything? It is a question that kept coming into mind at many meetings I attended. Avon is broken down into thirty-two different businesses, each of them a company in itself. No one person could possibly be expert in all of them. Yet "no surprises" is a favorite phrase around the chief executive office.

This is how Waldron explained what he expected of subordinates: "Let me see your plan and let me get into the hearts and the minds of your people and if we have a handshake on your business plan and your people plan, then go away and deliver the profits you promised. Let me know if you need my help and please send me your measurements every week."

I asked Waldron how much he needed to be aware of?

"The company probably has thirty-five lawsuits against it and I know of one—the radiation situation in St. Louis with Mallinckrodt. [This was a suit filed by a neighboring property owner seeking damages allegedly stemming from emissions from Mallinckrodt's radiopharmaceutical facility in Maryland Heights, Missouri. The suit was dismissed in St. Louis County Circuit Court and an appeal was pending. There is a steady flow of product claims. People periodically contend that they're going bald from an Avon shampoo. Or their vision is blurring from an Avon eyeshadow. Waldron wouldn't be told of these.] If somebody is going to lay off five people in Atlanta, I wouldn't know about it. But if fifty people are being laid off, I'd probably be informed. If it were a couple of hundred, I'd probably be asked for my approval. Jules Zimmerman [the chief financial officer] wouldn't set up a revolving credit arrangement without clearing it with me. John Cox wouldn't issue a press release without clearing it with me. New products? I would have the right of veto. There is a group of people who I keep track of. Those people don't get touched, moved, or their pay increased or decreased without my awareness or approval." This body consists of 115 people: all 20 corporate officers; any division executive who makes at least $75,000 (30 people); and anyone else whose salary is at least $125,000 (65 people).

In a speech he gave once, Waldron said that his management philosophy can be broken down into seven elements. The central one is planning.

"Freakish about planning," is a phrase often applied by underlings to Waldron. Another favorite remark of Waldron's meant to underscore the importance of planning—I had it repeated to me by several top executives in the company—is, "You want to avoid being at the airport when the ship arrives." His second ingredient is, "I will be involved in every major decision involving our top-level people, and I'll be continuously involved in the process of recruiting, training and developing, motivating and rewarding all of our people throughout the entire organization." The third is decision making: "The guidelines that I like to follow include identification of all pertinent information, and then a fast decision. And I would emphasize the word 'pertinent,' and not the word 'all.' If you waited until you had every scrap of information, the world would pass you by while you were sorting out all the nitty-gritty . . . Another point about decision making. I've never seen a good decision made by a committee . . . Decisions are made by individuals." Fourth is communications: "It's been said that a company's growth rate can be tracked directly to its ability to communicate . . . both internally and externally. And this is an area that I really work at." Fifth, standards: "One personal hangup I've always had, even back at Green Mountain College, is that I can't think of a single reason why anybody should ever set an objective of being anything but first." Sixth, measurements: "Over the years I've been called, among other things, measurement-happy. But in this competitive world, I think it's terribly important to know, as precisely as we can, just where we stand vis-à-vis our competition, and where we stand vis-à-vis the standards of performance that we set for ourselves." The final element is relationships: "I'm a relatively informal character. I don't stand on ceremony . . . All the cards are face up on the table at all times. And I have asked for that same treatment in reverse. No cleverness, no politics, and even more importantly, no yes-men or yes-women."

☐ ☐ ☐

I LEAVE WALDRON FOR A WHILE, so he can tend to some private sessions. When I check back with him later on, he is at his desk, jacketless, examining the "Thursday report." This is a famous institution inside Avon. It reveals the latest week's representative count for the beauty business, as well as the order count and the number of representatives appointed and those who left, and so serves as the main barometric measuring device Waldron gets of how beauty is doing. The new report is full of unlovely numbers. Domestic beauty is slipping off plan, and at a rather dismaying rate. Nobody seems to know why. Here it is mid-March, and the tally is off 14 percent and showing no signs of hitting bottom. Waldron tends to see problems in terms of the bottom line, and this unexpected malaise threatens the entire corporation's profits. A problem in a core business of a big corporation, if not corrected, can spread like a prairie fire.

Jim Preston, the head of the beauty division, a pleasant man with a pixyish countenance, has in particular been living with the gun to his head. Preston is a carryover from the old regime, and even though some of the directors themselves have worried that Preston may be overzealous about how quickly the beauty business can be shaken out of its torpor, Waldron has placed total faith in him. The pressure collects in his stomach.

"I feel the pressure," Preston told me one day. "I feel the pressure every day."

One thing that has been going on is Waldron has insisted on having a meeting, usually of about an hour's duration, every week with Preston. What's happening? What are you doing? Part of it is a coaching exercise, keeping Preston's spirits up when they sag. At the same time, when these weekly powwows take place, there is always a cautionary and sobering fillip. "He was under pressure from me from day one," Waldron told me. "He knew that if this didn't turn around his career was in jeopardy. He wouldn't be here. We would have that discussion. And it was also pretty implicit that if that happened I wouldn't be very damn far behind him."

For the time being, Waldron decides that any shortcomings in domestic beauty can be made up for by trimming expenses elsewhere in the corporation. No reason to panic. He will stay the course. But he knows that strategic plans have an element of wizardry. There is as much art as science to them. So he decides to fix an October deadline. If no sure progress is seen by October, then alternative plans will have to be put into motion. Waldron seems confident that none of that will ever happen. Any doubts he might have remain solely his own.

5 □ STRIKING POSTURES

"**W**HY DON'T you read the speech as you would at the meeting, so we can time it?"

"Gosh, I haven't even skimmed it yet," Waldron says.

"That's okay," somebody says.

"All right. Here goes."

The purpose of this meeting, held in a small conference room near Waldron's office, is to run down the final details for a large employee gathering to be held in mid-March, four days from now, in the Hilton Hotel. The convocation, the second of its kind, is something Waldron thought up as an annual ritual. It is perhaps sufficient to characterize it as a corporate pep rally. Waldron will deliver a speech (sermon?) reviewing Avon's problems and how management and the hard toil of employees will conquer them. Avon, of course, is scattered all over the country and the world, and so, in this age of high technology and deep corporate pockets, the company has seen fit to rent satellite time so that it can beam the meeting to nine locations throughout the Avon empire.

Waldron has expectations of a grand sort—that the meeting will give the employees new energy and a morale lift. A cheerless pall has been hanging over Avon. Faces seem pinched. Bad temper is often the prevailing mood. A few months ago, Waldron had sent a memo to all officers and managers offering an anatomy of a turnaround, broken down into four stages. Phase one is characterized by "unproductive anger and finger pointing, in a useless attempt to fix blame for being in the position of needing to turn around." The end of the phase is marked by the creation of a plan. Then follows a second painful phase of slashing expenses and firing unneeded workers. The third phase is one of "doubt, disappointments, and uncertainty," in which everyone wonders if the new strategies are right, and when "even those of you with the stoutest of hearts will be tempted to deviate from the plan." Then the final happy phase comes when "sales turn up and profits increase at an even faster rate . . . and you'll know a satisfaction that's unmatched in business." There is little question that Avon is very much mired in phase three. Doubts are everywhere. The stoutest of hearts are indeed being tested.

Attending this preparatory meeting are Len Edwards, the director of the Avon Video Communications Center, which handles training films and sales meeting videos for the company; Karen Palancia, a producer in the center; Trish Hogan, director of employee communications; and two people from Bob Ahrens Productions, an outside firm hired to do the videotaping, Bob Ahrens himself and Michael Bernhardt.

Waldron, stumbling occasionally, reads the speech. He pauses at times to correct things. He changes Avon International, for instance, to Avon Division International. He changes the wording "conducted the biggest marketing survey ever" to add "as far as I know." He says, "I think the lawyers would want that in there."

Waldron finishes reading his remarks and someone says, "Twenty-eight minutes."

Palancia says, "Twenty-nine."

"Is that where we're supposed to be?" Waldron says.

"We were supposed to be at thirty minutes, so that's great," Len Edwards says.

Then Waldron reads through a question-and-answer section so that can be timed.

As he reads, he edits: "That has to come out of there." "That baby has to be reworked." "That needs some retouching."

"Eleven minutes," someone says.

Then he reads the closing remarks.

"Three minutes."

Edwards says, "Let me give you some time constraints that are absolute drop-dead, if I may use that word. After one hour and twenty-nine minutes we go off the satellite. The bird goes away."

The group talks for a while about time. Should Waldron have a three-minute clock to tell him when to be done with questions from the floor? No. Should some questions be trimmed for safety's sake? Yes. What about the question concerning the dividend? Waldron says, "I'd say let's excise that mother right now."

Someone suggests cutting the question about salary delays that have plagued the Mallinckrodt division.

Waldron says, "I like my answer. That's a great idea! Why don't we do it for the whole company?"

The question gets condensed.

Some discussion ensues about how to handle last-minute questions from the live audience. Should they be put on the TelePrompTer? Should someone hold up cue cards? Should someone walk

across the stage and hand them to Waldron? Waldron says that one of the public relations functionaries should be given a microphone and read the
questions.

Then the topic shifts to questions arriving by
phone from other locations. Should they be
screened?

Waldron says, "I like the idea of just taking the
calls. If someone asks a nasty question, I'll give him
a nasty answer. You know, at the annual meeting,
the chairman is more beloved the more he's heck-
led. Or not beloved—less hated."

Waldron asks, "What do I do if something goes
wrong that nobody sitting here can anticipate?"

Palancia says, "We'll put them on the Tele-
PrompTer. So what you need to do is periodically
check the TelePrompTer for messages."

Waldron says, "Like my wife called. Bring home
a quart of milk."

"What should I wear?" Waldron asks.

Edwards says, "Blue shirt. A nonbusy tie. A suit
of a color like you have on [dark gray] is fine."

Palancia says, "The dressing room is backstage.
We'll make you up at noon so you'll be ready at
twelve-thirty."

☐   ☐   ☐

GOOD FOOT-TAPPING MUSIC. But, then again, not too
loud to still conversation. The jazz combo plays en-
ergetically, merrily, here in the Terrace Room of
the Plaza Hotel. Meanwhile, the tuxedos and glittery gowns worm their way in for the annual dinner
of the National Urban League, sponsored by Chris-
Craft Industries, Revlon, Joseph E. Seagram &
Sons, and Avon Products.

Hicks Waldron, in a perfectly fitted tuxedo, slith-

ers through the crowd in the company of his wife,
Evelyn, dressed to the teeth in a stylish short black
dinner dress. Mrs. Waldron is a light-haired woman
of pleasant good looks. The Waldrons go to get a
drink. They seem to be relaxed and imbibing the
garden-party atmosphere.

Chief executives must strike postures a lot. Now
he has on his public plumage, as he does roughly
twenty times a year (Joint Center for Political Studies Benefit Dinner, Stonehill College Benefit,
YMCA City of New York Salute Luncheon, Salvation Army Benefit Dinner, being among the events
he went to last year out of 154 benefits and events
that Avon supported out of 573 requests). This is a
different world for him. Faces that he has seen
once, maybe twice, the names teasing the tip of his
tongue, or nowhere near it. Many people who
themselves can do him no good—either personally
or professionally—but it is his presence here that
matters. Charitable affairs are important to chief executives as concrete signs that they believe in
causes; all their presence really signifies, of course,
is that they have had their companies put up the
several thousand dollars to buy a table for ten at the
event, but money is enough for the charities, naturally. Waldron, when asked, makes much of his sincere commitment to minority rights. There is not
necessarily any reason to question that. But I have
to wonder whether Hicks Waldron would rather be
bowling or having a pizza at home than be here.

Waldron is a grinner—his grin is boyish, engag-
ing—and the grin is out now, doing its work, capti-
vating, drawing others under its spell. Part of being
a CEO, however, means listening to tedious jokes
and dull speeches and tasting all kinds of gruesome
food. He establishes himself in one corner of the
room, sitting down at a table there, and stays there.

He spies me and beckons me over, confessing a bit of a problem. "All these people who I've been introduced to once and I can almost remember their first name, but that's about it," he says.

I told him it was worse for me: "I didn't recognize anyone."

"I think I'd rather be in your shoes," he says.

Waldron is greeted with deference by twenty or thirty people. He returns the greetings with a jovial grace. The other Avon guests straggle in. They pull up chairs and gather around the same table. Waldron doesn't manage to stay put more than a few minutes at a time, since somebody new keeps spotting him and coming by to say hello. With some of them, he is rather friendly. Others seem to bounce off him.

In the Grand Ballroom, the Avon tablemates loiter around Table 37, to which they have been assigned, awaiting word from the man. Waldron looks over the assemblage and says, "We'll do it boy, girl, boy, girl," and then he points to people and seats. All obediently follow his instructions.

I settle next to Mrs. Waldron, who informs me that she and her husband too often wind up at some incredibly boring dinners—endless dreary speeches, ghastly entertainment, insipid guests—but that this dinner is one of the better ones.

Why?

"No speeches," she says.

(Waldron has told me, "I hate these dinners. I try to avoid them like the plague. I want some day to have a nondinner. I'll send out an invitation and say this is an invitation to a nondinner at the nondinner hotel. Normally, a ticket would cost seventy-five dollars each, seventeen hundred and fifty dollars a table. Please don't attend this dinner. Instead, send me a check for eighty-five bucks, all of which will go to the Salvation Army or whatever and you don't have to get all gussied up and can stay home with your wife and keep the American way of life alive. I'm very tempted to do this some day.")

A loud band plays, for the most part, contemporary rock music, and there is a good amount of sedately athletic dancing. Waldron stays put, since he is nursing a leg he damaged in a recent spill. At one point, he drops into the seat next to his wife and says, "I'd be out there spinning if my leg weren't still bothering me."

"I know," she says, and rubs his leg soothingly.

Dinner is served, consisting of mousse of turbot, petite marmite Henri IV, cheese straws, roast prime ribs of beef au jus, whole tomato cored and filled with broccoli and cauliflower fleurets, Red Bliss potatoes, mixed green salad, soufflé glacé au Grand Marnier with fresh strawberries.

The band never seems to give up, and neither do the dancers. Everybody on the floor appears to be doing a synchronized rock dance.

Past eleven, and now there is a drawing for some rather glitzy prizes—a diamond ring, a mink jacket, diamond earrings, some luggage. The ring goes to an elderly, quite excited lady who half runs from her table to fetch it. Then the jacket goes to her husband, touching off a good deal of murmuring and tittering at the tables. What are the odds of that? Is this really on the up-and-up?

"Good Lord, can you believe that?" Waldron says.

No one wins anything at the Avon table, and now, after midnight and with a seven-thirty meeting awaiting him the next morning, Waldron and his wife prepare to leave.

"Well, this thing is rigged," he says facetiously. "I'm not coming to this party again."

Then he and Evelyn retrieve their coats and dissolve into the night.

□   □   □

GLENN CLARKE, A STOLID, matter-of-fact man who seems to find it difficult to keep a worried look off his face for more than a few seconds at a time, is the president of the Avon Products Foundation, in which capacity he is charged with sifting through the morass of charitable dinner invitations sent to Waldron and recommending which ones to attend and which to politely decline. One morning, he talks about the dinner circuit.

"Dinners fall into three categories," he says. "The easiest ones are the nos. Then there are the ones we need to go to because we're committed to the cause—health, women, minorities. Then there are the ones that they want him to take a leadership role in. We turn down three hundred to four hundred dinners a year. Hicks could be out five times a night with no problem at all. He never has to buy a dinner if he doesn't want to.

"Hicks wants to be sure that we get the bang for the buck here. One of his concerns is that the dinners are profitable for the organization. A lot of dinners don't make money. Some of them decide to spend a lot of money on entertainment. If they have Frank Sinatra and so and so, that's going to bring the cost way up. New York is very jaded to dinners, and so big wheels to sing some songs may not mean anything at all. Hicks thinks that the strength of the organization matters the most. When he chairs a dinner—he's invited to chair ten to twenty dinners a year and be vice-chairman of maybe a hundred and fifty—he's looking for dinners that will bring in people from his name and the company name. You can't chair too many. If you chair too many dinners, then when people see the invitation with your name on it, it's an automatic no.

"What Hicks gets out of the dinners is corporate identification with a cause. He gets a chance to talk to people he knows. It's an important networking opportunity.

"The dinner circuit is a relentless circuit. New York City must be the dinner capital of the world. It's a means for groups to raise revenues. It's not necessarily a cost-effective way to do it. But we are necessarily resigned to it. I call tickets grants, because they've gotten out of the price of dinners. A hundred and fifty dollars is the cheapest. There was one dinner out on the West Coast where you got to go to the inner sanctum and get close to someone big. It was about a thousand dollars a person. We turned that right down.

"Some dinners are fun. The Urban League is good. The Salvation Army is a good one. A prerequisite for us to go is no speeches. It helps if there are no awards, either. Everyone's got walls full of awards. Believe me, we don't need any awards. But most dinners are hardly memorable. I've gone to a hell of a lot of dinners. You can put a gun to my head and I can't tell you one line from one speech I've heard over the years."

□   □   □

"WELL, WHAT DO I have to do to improve?" Waldron asks.

"Look straight ahead when you talk," Cox says. "You were looking around too much. It's distracting."

One hour before the big employee meeting at the Hilton Hotel is supposed to start, Waldron is sitting, both of his legs outstretched, in the backstage dressing room talking with his public relations chief about how the just-completed rehearsal went. It is a hit of a day—unseasonably warm, the sun out bright.

"It's so long, I get bored with myself," Waldron says, nibbling his nails absentmindedly. "I'm reading along and I say, 'I've got to stop. This is boring.' Did you pick that up?"

"Well, I thought you weren't up," Cox says. "But I figured that was just because it was the rehearsal."

Waldron says, "I hope that we don't overtechnologize this. Have too much technology and foul the thing up."

There is just enough time to grab a quick bite to eat, so Waldron and Cox head upstairs, where a private dining room awaits with a plentiful buffet. When you're the CEO, no matter where you are, meals seem to appear like magic out of thin air. On the way, Waldron gazes out from the balcony at technicians working like beavers on the stage. He says, "You know the only thing that gets me nervous? Look at those guys screwing around with that podium. It couldn't possibly be the way I left it."

Upstairs, the nourishment includes roast beef and tuna fish. As Waldron hungrily demolishes a tuna sandwich, Cox shoves over for his perusal a proposal inviting Avon sponsorship of a Boys Club conference in Puerto Rico. Waldron takes the paper and screws up his face in an expression of concentration.

"It looks like a boondoggle to me," he says, "unless there are lots of underprivileged boys in Puerto Rico."

Cox says he thinks it's more likely that the underprivileged people are some businessmen who would not object to a paid vacation to Puerto Rico.

"Well, check into it and see what kind of visibility we can get."

Time is starting to get short. Waldron politely excuses himself and heads back to the dressing room for his primping session. Linda Grimes, a pert, slender young woman, is waiting to make him up. Waldron greets her warmly; he has been the recipient of her skills four or five times before. Grimes is a freelance make-up artist who has been coating faces with cosmetics since 1976. She says she has worked with Diana Ross, Liza Minelli, and Steve Allen, as well as a galaxy of corporate faces.

She begins putting on splashes of powder.

Waldron says, "All Avon products?"

Grimes says, "But of course."

(Last year, Waldron began to demand that all Avon employees use Avon products as much as possible. "If you're going to use a product Avon sells," he likes to say, "it had better be ours." Waldron, in trying to adhere to his own stricture, uses Avon's Cordovan After Shave, On Duty 24 Deodorant, Twice Fresh Mouthwash, and Naturally Gentle Shampoo. Right now, he has on a James River Traders tie. So does John Cox. One problem of this edict, conveyed to me by Cox, is that James River Traders is not known for the exceptional breadth of its tie collection and Avon executives sometimes show up at a meeting all sporting identical neckwear.)

Waldron says, "I have a bruise from a shaving cut there." He points to a scab on his chin.

Grimes says, "Okay. Does that sting?"

Waldron says, "No."

An assistant producer of the event looks in and asks Waldron, "Do you want a prepoured glass of water on the lectern?"

Waldron says, "Yes, that'd be good."

Grimes says, "You know I've been working with Steve Allen all this week."

Waldron says, "Absolute riot."

Grimes says, "Well, on stage I'm sure he is."

Waldron says, "They were having a test of the satellite hookup and they said, 'Okay, come in Pasadena.' Silence. Then they said, 'Okay, come in Rye,' figuring that's only five miles away. Silence."

Waldron laughs.

Grimes says, "I'm sure that's straightened out now."

Waldron says, "It better be."

Grimes says, "Do you gesture very much with your hands?"

Waldron says, "Yeah, I guess I do."

Grimes says, "Okay, put your hands up."

She begins covering them with makeup.

Waldron says, "I threw some hair spray on them. I didn't really know how to do it."

Grimes says, "It looks pretty good."

She continues coating them, then says, "Just don't put your hands in your pockets too much or too roughly, because some of it may come off on your suit."

Grimes dusts his face and then his hands with a soft brush.

Waldron checks the mirror and says, "Boy, it would be nice to look this way all the time."

Grimes says, "Been able to take any vacations?"

Waldron says, "Oh, yes, we've been out to Vail skiing. After just screaming down those slopes, I slipped on the ice in front of my apartment and tore all the ligaments in my leg. That's why nobody will dare say break a leg to me today. I won't have any left."

Grimes, just about done, says, "What do you think?"

Waldron inspects himself in the mirror and says, "Terrific. I hate to go back to the old me. You ought to bake it on."

Grimes peers at Waldron critically but with a smile of approval.

She says, "Wait, you have one hair sticking up there. Can I pull it?"

"Go ahead," Waldron says. "Make a wish."

□ □ □

THE BALLROOM IS JAMMED to the walls with fifteen hundred Avon employees (another two thousand are sitting in Holiday Inns watching Waldron's visage on a screen). The steady murmur in the room abruptly comes to a halt as Waldron reaches the lectern.

In his effort to coax and jolly the attending employees into a sense of contentment, Waldron starts off by reviewing 1984. He mentions that strategic plans were mapped out and the company's earnings turned up, though there were some bad portents: Both the domestic beauty products business and the direct response division had stormy years. However, he goes on, "During the year, the beauty products division made great progress in converting from a distribution-driven to a consumer-driven business. Let's see if I can explain the difference. As a distribution-driven business, we relied on pushing our products through the representatives to consumers. As a consumer-driven business, on the other hand, we try to understand what the consumer wants, match our products to those wants and create consumer demand. A distribution-driven tool manufacturer, for instance, tries to sell quarter-inch drills. A consumer-driven tool manufacturer understands that people don't want quarter-inch drills, they want quarter-inch holes. Consumer-driven companies don't sell lawnmowers, they sell beautiful lawns. They don't sell microwave ovens, they sell instant meals. They don't sell cosmetics, they sell beauty."

He talks about why strategic plans are needed. Slides are shown of the company's earnings from 1979 through 1983. Down every year. "We're not looking at a one-year aberration. We see a company that's headed for trouble. Not in trouble, in the sense of losing money—like Chrysler and International Harvester when they were in the news—but we were well on our way. Declining profitability severely limits a company's alternatives, and declines tend to accelerate."

Then he says, "Now let's look at Avon from the point of view of our owners, the shareholders of the company. In 1979, Avon stock was selling at forty-eight dollars per share. If we'd simply kept pace with all the other public companies on Standard & Poor's register, our stock would be worth seventy-two dollars a share today. In fact, our stock is trading for less than a third of that."

He says that extensive studies showed that the company is "critically dependent" on seven businesses and he lists the Magnificent Seven. The top priority, he says, is turning around the domestic beauty business. "It's our flagship—but it got hung up on a sandbar of changing demographics. What happened was that we regarded the business as primarily a direct selling business. Growth had come, and was to come in the future, from continually increasing the number of representatives. But as more women entered the work force, there were fewer of them to recruit as representatives and fewer at home to sell to. We spent more and more money trying to recruit, but it was a losing cause.

One study we did showed that if we were to meet our sales objectives with our present system, by 1995 every woman over the age of nineteen either would be working for Avon or would have been a representative. We also tried to prop up sales by adding more and more nonbeauty products to the line and by offering deep-deep discounts. Sales didn't go up, but profits went down."

He talks about findings of a consumer research study that Avon commissioned: "Consumers like Avon, but they thought our products were behind the times. There is a reservoir of good will toward Avon, although our image is a little tarnished. But that's good news, because we can fix the image. And we've already begun . . . In our consumer research study we found another exciting thing—that our customers buy only about a quarter of their makeup, skin care, and fragrances from us. That means we have a potential to dramatically increase our sales to our existing customers."

Then he says, "Our new sales strategies—and there are two of them—derive from the reluctant realization that we simply are not going to be able to get to the six hundred and fifty thousand representative force we'd dreamed of three years ago. The first new sales strategy emphasizes improving representative productivity. Although we can't get fifty percent more representatives, we can—over time—help each representative we do have to get slightly more sales. One of the keys to this is more and better training, training tailored to the individual representative. Another key is recruiting better-qualified representatives, and we have a new screening tool that will help identify high-potential candidates, who will get extra training and extra territories . . . At the same time, we will be testing a new approach in direct sales—employee repre-

sentatives called personal beauty advisors, assigned to territories not being covered by a
representative. These will be full-time employees
who will receive a salary, benefits, and commissions. We expect they will cover three hundred to
five hundred households and our target is for them
to generate twelve hundred dollars to fifteen
hundred dollars a campaign in sales . . . The other
sales strategy involves finding ways to serve those
potential customers that we're not currently reaching. We know from our study that there are, right
now, ten million women who would buy from us if
they could. That's one billion dollars in potential
business."

He goes on to talk about how great the future is
for Mallinckrodt's critical-care business, how great
the future is for Foster's home-health-care business.

Then he says, "Those are the plans. They're terrific plans. But as that great philosopher, Yogi
Berra, has said, 'The game's not over 'til it's over.'
Well, in our case, it's not over until the plans are
implemented. And implementation will not be
easy. Plans don't mean a thing until they're exe-
cuted well. And that is going to take the best efforts
of you and me and every Avon employee."

A curious sort of excitement seems to have been
stirred up. But why? Little of what Waldron is saying here today is particularly new, especially
couched in the corporate hype and flatness of the
speech. Perhaps it is nothing more than the sight of
him up there saying everything is going to be all
right, even if no one is altogether sure it is.

Linda Grimes has positioned herself at the rear
of the balcony, where she now studies Waldron
talking at the lectern and says, "He's a little shiny.
The perspiration is starting to come through. The

Avon makeup is meant to be a fashion makeup, and so it's not quite as thick as the theatrical makeup I would normally use. Oh well."

Waldron takes questions from the audience now, and very coolly answers them. Several people ask about benefits. Waldron says Avon's benefits programs are "very strong." Several people ask about morale, saying it is low. Waldron says it will pick up as soon as profits do. Someone asks how much the meeting is costing. Waldron says the price tag is roughly $140,000, or about $3.90 per employee. Someone wonders about job security. Waldron says, "I am surprised to hear that the words 'job security' were ever part of the Avon vocabulary. I can't imagine any sales and marketing organization promising job security. The supply of people depends on the demand for their goods and services. The best way to secure your job is to make yourself indispensable—or marry the boss's daughter, and mine is already married."

Time is running short, so Waldron segues into his closing: "We must continue to adjust to a changing world. Our failure to evolve in the recent past has forced us to make more changes in the last year than would otherwise have been necessary. We are in the process of turning around a corporate earnings performance that you saw earlier and that must still be vividly emblazoned in your mind. Turning a company around is an experience that you'll never forget—and will never want to live through again . . . We are now aimed in the right strategic direction, and I believe that we will begin to see tangible results within the next six months. Avon is on the go and nothing can stop us. We're succeeding. We're winning. And we're doing it the old-fashioned way—we're earning it."

Waldron receives a dutiful round of applause,

music engulfs the room, and he walks off the stage and files back to the sanctuary of his dressing room. He appears to be very much pleased, very much up, as if his words have lifted him to a greater level of belief in the Avon cause.

Waldron says to one of the technicians, "Seems to have gone well. You guys did a great job putting it all together."

The technician says, "You carried the ball."

Another technician pokes his head in and says, "Nice job. You were terrific. Like a pro."

Still another technician says, "It really was great."

Waldron says, "You guys were terrific."

The admiring men leave and Linda Grimes begins removing Waldron's makeup with the help of a blizzard of tissues and cotton swabs.

The chief executive says, "Now the ugly Waldron reemerges."

□   □   □

WALDRON SHUFFLES THROUGH PAPERS. It is afternoon, some days later. He says the problems at the beauty business are worse than he anticipated when he took the job. Every week, the numbers come in, and every week they are worse.

"I know we have to hit bottom," he says. "I know there is a figure called minus one hundred. Sooner or later, we have to hit bottom."

"It's hard to get people to leave the office feeling good," he goes on. "I have to provide optimism without looking like a fop, without looking like I'm not facing up to reality. 'Look, Waldron, I don't know where you've spent the last five minutes, but the business is going to pot.' I get some of that."

He tells me that he occasionally begins to feel as

if he is adrift in some kind of lunar world. "Sometimes you find it hard to believe that you're looking at those numbers over there," and he points to a chart of a downward-sloping red line, "and then you're having coffee over here with the Twenty-Five Year Club, one of those wonderful things I have to do. Sometimes it just doesn't seem to make a bit of sense."

"Shouldn't you be spending more of your time, all of your time, on the beauty business?" I ask.

"There's an awful temptation to become preoccupied with a major artery severing," he says. "You have to resist it. You have such responsibilities. If someone is going to sit in that chair [and he motions towards his chair] and call himself a leader, he has to be a full-time leader and be a consistent leader and not cry or laugh or fly off the handle when that's not the right thing to do. Anyone who lets a personal problem or a business problem get to him and interfere with how he runs the company is not doing the job the way it ought to be done. So you have to go out to the dinners and look after the other children in the family and laugh and slap backs, even though you know there's an engine fire going."

6 □ ZIGZAGGING UP THE PYRAMID

Hicks Benjamin Waldron was born in Amsterdam, New York, on Halloween Day in 1923. His father, whose name was also Hicks, owned a small foundry that made gears and belt drives chiefly for the carpet mills that were pervasive in Amsterdam. He had a sister, Louise, who was two years younger than he. Waldron remembers himself as being fairly typical. "I was a very standard, average American kid who got into his share of mischief," he says. "Once in a while, for example, I'd try one of those corn-silk cigarettes behind the garage. You know, you roll up some toilet paper with corn silk and smoke away." In high school, he was an average student and played fullback on the football team. "I'll tell you an anecdote that will have me crying by the time I finish it. My senior year, we had lost almost every game of the season. The final game was against Johnstown, New York, a town about nine miles away. It was a night game. Both cities turned out. It was like the goddamn Rose Bowl. It was zero-zero late in the game. I was the quarterback, because the regular quarterback had gotten hurt. The coach sent in a play and it was for me to carry the ball. I carried it and went into the end zone and just then I fumbled and the other team recovered it. The game ended zero-zero. As we drove away, all the kids were throwing tomatoes at the bus and calling me all sorts of names. So if you ask me when did I learn humility, that was when."

Waldron had a cousin named Jack Waldron, and he was just bowled over by him. As far back as he can remember, Jack Waldron was his success model. "He was five years older," Waldron says. "He always had a bicycle when I had a tricycle. He had a car when I had a bicycle. Jack's father had died and he was of very modest means, as I was. He had gone to Green Mountain Junior College in Poultney, Vermont, and to the University of Michigan to become an engineer, and then had gone on to General Electric. When it was time for me to go to school, we didn't have anywhere near enough money. So I went to Green Mountain for two reasons: Jack had gone there and I got a football scholarship of about two hundred and fifty dollars a year and they offered me a work program." (Green Mountain subsequently became an all-girls school, which has sometimes made it ticklish for Waldron to explain why it was that he went there.) Waldron, as he puts it, "almost fizzled out my freshman year and ended up on the Dean's List my second year."

Since his cousin Jack had gone on to the University of Michigan to study engineering, that was what Waldron wanted for himself. He took up mechanical engineering and made fullback on the second team. In the summer, he worked in one of the Amsterdam rug mills, yanking huge rolls of wool off freight cars with big bale hooks. At this point, the Second World War was going on, and Waldron knew that he was shortly going to be drafted. He far preferred the Navy to any other branch of the service, so to insure his assignment he enlisted. He was in a rush to go play golf when he filled out his service application, and when he came to the final question, asking the school of choice at which he wanted to get his officers' training, he scribbled down the abbreviation that everyone knew Michigan as: UM. Not long afterward, he got his Navy orders instructing him to report to the University of Minnesota in Minneapolis. "It was one of the great mistakes of my life," Waldron says.

At Minnesota, Waldron was a reasonably good student. He did quite well in Navy courses. And it was at this time that he married his first wife, a woman named Peg whom he had met at Green Mountain College and who was now a secretary. He borrowed money from her to buy her a ring.

After he graduated, Waldron was assigned by the Navy to Cornell University for officers' training. There he learned the advantage of having one's name start with a letter deep into the alphabet. "I was always at the end of everything, since I was a *w*. The Navy cut orders—they were all the same—by calling out the names in alphabetical order and then giving out these identical orders. They got to the guy before me and he took the last set of orders. So they got to me and they had to call the other guy back and make a copy of his orders and give them to me. Ninety days later, I'm an officer and the same routine happened. They shipped out everyone to the Philippines, many of them never to come back, and they got to Waldron and there were no orders. So the top guy said he'll invent some orders—twenty days leave and come back to Cornell in the engineering school. See, I had finished second in my officers' class and had an engineering degree. But if I hadn't been a *w* I'm not sure I'd be sitting here right now."

Waldron spent time on some ships but he never saw any combat. He once got a chance to dock a ship; he crashed it into the pier. In 1946, he was discharged from the Navy. Again following the path of his cousin Jack, he went off to the General Electric Company to start his business career. He and his wife moved into the upstairs of someone's private house. The back porch was their kitchen. The appliances consisted of a hot plate and a sink. Waldron's goal was nothing grander than to design jet engines, which were as romantic and sexy a product then as computers are today.

Waldron began at the absolute bottom of the GE ladder. His first job assignment was in the jet engine testing department, where he was to test a jet fuel relief valve. When the fuel pressure got too high, the valve opened and jet fuel dripped out. Waldron's job was to count the drips. Eight hours a day, five days a week, he counted drips. "I remember clearly that it dripped every six seconds. That's ten drips a minute, six hundred drips an hour, and four thousand eight hundred drips a day." After he had done this for three weeks—seventy-two thousand drips worth—he got fed up and figured that his engineering degree was worth more than a job counting drips. Rather than protest to his immediate boss, though, he complained to the general foreman. He was put on a job testing electric motors. But he was put on the third shift—eleven at night to seven in the morning—as a way of being told that he had done the right thing, but done it the wrong way. His next assignment was to clean out the grooves in the floors of a GE factory. "There were acres of them—that floor was hundreds of feet long—and you had to get down and shine them with a file and brush. It was total disillusionment. But humility is lesson number 1 wherever you go. 'Let's teach the bastard how the cows eat the cabbage and then we'll let him loose a little bit,' I guess was the message. Somebody had to clean the cracks and I was the lowest-paid guy. I think I was paid forty-seven dollars a week. But I made the decision that my cracks were going to be as clean as anyone's."

His horizons brightened after that, and he zigzagged his way up the pyramid, in the standard and physically punishing way that managerial talent is groomed in big corporations, by changing jobs and mailing addresses thirteen times. He moved from sales training to marketing to purchasing to manufacturing and then to his first major job: as general manager of a plant that built record players in Decatur, Illinois. "That was probably the best job I ever had. I was on the bonus plan for the first time. I had eight hundred employees working for me. It was my first exposure to consumer products. And it was remote. I was not bothered by superiors. My boss was the bottom line."

The idea of being the chief executive suggested itself as he continued to move up and discovered the intense pleasure of managing other people and being responsible for a division's fortunes. He became a vice-president in 1970 and then, the next year, was promoted to group executive for consumer products. "There was no question that he was one of the most effective managers in the company," Reginald Jones, who was GE's CEO at the time and is now retired, told me. "As an anecdote, I remember when we had a chance to divest ourselves of our television business in Germany. It was giving us some problems. Profitability was just nonexistent. I told Hicks to go over there and try to move this off our books. I told him this was important and not to hesitate to call me at any time. There was a six-hour time difference. And he took me at my word. Several times, I would get a call at five o'clock in the morning and it was him. That was typical of his tenacity. But he moved it off the books. He got things done."

Waldron thought he was very much in the running for GE's top slot. But would he get it? There were maybe eight hot prospects.

Someone I know who was high up at GE at the time and close to the jockeying for the GE chairmanship told me something about the nature of the competition: "When you get that close, anything can knock you out of the running. If you comb your hair the wrong way, that can do it. One executive was right in the thick of it and he did this interview with *Fortune* magazine. And it was a really positive story. The problem was the article implied that he was a possible heir apparent. The board members read it and they didn't like it one bit, because they felt he was promoting himself, starting a campaign to get the job, and one of the rules is you don't run a campaign. So that finished him. Another guy could have gotten it, but he wasn't terribly warm. People were turned off. The chief executive knew this. He knows everything. I tell you, the contenders have to walk on eggshells. They have to do their job and not do anything out of the ordinary, because that might be perceived in the wrong light. And, of course, they work like hell not to mess up. No mistakes at this juncture."

One day, while the race was still at a high pitch, Waldron got a call from a headhunter named Spencer Stuart who invited him to lunch at the Greenwich Yacht Club. He said the top job at Heublein, the wine and food company which, among other things, owned the Kentucky Fried Chicken empire, was available. Stuart was most impressed with Waldron. As he told me, "Some people are the creative leader, contributing to the business. Some are strong financiers. Some are business developers.

They don't operate what's there too well, but they're good at making acquisitions and putting two and two together and getting six. Hicks can do all of those things, but I think Hicks's mark is his ability to deal with people and get them to move the ball. He's not a guy to take a secondary role. He's a natural leader. On occasion, I suppose that take-charge, go-for-it mechanism that's built into him might push somebody out of the way who isn't as strong or who's sensitive. Some people would say he takes over."

For all the flattery Stuart heaped on Waldron, he didn't want the job. "I said no and no and no and he kept coming back at me. I didn't want it because I thought I had a shot at the top job at GE."

One evening, overhearing his father and mother discussing the Heublein opportunity, Waldron's son, Ben, interrupted and said, "Why don't you do it. After all, look at what happened to Jonathan Livingston Seagull."

Waldron didn't know what had happened to the talking seagull, but he went out and read the book. "It was like a catalyst. I said, all right, let's do it."

After twenty-seven years at GE, Waldron in the summer of 1973 became president and chief operating officer of Heublein, Inc. Two years later, he assumed the added responsibility of chief executive officer.

"Things were going okay until one day I picked up the phone at home and the person on the other end said, 'Mr. Waldron, I'm Richard Smith. I'm chairman of General Cinema. We own 9.7 percent of your company.' That was the first phone call."

Smith and his relatives collectively held about forty-five percent of General Cinema, which owned movie theaters and bottling companies. It was a well-run money machine. "They were looking for

some place to put their cash. He told me that they
didn't have the money to go out and buy a big liquor or fast-food company. So they decided to buy
a piece of a big company and so he wanted only an
investment in Heublein. And he was just cocky
enough to say that he thought he could help manage the company better. I had him to my office that
Sunday and had Goldman Sachs sit in with me and
I went through the whole litany of we want to stay
independent and go away and peddle your beans
somewhere else. This was February. It went on for
eight months. They kept buying more and more—
it got up to 18.9 percent. We had a meeting—I had
two or three meetings with him—in some little
shabby motel in Springfield, so we wouldn't be
found out. I didn't want anyone to discover in any
way that we were talking. One of the postures we
keep is stay away. The meetings were pretty ugly
with him. We were grown, mature men. We didn't
swing at each other. But they were rather unpleas-
ant encounters. One offer I made was we'd trade
our wine business for all of his shares. He said
great. So we gave him the wine business numbers
and he said forget it. The wine business wasn't
worth it. So he said I'm going to keep buying the
company. We said we're not going to let you do it.
We tried to negotiate a standstill agreement but his
demands were outrageous. We went out and bought
a ton of his shares and it put the squeeze on his
balance sheet. He had to buy shares to keep the 50
percent ownership. Our lawyers said that if he got
up to 20 or 25 percent, he'd pretty soon end up
owning Heublein and wouldn't pay a nickel for it.
I had some discussions with Paul Sticht of R. J.
Reynolds. So I called Paul and made a deal to sell
the company at sixty dollars a share. I made the deal
only to avoid the creeping tentacles. Those were

very trying times. But it was a good deal for the shareholders."

I asked what the effect was on Waldron and the company during this acrimonious battle?

"From a health standpoint, my doctor kept saying, stop all this. But I was really thriving on it. I was eating well. It was challenging. If things were only heading in the right direction, it would have been the best period in my life. I set up a crisis team, as we called it, that met at least once a day. The company was being run by two vice-presidents. All I did was fight this battle. It really cramped our style. We worked every weekend. There was never any doubt that Saturday and Sunday were like Monday and Tuesday."

"How worried were you?" I asked him.

"I would have to say that it was clear that we would probably lose. I had that fear. They had an unbeatable strategy. The only strategy was to buy them, but they owned too much of their stock. It was kind of a sad day for Heublein. You know, I always resented it—I resent it to this day—that that goddamn guy came in and tried to buy us for peanuts and then just be cocky enough to say he thought he could run the company. It was just a zero contribution. He made a pile of money. For what? For a zero contribution."

(Mr. Smith, when I asked him if he cared to talk about his side of events, politely declined.)

When Heublein was swallowed up by R. J. Reynolds Industries, the tobacco conglomerate famous for its Winston and Camel cigarette brands, Waldron was in effect demoted from chief executive of a company to head of a large subsidiary. His title was executive vice-president of the Reynolds food and beverage group, a combination of Heublein and the Del Monte Corporation. Waldron didn't like no longer being the boss. As he would express it, "It's like having a seventy-five horsepower engine and only going half-speed, or being able to dive to a hundred feet and only diving to ten." What's more, he wasn't thrilled about selling cigarettes. "I had trouble with the cigarette business. I have to get up and shout my product. I didn't have trouble with the liquor business or the wine business. But cigarettes bothered me. I remember for our annual meeting at Heublein, when we were talking about our sale to Reynolds, I told our public relations man to call Winston-Salem and get the company line on cigarettes and health. He called and I couldn't believe it. They said there was no company line and that there was no connection between cigarettes and health."

In the middle of 1982, Waldron got a call from David Mitchell, the chairman and chief executive of Avon. Mitchell said he was getting divorced for the second time and wanted to marry again and to spend the rest of his life having the fun he never had found the time for. He said Avon was in trouble, its earnings were going down and down, and he was tired and out of ideas. He thought Waldron might have the lust to be a CEO again. Waldron mulled over the opportunity. He thought, "I could move to New York and sell a product that's intended to make you smell good, feel good, and look good. That's a hell of a lot better than trying to peddle cigarettes." Plus Waldron was antsy to be at the top again. "Once you get chief executive into your blood," he says, "it's hard to get it out." He packed his bags.

7 □ CONSTITUENCIES

TOO EARLY, almost, to be working, but it is coffee klatch time. Eight-thirty, a Wednesday, in the small but tasteful thirty-sixth-floor conference room.

Waldron, in shirt-sleeves, ambles in to greet five middle-management Avon people invited from various divisions of the company. These are managers whom he does not often come into contact with. In many ways, Waldron's brushes with ordinary life in the corporation are limited. From time to time, therefore, he assembles such a group to see what they have to say.

In explaining these sessions, Waldron has told me, "The notion is availability, accessibility, candor, and to get ideas. There's an old adage. It's called 'MWA,' instead of 'MBO'—management by walking around instead of management by objective. We have twenty-six floors here, and I started going up and down the elevators. It was very inefficient. I found that I had to really force myself to get out of my office and press the elevator buttons. And then I'd walk down the hall and eighteen people would be in a meeting. So this is an alternative to that. We also have an open-door policy. It's rarely taken advantage of, though occasionally it will get to be too much and I won't see someone. But I see on my schedule that I have five minutes today for a waitress in the cafeteria. I don't know what the hell she wants to see me about." (I found out later that she stopped by to seek some investment counsel: She had some money saved up. What should she do with it? Waldron told her he really wasn't in a position to give advice but cautioned her against sinking it into anything risky.)

Everyone—four men and a woman—pours some coffee into a mug, chooses something of interest from a tray amply filled with pastry, and sits down around the conference table. There is some horsing around, and then Waldron begins the session.

Waldron: "One subject I'm interested in is what you're hearing back about me." (He is referring to commentary on his performance at the big Hilton Hotel employee gathering.)

One of the men, who is smoking a steady procession of Kent cigarettes, says that some of his underlings thought that Waldron was perhaps too candid.

The woman says that one person told her he was uncomfortable hearing the takeover discussion.

Waldron: "It's like talking about teenage pregnancies."

Woman: "He felt that, the way you put it, no one wanted to take us over, we were in such bad shape."

Waldron: "They haven't made a pass at me in three years because I'm so uncomfortable, that sort of thing?"

Woman: "Yeah, I guess so."

One of the men says, "I hear from several people that we need to do more on affirmative action. We need to do more."

Waldron: "Well, they're right. It requires a hell of a lot of effort and we're not getting to church on time."

The man then suggests that Waldron should spend more time going to meetings and dinners peopled by black leaders.

Waldron: "I don't like to pat myself on the back, but there probably isn't a chief executive who is better known to black leaders than me."

Some more discussion ensues on the black issue.

Waldron: "I remember when I was at Heublein and we were really in serious trouble. We didn't have any blacks. There was talk about how twenty-five percent of Kentucky Fried Chicken was consumed by blacks and they were going to stop eating it if we didn't do something. So I put in a rule that nobody is going to be hired unless they're black. There was a lot of screaming, and hiring came to a screeching halt. Greatest method of reducing corporate overhead ever. [Everyone laughs.] Then when hiring started again, it was all blacks. The problem was we put a lot of people on the payroll who shouldn't have been there. So you can get into overkill."

Another man says, "When you talk to analysts, what do they ask you about?"

Waldron: "The dividend. Can you really turn it around? Why don't you fire Preston and his people? Why did you pay so much for Mallinckrodt, and when are you going to sell Mallinckrodt?"

Then the man says, "Do they ask about direct selling?"

Waldron: "Oh, yes. We try to get them away from that as quick as we can. I think our personal beauty advisor speaks to that. It's still direct selling but it gets us into the real world. Women don't want a honky-tonk job from ten to two. They want something to take home. They want benefits. But to answer your question, the Street is down on direct selling and they question whether Avon can go on with direct selling. That, of course, flies right in the face of our strategy."

Then the assembled group talks about a sales meeting in Atlanta last month and pours forth stories about corporate speakers.

Waldron: "We had in Atlanta as a motivational speaker Larry Wilson, the coauthor of *The One Minute Sales Person.* He said that, talking of the Fiddler on the Roof, that the fiddler hung onto the roof ninety-five percent of the time and fiddled five percent of the time. He said he'd hang on fifty percent of the time and fiddle fifty percent of the time and risk falling off the roof. That's the way I feel."

The Kent cigarette man says, "We had Peggy Fleming, too, recently. There must be a lot of money in this speaking racket because everyone seems to be doing it."

Waldron: "Well, if we fizzle here, we're going into that next year. I'll make the deals and you do the speaking."

The woman says, "I never thought of Peggy Fleming speaking."

The Kent man: "She's a very shy person. And she gets up there and talks about how she overcame her shyness. She's not a pro, but she's getting better at it."

Waldron: "One of the best I heard was Joe Paterno. He talks only about football. He says our team wears the ugliest football shoes in the country. And, boy, are we proud of them. I tell my team, you go out and make those boys eat your ugly shoes."

One of the men brings up the subject of Mallinckrodt. What sort of return is Avon getting for the big purchase price it paid for it?

Waldron: "I'm having Jules [the chief financial officer] work up a figure for the analysts. If it's a good one, I'll use it."

One of the others says, "Are there any acquisition possibilities in direct mail?"

Waldron: "We get things thrown at us. I don't know how many go broke every hour. Ten an hour or something like that."

Waldron checks his watch now, and realizes that it is nine-thirty. He peers around the table and brings the session to an abrupt close by saying, "Anybody have nine-thirties? And if not, why the hell not?"

☐ ☐ ☐

RAIN HAS BEGUN to beat down when Waldron returns to his office, but, never mind, the view is still dizzying. Waiting for him are Jules Zimmerman, the chief financial officer, Margro Long, vice-president of investor relations, Sabine Hugueny, director of investor relations, and the ubiquitous John Cox.

The topic of discussion is the 1985 investor relations program. This meeting, in essence, is a strategy session to map out what posture to assume with the investment community, most particularly the securities analysts employed by the mighty Wall Street brokerage houses who follow Avon's stock and issue buy or sell recommendations to the world. Next week, in fact, Waldron will be making one of his periodic appearances before a group of analysts to try to win their favor. The Wall Street posture of every corporation basically comes down to: Every Aspect Of Our Business Is Great And Is Getting Even Better; Anyone Who Doesn't Buy Our Stock Now Will Look Like A Jerk Tomorrow. Securities analysts matter quite a lot: Their buy, sell or hold proclamations have wide influence on investors, especially the big institutions—the pension funds, mutual funds, and insurance companies —that engage in most stock trading. Analysts originally used to be introverted scholars who sat in their cubicles, scratched their heads a lot, and wrote research reports of novella length. In more recent times, however, they have been pressured to become marketers, and they roam the country singing the praises of the companies they follow to institutional clients. Needless to say, managements find it quite useful to have them on their side. Waldron likes to say that winning the favor of Wall Street analysts is "like going to heaven without the inconvenience of dying."

The stock price of a company is important, for the higher the price of a stock, the more easily a company can raise money, since it can sell stock that it holds or borrow against its stock. What's more, in this age of takeover mania, a company's stock price can serve as a potent defensive tool. Corporate raiders look for companies that are selling cheap. Nobody wants to buy a company that is selling dear. Besides all this, chief executives are macho and what their stock is selling at is one of the most visible report cards that they get. It can be downright embarrassing to run into, say, the head of GM or IBM when your stock is stinking up the market.

One of the arts a CEO must master is the art of analyst persuasion. CEOs vary a great deal about how accessible they make themselves to analysts. Waldron has been making himself exceedingly accessible, expecting to meet over the course of the year individually with about thirty of the leading soothsayers and to hold a number of regional analysts' sessions in places like Chicago and Philadelphia. (Waldron also periodically personally visits major institutional stockholders, such as Delaware

Investment Management in Philadelphia, and
United Capital Management, a group of banks
based in Denver that is Avon's largest single share-
owner.) He has little choice. Avon has a badly tarnished reputation on Wall Street, and Waldron
knows he needs to restore it if he's going to turn the
company around. Something like three hundred analysts regularly follow Avon, and their power is
never underestimated by Waldron. "He is very sup-
portive of investor relations and dealing with the
analysts," Margro Long had told me. "He fully ap-
preciates the benefits that can be gotten from it.
And that's an intangible. It's very hard to calculate
the benefit. Frankly, the previous management had
poor credibility with analysts. We had four years of
down earnings. Yet if you read the previous communications to analysts, it was that we were expecting to have good performance. And we didn't.
Hicks was very sensitive to our credibility problem.
If Wall Street thinks management doesn't have a
handle on earnings, that colors their reports. If you
have one highly respected analyst who puts out a
buy order, you can see it in the price of the stock.
So we take this group very seriously."

There is a written report of twenty pages to allow
Waldron to follow the oral presentation. Like others
I have seen, it's pretty simplistic stuff.

Hugueny has been nominated to do the talking,
and she races through the opening pages until she
gets to a point on page four where it's suggested
that, according to a Yankelovich study, Avon's
image is poor with analysts.

"Whoa," Waldron says. "Amplify that a little bit."

Hugueny says, "Well, there was some concern in
the study about Mallinckrodt and so forth."

Waldron says, "So these are sins of the past that
are converted into the future?"

Cox says, "I think there's been some concern about Foster, that we overpaid for Foster."

Waldron looks at Zimmerman and says, "Is there something, Jules, that we can present at the meeting about Foster to prove it's been a good purchase price?"

Zimmerman says, "Yes, I suppose there is something about sales and earnings of Foster. Let me see if we can pull together a paragraph."

"But we have to be sure to tie it in to the purchse price," Waldron says. "The return on investment or something."

"Okay," Zimmerman says. "Will do."

Hugueny continues her presentation. She notes that Avon is considered by analysts to be fully priced or overpriced, because of slow anticipated per-share earnings growth and because of the perceived insecurity of the dividend. She says that attitudes toward the beauty industry have become less favorable, that Avon's diversification and acquisition strategies remain controversial, that the competence of Avon's new management is recognized but there is interest in learning more about the corporate strategic direction.

Hugueny mentions, at one point, that the mix of Avon shareholders has changed such that institutional holders, as opposed to individuals, represent 56.3 percent of holders, compared to 61.4 percent in 1980. Companies prefer individual holders, since they are less fickle and don't turn over their shares frequently, causing instability in the price.

"That's great," Waldron says. "Now why has it happened? I'd like to say that we had a hell of a strategy, but if we did I don't know what it is."

Hugueny says, "We've been talking to retail brokers whom we haven't talked to before. Plus we haven't cut the dividend."

Waldron, obviously dissatisfied with what is clearly an unsatisfactory answer, says, "But the dividend is not related to share price. Many companies spend tons of money trying to get their individual mix up. I'd like to know how we did it and do more of it."

Hugueny says she will explore the subject and try to do more of whatever they've been doing.

Margro Long now finishes up the presentation with few interruptions from Waldron. She says that the key elements of the 1985 strategy are to maintain interest in Avon among analysts and sustain turnaround expectations and to gradually diversify the ownership of Avon shares so that a smaller portion of the stock is held by institutions. She says that the company should inform analysts and institutional holders on a timely basis of strategies and progress through "open, candid, and responsive communications."

Then Long says, "We'll be happy to discuss any questions."

"I think we're right on target, ladies," Waldron says.

8 □ OFFICE ROUTINES

WALDRON HAS two secretaries. They sit at the portals of authority, each in her own office, directly adjacent to Waldron's. The lead secretary is Maureen Ivory, a middle-aged woman whom Waldron inherited from David Mitchell. Second in command is Eileen Walsh, who is a younger, heavier-set woman with a relentlessly friendly demeanor.

Ivory spends a lot of her time with a phone receiver warming her ear. By Ivory's count, some sixty-five to seventy calls arrive each day, few of which are ever taken by Waldron. In eighteen years at Avon, though, Ivory has had only one obscene call.

One afternoon between phone calls and letters, Ivory talks with me over fish in one of the corporate dining rooms. She is a small, trig woman with an abiding gentleness about her. Waldron says that she is a walking advertisement for a beauty products and fashion company—always impeccably dressed, always wearing just the right dosage of makeup. She is a little shy, and it takes some gentle coaxing to get her talking.

She says of her chores: "I have to be his support. And that encompasses all the normal secretarial duties. Keeping the flow of the office steady. Scheduling his trips. Directing the flow of traffic.

Protecting him. I'm his protector. I belong to a society called 'The Seraphics,' which is made up of
secretaries of presidents or chief executive officers.
A seraphic is a guardian angel. And that's pretty
much what we are. We try to save him from unnec-
essary calls or people who want to see him. My
major job is seeing that Mr. Waldron's life is made
easier. All sorts of people call him. They want to do
everything from sell him insurance to really non-
sense things. They have screwy ideas to give him.
They want jobs. You get all sorts of hard-luck stories. We have people who are in jail writing for jobs.
We've had people from leper colonies who want
jobs. A woman called with a phony accent who gave
herself the title of princess. A Queen Victoria once
called. You do get all sorts of strange calls. So I
protect him. And I take a lot of abuse."

"He has no idiosyncracies," she goes on. "He
drinks a lot of coffee. We have to watch that he
doesn't drink too much. He drinks decaffeinated, so
he's not climbing the wall. He drinks it black.
Sometimes he'll ask for some juice. That's it. He's a
very simple man in taste."

She says that there is no approved list of callers
who will automatically be put through to him, but
that she has picked up who are his friends and
whom he always talks to. Many of the callers are
CEOs.

"It's sort of like a fraternity," she said. "You recognize other CEOs. You always give them every
courtesy. You always return those calls. Very few
calls go right through, because he's not there or he's
in a meeting. It's telephone Ping-Pong. All these
men that he talks to are very busy. And he's very
busy. So it can be days or weeks before a call gets
returned. Sometimes—it happens rather frequently
—one of the CEOs or Mr. Waldron gets on the

phone and there's dead silence. Neither one knows who's calling whom or what they're calling about."

One of her regular duties, she continues, is to advise Waldron twice a day—at eleven and at four —of Avon's stock price on the New York Stock Exchange.

"How does he react?" I ask.

"When it's down," she says, "he'll be mad. He'll say, 'Goddamn it, down again.' "

□   □   □

THE MAIL ARRIVES twice a day. On a Monday, the heaviest day, the letters frequently exceed fifty pieces. Other weekdays, as many as twenty or thirty letters come in seeking the attention of Hicks Waldron. Two screenings take place that assure that most of it, perhaps as much as three-quarters of it, will never come before his eyes.

One Monday afternoon, after both of the day's deliveries are in, I sit down with Eileen Walsh to open Hicks Waldron mail and see for myself who wrote to him and what they had to say. When the mail arrives, Walsh sifts through it and weeds out the materials that ought to be routed to someone else in Avon, passing on what strikes her as essential to Waldron for his understanding of the state of the business.

She explains her criteria: "As you can see if you look at this pile, everything from soup to nuts is sent to his attention. So there's a lot of sorting to do. Most of it gets referred elsewhere. Usually anything that says, 'Dear Hicks' that looks like he knows the person or that refers to a company that he was at I send through to him. Or if it's from one of the people he regularly corresponds with, like Bob Frederick, the chief executive officer at RCA, who is a friend, that goes through. He gets letters from boards of directors he's on or charities he's involved with. He never gets customer complaints."

Once the Waldron mail is winnowed out, it is turned over to Ivory, who separates it into manila folders by category: Avon division mail, Direct Response, Outside Boards, Foster Medical, Mallinckrodt, and Personal Mail. All his bills and reports on his personal investments, come to the office. The reason is that he has several homes and is so often on the road that the one sure place to reach him is at Avon. Because of the time constraints, he has Ivory take care of his bills. She writes the checks and all he does is sign them. Dozens of bills come in weekly: mortgage payments, phone bills, electric bills, credit card bills. "He has a very heavy checking account," Ivory says. Waldron banks at the Connecticut Bank and Trust Company in Hartford; he has a weekend house nearby and is a member of the bank's board.

On this day, among the letters that get through to him are: a confirmation of a breakfast date with Ed Ney, the head of Young & Rubicam, the big advertising agency; a thank-you note for making a contribution to the Jackie Robinson Foundation; two responses from people whom Waldron invited to the Salvation Army dinner dance that he is chairing this year; a letter from someone at Salomon Brothers outlining a corporate takeover defense; a letter from James Robinson, the chairman of American Express, inviting him to a dinner for the Burden Center for the Aging; a letter from William Butcher, chairman of Chase Manhattan, inviting him to an affair held by the New York Botanical Gardens honoring James Ferguson, the chairman of General Foods ("I just laugh," Ivory says. "I see a lot of letters to dinners from Mr. Butcher. Mr. Butcher is very good-natured, obviously"); a report on Revlon put out by the brokerage house of Smith Barney; and a letter from a first-grade student in Pittsburgh who, as part of a class project, had to write to somebody out of town and chose Waldron, asking him to come visit him. ("He loves children," Ivory explains. "So I usually put through things like that.")

There is also a stack of internal memorandums and reports. These include proofs of the 1985 Avon annual report and proxy statement; a memo from J. E. Donaldson saying that commercial paper outstanding is $30.2 million, though the 1985 plan called for no commercial paper indebtedness at this time; a report on the number of Avon representatives and on the orders for Avon beauty products; a monthly operations review from the Direct Response division; a report from Human Resources examining compensation of senior-level people at Avon.

Then there is a bunch of magazines: *People, Manhattan Inc., Business Week, Dun's Business Monthly, Forbes, Stratton-Bromley Magazine* (Waldron owns a home in Stratton, Vermont), and *Focal Spot Magazine* (a publication from a radiology institute that is partly owned by Avon).

Walsh keeps a logbook that summarizes every letter referred elsewhere to lower-level eyes by either her or Waldron, so that if follow-up letters arrive it is clear where to shuttle them. I went through the log to get a sense of who was writing Waldron and what they wanted. By far the preponderance of letters were invitations to charitable events and resumes from job seekers.

Samples:

A woman from Ridgefield, Connecticut, wrote to say that her mother was an Avon representative who was unhappy with "retirement."

A letter from Stan and Jan Berenstain, authors of the children's books featuring the Berenstain Bears, wrote to see if Avon would be interested in selling the bear books through its door-to-door network.

A man from *Focus* magazine wanted Avon to advertise in their upcoming special edition.

Someone who works at IBM wrote to claim that his relatives founded Avon.

A terminated Avon employee complained about his pension.

A New York Stock Exchange official urged Avon to hold some of its corporate meetings at the Exchange's meeting rooms.

A man from Kentucky Fried Chicken in Louisville wrote to say that while vacationing in Hilton Head, South Carolina, he saw the Avon SSS product displayed with a sign saying "gnat repellant" in a local drugstore.

A functionary from the market research firm of Yankelovich, Skelley & White wrote inviting Waldron to participate in a CEO survey.

A man from Wichita, Kansas, wrote asking that Avon not sell any products to his mother-in-law, because she is ill and not in full control of her mental powers.

A customer said he returned some Avon products three months ago and never received his refund of twenty dollars. A similar letter came in the same day from some other customer.

The Metropolitan Opera Club wanted Avon to advertise in its journal.

The Ethiopian Hunger Fund wanted Avon to distribute an appeal letter to its employees.

Jerry Falwell wrote complaining about some of the places where Avon advertised.

An employee wrote to complain that he was fired because he smoked pot.

A woman wrote saying that she had bought some ceramic birds for $14.95 and then discovered that they were on sale later at a price of four for $50.00.

Someone from the Gulfstream Aerospace Corporation wanted to sell Avon a Gulfstream IV corporate jet.

A prison inmate wrote who was interested in a discontinued item from the Avon jewelry line.

A woman wrote to say that she sent an idea to Avon for a product that was used and she was never paid for it.

A woman wrote to say that her daughter, Jackie, under eighteen years old, was an Avon representative and has had to pay tax on her earnings when Avon originally told her she wouldn't have to.

A letter complained about animal testing. (This is a periodic complaint and highly sensitive issue at cosmetics companies. They kill animals, especially rabbits, to test new cosmetics. Avon has tried to defuse some of the attacks by donating money to animal agencies.)

A man from Interscan Ltd. wanted to know if Avon needed his firm's services. It specializes in preventive security and bomb detection.

A company wondered if Avon was interested in using the Rolling Stones license for any of its products.

A woman wanted more recognition for making the top ten producers in her first year as an Avon representative.

A man wrote from Columbia, Missouri, suggesting that the town be considered in the event that Avon is relocating or expanding.

Two boys from New Zealand asked for a car.

A California employee wrote offering his apologies for an "outlandish" accusation in a previous letter that blamed Avon and the Pasadena division for this employee's marital problem. He wanted to recant his "boorish behavior."

A customer wrote reporting a terrible rash she suffered after using Wardrobe Freshner in her closet.

A model wrote to offer her services.

A woman claimed her face got sunburned after using Avon's Avocado Face Mask.

An elderly woman wrote to tell about her holidays. She said she loved the new Avon Christmas plate.

9 □ PRESENTATIONS

THE CONFERENCE TABLE of the boardroom is ringed by seven sober-suited, white-shirted individuals—managerial talent in the Avon Fashions group. It is incredibly hot in the room. Two wooden easels, with large white cardboard charts perched on them, stand at the far end of the table, as if awaiting students in an art class. The lead man here, the one on the spot, is William Willett, the head of the Direct Response division, which embraces Avon Fashions. This is a meeting to tell Waldron about how Avon Fashions is positioning itself in the marketplace.

One of Willett's underlings, a man named Martin Smith, who speaks with a strong English accent, starts the presentation. He goes up to the easel and shows some charts and says some things about them. He shows a pie chart of the $58-billion women's apparel market, indicating that 8 percent, or $4.64 billion, is the mail order slice that Avon competes in. Avon Fashion likes to say that its arena is the mailbox. A chart reveals that the average woman spends $550 a year on clothes.

Waldron peers over his half-glasses and says, "Then I have a problem at home. That's the most important statistic I'm going to hear today."

Then Waldron asks, "Doesn't your research sug-

89

gest that the consumer considers the Bloomingdale's store to be a competitor to Avon Fashions?"

Smith says, "Clearly not. Because they're aimed at a different customer."

Someone else says, "Customers buying from us are buying eighty percent of their clothes from department stores. So clearly they do consider stores competition."

Waldron says, "Someone from Bloomingdale's was telling me the other day that women walk through the stores with catalogues they got in the mail, comparing the prices, and if they're cheaper in the catalogue then they go home and order it from whomever."

After a bit more discussion on that point, Smith turns to a demographics chart detailing the Avon customer: young, average income, employed, has a high school education, married. A lifestyle chart suggests that she tends to live in the suburbs, works in an administration/clerical position, spends eight hundred dollars a year on clothes (almost 50 percent higher than the national average), buys more than twice as much from catalogues (20 percent) as the national average, has credit cards, has an active social life, lists shopping for clothes as a favorite pastime. Then there is a heavy-user chart. For this person, clothes are a manner of self-expression; she looks for fit, price/value, overall style, does not like to repeat an outfit within a two-week period, is an impulse buyer, is less likely to upgrade to higher prices for better quality, finds catalogues great fun to read through.

Then there is a chart that offers a word portrait of the typical Avon customer: "She is a twenty-two-year-old secretary living in La Grange, Illinois. She is married with a household income of twenty-six thousand dollars and she drives a Chevrolet. She loves clothes, the more the better, and she buys more from Avon Fashions than any single store."

Smith is done now, and Waldron says, "Thank you. Very interesting."

A young woman named Judy stands up, goes over to the easel, and compares Avon customers to those of competitors. A chart shows that Avon has the youngest customers of all direct competitors and is in the mid-range in household income. Another chart shows that Avon customers are similar to those of J. C. Penney and Sears in terms of income, but they are younger. Another chart on "Cross Purchases by Avon Fashion Customer" shows that 13.6 percent of Avon customers also buy merchandise from J. C. Penney, and 13 percent also buy from Sears.

More charts are displayed and discarded, a mass of data, the marketplace in crushing detail:

"Fashion Orientation by Occupational Segment."

"Avon Fashions Profile."

"New Process."

"J. C. Penney."

"Sears."

"Spiegel."

"Just a minute," Waldron interrupts. "Who is going after the trendy person? I don't see anything up there."

Smith says, "No one is. No one is going after the back-office worker who wants trendy clothing."

Waldron says, "So that's an opportunity?"

Smith says, "Correct."

More charts:

"Price Range."

"Percent of Items $30 or Less."

"Fashion/Price Positioning."

Then a chart sums up customers' description of

the Avon Fashions customer: "A young woman in her twenties, warm and happy, up-to-date and active, vivacious, sociable and fun, somewhat conservative fashion tastes, conscientious about her fashion budget."

"Very interesting," Waldron says. "I could describe Evelyn like that except about being conscientious about her clothes budget. That just wouldn't fly."

Lots of laughter.

Then Waldron asks, "What did you learn from this exercise?"

Willett says, "I think what we learned is that to reinforce our marketing emphasis, I think we learned that the low-income, trendy is wide open. I don't know what else I learned from it. George, what did you learn from it?"

George says, "I think we learned a lot of things that we thought we knew. What I learned is we've got a great position. Better than I thought we did going in."

Waldron says, "One thing I hope you learned is, we've got to resist going upscale and trying to be with The Talbots and so forth. We have to be what we are and resist like hell going upscale."

Willett says, "Right. Be who we are."

Waldron says, "Now, if you'll just put pockets in your men's golf shirts and make your neckties a little longer, then you'll be all set."

The atmosphere of this encounter has been marked by a certain amount of bonhomie. But now it is summing-up time, and it takes a more critical turn.

A planning officer says, "I think we need to know more about our competition, who we are defending against. More about who doesn't buy from us, why they don't buy, where do they go to, and why. Here are the ones we have to worry about, here are the ones we don't worry about, here are the ones we could go after."

Waldron says, "I think what we have to do here is think in a little different way. 'Here's how we can take more share from this guy and that guy by offering more consumer value.' So let's be less protective of our share and more aggressive. That stretches a different part of the thinking process than saying, 'We're here now and we're fine,' to 'We're here and we're going to murder them.'"

On that note, the meeting breaks up. Outside his office, Waldron puts it in some perspective for me: "That's typical of about two meetings a month. We have one of the areas of business come in so I can check it out. Either one division or a piece of a division. We had a meeting of gifts and decorative products in the other day. We have thirty-two different business in four divisions, so I say to someone, Preston or somebody else, come in and tell me about the business. Let's talk about Japan. Or let's talk about home health care. This way I can keep an eye on the area's progress. In a couple of months, we'll bring fashions back and hit them again and see how they've carried out this strategy."

Waiting out in the hallway for an elevator to arrive, the Avon Fashions people huddle among themselves, apparently reviewing what has gone on. I overhear one of them say, "And you think he means that?" And then someone else says, "I'm really not sure he meant that."

A lot of time in corporations is spent by minions trying to interpret something that the chairman has said, words that once a meaning is settled on may dictate some not insignificant shift in strategy. The thing is, the words being deciphered may have been said with relatively little thought and mean absolutely nothing at all.

□   □   □

THE PARKER MERIDIEN HOTEL is one of those swank, glittery new towers, perched on Fifty-seventh Street between Sixth and Seventh Avenues, a short stroll from the Avon headquarters. Outside the third-floor banquet room, securities analysts are milling about. A good deal of superficial chatter goes on as the analysts drink wine and mixed cocktails that are being doled out at a rapid-fire clip. Waldron, looking hale and hearty and ready for just about anything, stands dutifully in the center of the chattering throng, sipping a glass of red wine, being nice as pie to everyone who comes up to say hello. Waldron works hard at the reception-line chores, shaking hands, expressing, with lively hand gestures, enthusiastic hopes for his company's future.

After a half hour of this, Waldron leads the handshakers into the banquet room for lunch. The meal is quickly served and quickly eaten. Everyone here is a busy person.

Waldron stands up now, peers at his audience, and then begins to speak slowly. He spells out the new corporation mission of Avon. As he talks, slides flick away on a screen in the center of the far wall. He says that the central focus is "creating shareholder value. I realize that has a 'mom and apple pie' ring to it, but it represents a unifying principle that I want all our managers to firmly have in mind at all times." He says the goal is to "more than double—substantially more than double—the market value of Avon's stock over the next four years." To do that, he goes on, sales will have to increase at an average growth rate of more than 10 percent and earnings per share will have to grow at an annual rate of 14 percent.

Slide follows slide. The audience seems interested but not rapt. The speech is manifestly upbeat, promising that the times of tribulation are ending and the attestation will come in third-quarter results of sales and earnings.

He says, "Despite the high awareness of the Avon name, our beauty image has been eroding, particularly in the United States. Work has already begun to correct that . . . The brochure has been improved. Our powerful new advertising campaign started just last week. We've stopped the deep-deep discounts that hurt image. We have upgraded our jewelry line. We're bringing out some state-of-the-art new products. We've begun a program to better train our representatives, who are the first line of our image."

He goes on to say, "The overall corporate performance is critically dependent on seven businesses. These seven account for two-thirds of the current market value of the company and a large percentage of our planned value improvement.

"The domestic beauty business is far and away the most important—today and tomorrow. It's followed by Foster Home Health Care, Mallinckrodt's Critical Care, Direct Response, Avon Japan, Avon Mexico, and Avon United Kingdom."

Then he says, "Based on these conclusions, you won't be surprised by Avon's strategic direction, which has four major elements.

"The top corporate priority is to turn around the domestic beauty products division.

"The second is to support the other six key businesses. The corporation needs to do everything it can to insure that these businesses come close to reaching their aggressive performance objectives.

"The third is to improve Avon's portfolio by improving the mix of businesses, divesting some and constraining the growth of others while continuing to support the aggressive growth plans of the current high performers and future winners.

"The fourth is to develop new business opportunities, largely building on existing strengths in core consumer and health care businesses. This will involve acquisitions."

The question period is short.

One analyst asks what is being done to prod managers to be concerned about the stock price.

Waldron says, "There are two levers to pull here. There is a changing culture. Avon has been a sales-increase company. The whole culture has been moved to a profitability emphasis. Secondly, we are in the middle of a brand-new compensation program. If targets are met, you get bonuses. Another thing we have at Avon is stock options. I can't think of a person at Avon who is still alive who has ever exercised one. So there's an incentive there."

Someone else asks, "Based on your need for cash, how can you justify keeping the dividend?"

Waldron says, "Well, you've made an erroneous assumption, my good friend. We don't have a need for cash."

An analyst asks, "What about the kiosk test?"

Waldron says, "The kiosk is an electronic telephone booth, I guess, is one way of describing it. What we're trying to find out—we're looking at videotex, we're looking at cable TV—is whether there's a possibility that zero-labor distribution systems may be useful. Florsheim Shoes is one who has tried it, and I think there may be something to it. But let me say this—if Avon was going to rise or fall on kiosks, look out below! I can tell you that Bob Pratt and I went tromping through the Hartford Mall a couple of weekends ago looking for our kiosks and couldn't find them. So there are a lot of bugs to work out."

Then Waldron says, "Let me answer one question that nobody asked. There was a story in *The Wall Street Journal* today [it concerned the perils of doing business in Brazil, and reported that Avon sales in Brazil were off by 20 percent]. I have never been shot at in Rio de Janeiro. Our sales are not down twenty percent. They're not down anything. Our sales are up six percent this year. One of our people did agree to talk to *The Wall Street Journal* and he said three things. There are some danger areas where sales are down twenty percent. But those represent three percent of our total coverage. Our sales are up. So please disregard that."

After the meeting, a *Wall Street Journal* reporter (though not the one who prepared the article on Brazil) corners Waldron for some further interrogation. Waldron takes the opportunity to needle him a bit. "Why don't you write about Brazil?" he says. He pulls out a copy of the *Journal* story and shows it to him, repeats again that it is completely false, hands it to him to take along.

The analysts having dispersed back to their offices, their stomachs full, Waldron now gives his coat check to a young woman reading a Sidney Sheldon novel. He says, "Did I win?"

She says, beaming, "Everyone wins."

Strolling down the street toward the office with Waldron and Jim Preston, I ask Waldron how he thought the meeting went.

"I thought it went just great," he says. "Couldn't have been better."

"Were there any questions that you didn't anticipate?"

"Not a one," he says.

Then he says to Preston, "You know, I thought the questions were a bit less nitty-gritty this time."

Preston says, "Yes, that's true. They were more general."

Waiting at Sixth Avenue for the light to change, Waldron says, "You know, when I was at Heublein, we used to go out drinking with these guys and have a lot of laughs. When I came here, we had an analyst meeting a year ago and I gave the presentation and eighty hands shot up, asking why did you do this, why did you do that. Boom. Boom. Boom. Boy, was it different! These people are combative."

10 □ GETTING THERE

ONE AFTERNOON when I was sitting outside Waldron's office, waiting for him to finish with a
private phone call I was wondering why some individuals become the chief executive and others
don't. Why is it that that man in the next office, who
wears the same dark pin-striped suits and has the
same IQ and works the same eighty-hour weeks, got
the nod and you didn't?

When Waldron signaled for me to come back in,
I said that in his managerial experience he must
have known a goodly number of extraordinarily
skilled executives, people every bit as smart as or
smarter than he is, every bit as charismatic as he is,
every bit as sharpened in the politicking and ma-
neuverings of the corporate suite as he is, but who
never sat in the chief executive officer's chair. What
was the difference? Why you?

"Another way of asking that," he said, "is what
are the qualities I'm glad I don't have or I wouldn't
have made it? One of these would be cynicism. The
opposite of that is to be the world's biggest patsy.
And I would be closer to the world's biggest patsy
than the world's greatest cynic. The guy with little
faith, I think, is immature. Being a cynic somehow
makes someone bigger, seems to be their feeling.
'Wouldn't it be great if U Conn could win the East-
ern Collegiate championship?' 'No way!' says the

99

cynic. That's one way of asserting your power and influence. 'No way!' Let me title this next concept, 'The cause!' The cause being bigger than yourself. Guys who consider the politics or the peripheral aspects of a situation to almost the same degree as the basic issue itself. When I have an issue to look at I want to get straight at that issue—get the absolute best solution on the table and then think about the ramifications. I think too many people start with the ramifications and then worry about the solution. Another quality I would put high on the list to have is a sense of humor. A lot of people can't laugh at themselves. Then the last one is my little plaque. [He gets up and picks up a plaque that sits on the table behind the desk.] Mr. Reagan and I share one thing. This sits on his desk: 'There is no limit to what a man can do and where he can go if he doesn't mind who gets the credit.' You and I know people who would rather turn that around the other way. You know, I have never in forty-six years ever asked for a job or a promotion or a raise—period. My assumption is if I'm offered something I'll either take it or not take it. I never would be comfortable asking for a raise and I'm never comfortable with people asking me for a raise. I think if I do my job properly I'll get rewarded. Another characteristic is candor. Some people can be candid and some can't. I'm always candid. That sometimes gets me in trouble, but I think it's better than not being candid."

Do you have to be the smartest person in the company?

"No," Waldron said. "I think you have to be a little bit street-smart. You have to be smart enough to surround yourself with people who are smarter than their counterparts at the competition. John Cox has to be smarter than his counterpart at Revlon. I think that's more important than me being smarter than my competitive counterparts. You can't be stupid. I don't think I'm stupid. But I'm not super-smart. I don't think I'm the smartest guy in the cosmetics industry. I know I'm not the smartest guy in Avon."

Psychologists who have studied the executive mind say that their research has repeatedly shown that although the best executives almost always do at least moderately well on IQ tests, their ranking on these tests is not the factor that distinguishes those who advance from those who don't. They have a "practical intelligence," as psychologists put it. Recent research suggests that the most successful corporate leaders think in a style notable for its complexities, according to Dr. Siegried Streufert, a behavorial scientist at the Pennsylvaina State University College of Medicine. This so-called cognitive complexity does not depend on IQ, instead, it describes a way of approaching decision making. Executives who think this way plan strategically without being rigidly locked into one course of events. They soak up ample information for decision making without being overwhelmed, and they are able to grasp relationships between rapidly changing events. Executives who do not think in this way see problems in isolation from each other, and often rigidly hold to a single overriding goal.

I asked Waldron how the chief executive has to think.

"I'll say it in two words," he replied. "Bottom line. Creative people contribute to the bottom line. But many creative people don't know how to execute or do strategic planning. The CEO has to be able first to say this is how we do it. He needs the concept as well, but he has the creative people to generate the how-abouts. It's the CEO's job to select the right how-abouts and put them into an executive plan."

Waldron went on to remark that, in order to get ahead, it's important to have a "rabbi," or mentor in the corporation. "I had three good mentors. In Plainville, it was Chuck Skinner, a maverick, really didn't give a damn what he said to anybody, yet never let me get into trouble while still giving me great freedom. Number two was Bob Wilson, eventually chairman and president of Memorex and bailed them out. Tough, no-nonsense, not popular vice-president at GE. He was considered to be unnecessarily tough. I thought he was, too. He was a nonfun guy to work for. But he was very bright. Almost everything he said was very bright and I learned an awful lot from Bob Wilson. Number three was Dave Dance, vice-chairman eventually of GE. I worked for him in Louisville, counselled with him before I went to Heublein. What did I learn from Dance? I guess more than anything, don't take yourself too seriously, get the job done, if you run into a stone wall step aside and move forward again. He was the radar who would help me through the minefield. You need people to help you stay out of trouble, because there are others who will try to get you into trouble."

I said that there was another ingredient that seemed to be important, and that was the matter of serendipity. It seemed to me that it wasn't enough, certainly it wasn't enough in a giant corporation, to simply have all the skills that it takes, but that it was necessary to have had the chance to display one's mettle. Many executives have reminisced about how they were dumped into some miserable situation, put in charge of a dog of a subsidiary, and then managed to pep it up. They were heroes and got promoted up the ranks.

Waldron nodded his head. He said that that was part of it, but that it isn't necessarily true that you have to work some miracle. Sometimes it is enough to have peculiar things happen to you that draw the attention of the top brass.

"It's getting into a position to be noticed," he said. "You know, when I was an engineering trainee right at the start at GE, there were thousands of us. There were all these heads out there and any time a better job came along you needed one of those heads. How did you pick the head? All you needed was one head sticking out a little taller than the others. It didn't have to be way taller, but just a little. The trick was to get your head up a little higher. I'll mention two screwy examples that got me the attention to prove myself. At the end of the sales-training session in Schenectady, I had a GE course called 'Effective Presentation of Business Ideas.' The fifteen best speakers in the course would get up at the end and each give a two-minute speech. You were given a subject as you walked to the podium and then you had to do an extemporaneous talk. I was one of those chosen. There's a technique we learned in giving a speech known as the 'ho-hum crasher.' When a speaker is introduced and walks to the podium, the audience is in a ho-hum mood. The first thing you have to do is crash through that ho-humness. So you introduce a joke or a long silence or the profound statement. Well, as I was walking to the podium to give my speech, I tripped. I didn't plan to trip. I just tripped. Everyone thought my tripping was an intentional part of my speech and was that attention-getter. I didn't win the competition, but I got honorable mention. That had something to do, I believe, with my going on to a better job in Lynn, Massachusetts, a couple of years later.

"The other time was when the president of GE came to Schenectady. Everyone was all excited. The whole town was fixed up and decorated. Part of the program was that five upcoming guys, and I was one of them, were to give minute-and-a-half speeches for him. My subject was cost reduction. We had to write our speeches and then get the approval of the boss and then the speeches were all bound in a manila binder. The idea was you did your speech and when you finished you turned the page so that the next guy would have his speech all ready for him when he got to the podium. We practiced that and practiced that—it was stupid as hell. I was number three in the order. The big day came and the first guy did his speech and turned the page. Number two went up there, gave his speech, closed the binder, and walked off with it. I went up there and I couldn't remember a word of what I was supposed to say. So I yelled, 'Hey, Charlie, bring back the book.' The president of GE, I was told later, said that the only thing he could remember of the trip was that poor bastard who yelled, 'Bring back the book, Charlie.' It's pure bullshit, lucky things like that that can matter."

□   □   □

IT IS FOUR O'CLOCK on a warm mid-April afternoon and Waldron, stationed behind his desk, looks a little glum. The Thursday numbers depicting the domestic beauty situation are in. They're still bad. The first three months of the year have come and gone and the number of representatives keeps dwindling. Minus 16 percent. Minus 18 percent. Minus 20 percent. They are heading to never-never land.

Preston has been offering soothing replies. But

there's been no hard evidence of a turnaround. Comforting words are a dime a dozen; one could go on listening to them forever. There is a sense of time running out, backs against the wall.

His fog thickening, Waldron calls Preston into his office, the door is shut, and it is decided that in late April Preston will fly to Vienna and attend the Circle of Excellence celebration going on there. The district managers who perform the best in the last year get a fancy trip to Europe and are installed in the Circle of Excellence. It should be an ideal opportunity to take the pulse of the organization. Talk to the people there, Waldron tells Preston. See if you can ferret out what's happening, why this thing isn't turning. Something, quite clearly, is very wrong. "We ain't got forever," Waldron says. "Time's becoming our enemy."

11 □ GOING TO THE COUNTRY

"**B**OY, IS that rain or bugs on the windshield?" Waldron asks.

"Bugs," the driver says.

"You sure hit enough of them."

"I'm a good shot."

Waldron releases one of his hearty laughs.

Waldron and I are heading out, in a cozy, chauffeured London Towncar, to Connecticut early this Friday afternoon in April. He has an appointment for his yearly physical with his doctor in Hartford, then he will be spending the weekend at a home he owns in Farmington. I have been invited along to get a feel for how he unwinds and to chat with his wife. Waldron has told me that he really relaxes on his days off—but not completely; the engines of Avon must be kept running. He's always in touch with the office. He always takes some work with him in his briefcase. Among the contents, he tells me with a weak smile, are the latest beauty division numbers, which he wants to study a little deeper.

Just about everyone else in New York seems to be fleeing the city and to be leaving at precisely the same time as we are. Waldron shakes his head as a cab rockets through a red light at Sixty-first Street, barely avoiding getting decimated by the onrushing river of traffic.

"Boy, look at that cat," Waldron says.

Waldron tells me about a water problem he's been having at his house. It seems that it was recently discovered that for eight years, since the house was built, a line from the underground oil tank had been leaking oil through a small crack. As a result, both of the wells for the house have become contaminated. While a new well is being drilled, the Waldrons have been getting their water from a water truck. So he says not to be surprised by the large truck I'll see parked outside.

Waldron has made millions of dollars in his business career and he has held on to a large part of his earnings. Besides the Trump Plaza apartment he lives in in the city and his home in Farmington, he owns seven other residences. He has two condominiums in Florida that he bought for investment purposes; one of them is rented to his sister-in-law. He owns two other condominiums in Sugarbush, Vermont, which he rents out. Then he has a house in Stratton, Vermont, which he uses for ski weekends during the winter, as well as a condominium in Stratford that he rents. Finally, he owns a one-bedroom apartment in Manhattan in the Savoy, a building across the street from Trump Plaza.

Waldron describes himself as conservative with his personal investments. Besides real estate and a great deal of life insurance, most of his money is in the stock market. He has a personal adviser at Fiduciary Trust who does the selections, though Waldron will make a pick every so often. Once a month they chat on the phone and once every three months Waldron gets a report on how he's doing. Twice a year, they sit down to review strategy. "I'll bet I don't spend an hour a month in studying or analyzing my personal investments," Waldron says. "I don't have the time."

Remarking on his strategy, he says, "I want to be aggressive. I don't mind ending up the year with no profit. I much prefer ending up the year with no loss. But my objective is to end up the year making a lot of money. Mostly, I'm the one who puts me in the risky stocks. I forced him to buy a lot of MCI just before it fell apart. I told him to buy Life-Line Systems—down."

All of the Avon officers also get free financial advice and tax-preparation services from a company called Ayco, which is owned by American Express. "The man who does me knows me and Evelyn and my daughter intimately," Waldron says. "He has led me in and out of tax shelters that aren't worth a damn. But he's given me advice on how to protect my future and Evelyn's and my daughter's. I want complete protection in case I'm hit by a truck. And I have that now."

Waldron, who has taken off his jacket, leans forward and addresses the driver: "Could you turn down that air conditioner? It's freezing back here."

Once we escape the Manhattan crush and start moving, Waldron talks about security. Chief executives have their salaries and benefits published in proxy statements and, if the numbers have enough zeroes on the end, in the newspapers. Their pay makes them logical targets for extortionists, kidnappers, and the other shadowy crazies who lurk in the world. Besides their personal resources, of course, they are vital links in corporations with seemingly bottomless kitties. Kidnapped, they would be worth a pretty sum. Chief executives, moreover, make enemies. Someone has been fired; someone thinks that one of their company's products caused their nephew's ears to fall off. There are multiple reasons for a chief executive of any prominent company to think a little more than most about his own safety.

"Each officer at Avon has a home alarm system that the company puts in," Waldron says. "I don't want any of them to be hurt or to worry about getting home late at night and worry about the security of their family. Every CEO is taught certain lessons of how to help insure one's own safety—like don't develop a pattern. Take different routes when you walk to work. Often I'll come out of my apartment and go down Sixty-first Street. Once in a while, I'll peel over to Third Avenue and go down Fifty-ninth. Some days I'll leave the building on the Fifty-seventh Street side; other times, I'll go out on Fifty-eighth. When you go to church on Sunday, don't always leave at five to ten. Go different ways. If you have two cars, use them. I have a listed phone number in Farmington, but not my address. I encourage my daughter not to use her maiden name. Our offices are regularly swept for bugs. I have my apartment swept on a less frequent basis. I'm careful about foreign travel. Through the State Department, we monitor what's going on in foreign countries. The world is getting tough out there. Some companies wouldn't allow this, riding in a rented car like this. The CEO has to have a company car. Has to have communications with the office. Has to have an emergency button to alert home base to big trouble. I have an emergency button at the house, and I carry it around with me when I'm in the woods picking up sticks. The button sort of looks like a beeper. I always sleep with it next to the bed. Evelyn has two—one is kept in a secret place in the kitchen and the other is in the bedroom. Also, Evelyn and I have a password that only we know. So if she were to call me and there was a guy with a gun at her head and she says, 'Hey, honey, meet me at the movies,' she can slip in that word and it tells me that she's under duress. We've rehearsed it together face to face, but we've never had to use it."

The most serious threat Waldron has faced was in the middle 1970's, when he was running Heublein. An extortionist said that he was putting poison into bottles of Smirnoff vodka and A-1 steak sauce and he wouldn't stop until two and a half million dollars was deposited in a Mexican bank. He also posed threats against four or five other companies. He somehow managed to find out that the CEO of one of the companies was having a backyard party for his twins on a given day and he threatened to mine the yard. He told Waldron that he was going to mail him a letter—he would never know which one it was—and when he opened it bacteria would be discharged into the air. The FBI was called in. For six months, they staked out Waldron's office. All of his mail was opened by them first; all packages were X-rayed to insure that they weren't bombs. The Waldrons couldn't even open their own Christmas cards themselves. Finally, before he carried out any of his threats, the man was caught; he turned out to be a crazed individual from Denver. The episode has left its mark on Waldron. "I'm still careful today with the mail," he says. "When a package arrives at the apartment or the house, I look at it carefully. If it's a package with clothing, we make sure that it feels like a package with clothing and not a package with five or six hand grenades."

On another occasion about five years ago, the Waldrons had come back from an out-of-town trip on a Friday night. They called Waldron's daughter and son-in-law and suggested that they have dinner together at a local restaurant. No sooner did they sit down than the waiter came over and said there was a call for Waldron. The caller was a woman who had been in and out of several mental institutions and who had been making threatening calls to him at work, insisting that he hire her. He couldn't imagine how she knew where he would be eating. Waldron at once called the police and was given an escort home. Heublein's security department eventually got a picture of the woman and gave it to Mrs. Waldron to keep at home, so that if the doorbell rang and it was the woman in the picture, she wouldn't let her in. The woman, after a while, gave up. Waldron never heard from her again.

□   □   □

HARTFORD, CHOKED WITH the tail end of rush-hour traffic, looms. The driver leaves Waldron off at the doctor's office, then takes me to the house, where Mrs. Waldron is waiting. His orders then are to backtrack and retrieve Waldron.

The driveway cuts through dense woods, rises gently over a mound, and then plunges into a clearing where the house stands overlooking the Farmington River valley.

Mrs. Waldron greets me at the door and shows me my room, in the downstairs corner of the house. The house is on two levels and is quite spacious. There are rooms just about everywhere, and places to sit everywhere. The interior is exquisitely done up in predominantly modern furniture. It radiates class and radiates money. In the den, I notice there's a big picture of George Burns. (When I asked Waldron once who his heroes were, he replied, "Lou Gehrig, Henry the K Kissinger, and my all-time favorite, George Burns." Why Burns? "I just think he has so much talent. He never lets age bother him. He loves the women. He smokes cigars.") Mrs. Waldron apologizes, saying that she's almost done decorating the place, though to my eye it seems perfect. She tells me that Waldron thought it was done being decorated the day they moved in.

Mrs. Waldron makes some coffee and we talk in the breakfast nook adjacent to the kitchen, interrupted frequently by the unauthorized appearance of Yogi, the Waldrons' black German shepherd. He has been given stern instructions to stay in the laundry room. He's shedding heavily. To keep him at bay, Mrs. Waldron has constructed a blockade across the door consisting of a laundry basket. Yogi, however, has not found the blockade much of a deterrent.

Evelyn Rumstay grew up in the small town of Burling, Connecticut, about ten miles from Farmington. Her parents were divorced when she was quite young, and she has no recollection of her father. Her mother worked in the production department of a local company to support her and her brother and sister. Evelyn got married impetuously when she was nineteen, then divorced two years later. She decided she wanted to be an executive secretary, and eventually found a job at Heublein. After a while, she became the brand manager for Snappy Tom, a tomato cocktail. She was nominated as a "token woman" to serve on the Greater Hartford Arts Council. Soon afterward, Waldron became the head of the council.

Waldron, at the time, was slowly rebounding from a personal tragedy. On the Fourth of July, 1974, Hicks and Peg Waldron moved into a home in West Hartford, the seventeenth change of address for them. They couldn't have been happier. The house was beautiful, the commute to work for Waldron was shorter than from Darien, where they had been living.

Three days later, Waldron was in Louisville on a

business trip to Kentucky Fried Chicken when he got a telephone call from Peg. She hadn't been feeling well and had been in to see the family doctor; she said he thought there might be something seriously wrong. Waldron returned home. Peg was diagnosed as having cancer of the lining of the stomach. She was operated on and given nine months to live. Nine months later (in April 1975), right on schedule, she died.

("After twenty-nine years and eleven months of marriage, I was absolutely devastated," Waldron had told me. "She went downhill, downhill, downhill. I spent more of my time at home and wasn't giving my all to the business. But I picked up the pieces of my life. I became very close to my son, Ben. He moved back into the house and we would hit the bars at night together. In July, I met Evelyn Rumstay.")

Mrs. Waldron tells me how that first encounter went: "One day there was a meeting that we were both at. It was five o'clock. I had a date that night. Hicks was so pathetic. He was so lonely. You could see he had been devastated by the loss of his wife. Another person there said let's have drinks with Hicks. Then the other guy left. I didn't want to be alone with him, and I had a date, and so I said, if you'd like to, you can join me and my date for dinner, thinking he wouldn't. He said, oh no, he couldn't. Well, I said, if you want to have a drink with me, and he said all right, I'll have a drink. And so he came over to my apartment and we had a drink and my date arrived and we were sitting there and I said, well, if you'd like to you can join us for dinner and he said, sure. It was just so pathetic. I didn't hear from him for a while and then he called me up one Friday night and we started going out."

While she dated Waldron, she also went out with

the man she was seeing that first night. He lives in
Farmington now and all three of them are quite
good friends. He lives with his mother and has
never married. Sometimes, they go on vacations together.

By Christmas of 1975, less than six months after
they met, Waldron and Rumstay decided to get married and were wed the following May.

Tragedy, though, wasn't quite done with Hicks
Waldron. On December 11, 1976, at two-thirty in
the morning, Waldron got a phone call that he says
he will never get over. It was from the police. His
teenage son had been killed in an automobile acci-
dent. "And if Evelyn hadn't been there, I would
have been dead—out of it." Afterward, the two of
them went down to Marco Island, off the coast of
Florida, and rented a villa for a week. "We did
nothing. Just talked about it a lot. Realism is what
you miss. You just don't believe that your son—who
was with you just the day before—is dead. It's so
final. We had discussions about heaven and who's
in control. Without discussions like that, I think you
go out of your mind."

□   □   □

I ASK MRS. WALDRON about the life of a CEO's wife,
and she says, "It's a wonderful life in many ways.
We can afford to do all the things we like to do. But,
on the other hand, we don't have the time to do all
the things."

When I inquire about how she spends her day,
she replies, "My priority is Hicks, and has to be, I
feel. It's difficult when you're married to someone
who has a schedule like Hicks to make a marriage
work. I've often thought of going back to work—
I've threatened Hicks with that—but when he trav-

els I couldn't be with him, and if there's a function he'd want me to go and I wouldn't be able to. Hicks is not the sort who thinks I have to be on a committee or involved in something because it would be good for Avon. He's never demanded this. My role is not really a difficult one. He's very good at doing a minimal amount of business entertaining. I love to entertain, but most of it is friends. I go all the time to functions. I don't have to go, but he would prefer me to go. If I had my druthers, though, I wouldn't go. They're not fun."

The two of them share identical hobbies. They go scuba diving together (Waldron is the better diver), ski together in Vermont (she's an intermediate, he's an advanced intermediate), and play golf occasionally at the Hartford Golf Club (when playing regularly, both hold handicaps of around sixteen, though Mrs. Waldron suggests that her husband's is dishonest). Waldron likes to look at art, but he has failed to gain much appreciation for it. As Mrs. Waldron tells me, "He likes lighthouses. He would put paintings of lighthouses throughout the house. I wish he didn't like lighthouses."

Slam. It is Waldron, arriving home from the doctor's. He's in a chipper mood. He gives his wife a kiss, and she asks him, "What did he say?"

"He says I should hire a cook," Waldron says. "He says I'm seven or eight pounds overweight. I said Evelyn won't cook in New York. So he said, well, you can afford to hire a cook."

Mrs. Waldron says to me, "That's one of the advantages of being a CEO. You can afford to hire a cook."

"I told him I couldn't wait to get home to tell Evelyn," Waldron says.

"Very funny," Mrs. Waldron says. "Real funny."

The subject of eating at home is apparently a sore

point. Waldron had told me that, when they're in New York and don't have a business dinner, they can usually be found at Jacqueline's Restaurant and Champagne Bar, which is a few strides down the block from their apartment. Waldron likes to say that Jacqueline's is their kitchen.

Mrs. Waldron wants Waldron to come out to the back garden to see the daffodils, which have just bloomed.

"Okay," he says, "Take Yogi too?"

"Yes, Yogi too," Mrs. Waldron says.

Yogi frolics on the grass as we inspect the daffodils, which look just splendid. There is a wild whistling of birds. Some rain begins to patter down, and so we go back inside for a predinner drink.

"I've got two things to show you," Waldron says to his wife once we're settled in the house. "First there's this, which I cut out for Maureen." He shows her a cartoon from the *New Yorker*, which reads, "Maureen was built for the long haul."

"This I got from the nurses," he says, and he unfolds a sheet of paper that he gives to Mrs. Waldron. It is a rather obscene cartoon about chickens that she doesn't think is at all funny.

Waldron and I have a glass of red wine. Mrs. Waldron has a spritzer. The cocktail napkins say, "A Woman's Place is on the Golf Course." Waldron tells me that his wife is a terrific piano player and then insists that she play for me later. She begs off, saying all of her music is in New York. He says, "Oh, come on, I'll find some around here." She says, no, she hates to play for people: "I only like to play when I'm depressed."

"We can arrange that," Waldron says.

Yogi, who had been banished back to his room, has again escaped and trots in, making a racket.

"You're causing a lot of problems," Mrs. Waldron scolds him. "You're going back."

"That's the way it goes, Yog," Waldron says, stroking the dog's head. "You win some and you lose some."

"So nothing else exciting?" Mrs. Waldron says.

"No," Waldron says. "The only exciting thing that happened to me today is I couldn't have any lunch."

"Oh, the doctor said to get a cook and a Barcalounger," Waldron says. He explains that the doctor told him that by sitting upright a lot, as Waldron inevitably does, the circulation is cut off below the waist, and so a Barcalounger would be healthier for him to sit in. Waldron says he told the doctor that he tries to sit with his feet up as much as possible, but he was still adamant about the Barcalounger.

Mrs. Waldron does a mild double take and says, "If you get one for work, you'll fall asleep." She looks at me and says, "He can fall asleep in a minute anywhere."

She laughs and then says to Waldron, "I can just see you in a Barcalounger. You'll fall asleep."

Waldron glances at his wife and says, "Well, I guess we should tell him about our great business fiasco." Then he directs my attention to two special heating panels on the ceiling of the room, near the sliding glass doors. They run on electricity, he says, and are intended for weekend homes to provide instant heat while the oil burner is getting up to speed. Waldron says that he was so impressed by the presentation of the company that he installed the panels in the rental property he owns in Sugarbush. The first couple that rented the place moved out because they were so cold. The company told Waldron, no problem, put in a few more panels. His electric bill, he says, soared to something like $750 a month, at least double what oil heat would have cost him. The panels here don't work either, he says.

Then Mrs. Waldron tells about some rather peculiar happenings at the house they lived in before moving here. "There was a terrible odor that developed in the basement," she says. "I had everyone in and they couldn't find what it was. It was like *The Amityville Horror*. So we decided we were moving out, whether this house was done or not. Then the guy who bought it lost his job just before the sale and tried to back out, though he didn't. He left after a year and then the next buyer had a triple-bypass operation soon afterward and eventually died."

Waldron says, "It was rats."

"I had the exterminators in," Mrs. Waldron says. "They'd know rats. It wasn't rats. Something weird was going on in that house."

I mention that I wholeheartedly believe in unexplained forces and had once written about a parapsychologist, a professional ghost hunter, who it seemed to me had, in fact, come across mysterious forces that defied logical explanation.

Mrs. Waldron puckers her mouth and nods. "I know. Those things really do happen. Maybe that person who previously owned the house was murdered by his wife and is unhappily dead."

"Honey," Waldron says, "most people are unhappily dead."

We sit around and talk for a while more, and then Waldron sees that it is edging toward seven-thirty and he says, "Let's eat." Waldron owns two cars, a dark blue Lincoln and a white Mazda. We climb into the Lincoln, which is so big that, in less capable hands, it would certainly take some trees with it as it descended the driveway.

As we cruise along, Mrs. Waldron says, "So are we going to hire a cook?"

Waldron says, "I'm going to teach you where the stove is. It's the thing with the flames shooting up."

Mrs. Waldron says, "Well, what we agreed is, I'll cook every other night when we're home. But we're never home."

Waldron tells her that he had a good meal last night, while she was already out in Connecticut, at a Chinese restaurant on the West Side. Then he took a leisurely stroll home along the outskirts of Central Park.

Mrs. Waldron arches her eyebrows and says, "Honey, you know you shouldn't do that at that hour. It's really dangerous."

"It was all right," Waldron says. "Everyone thought I was a mugger."

We drive to a nearby restaurant called The Black Olive. It is one of the Waldrons' favorite spots. They inevitably end up there when they are in Connecticut. Once we get out of the car, the headlamps remain on, since the Lincoln is outfitted with a device that delays shutting off the lights, to help the passengers get indoors in a dark area. Waldron, however, waits in front of the car to make sure the lights do in fact go out. "They're supposed to go out in ten seconds," he says. "I guess it defeats the idea of the thing if you wait."

The Black Olive is nothing much—basically a pleasant, simple Italian place encased in a small shopping mall. It has a smoky bar when you come in and then an adjacent dining room. The place is about half full. Most of the diners are dressed in various states of dishabille.

After we sit down, the owner comes over to greet the Waldrons. He has obviously seen a lot of them. He suggests some wine possibilities, which Waldron mulls over before issuing his decision.

Once he has left, Waldron remarks that just about every wine on the restaurant's list is a Heublein product. The first time he dined here, he says, there weren't any Heublein wines. He made a note to himself, and the following week he called in the distributor and dressed him down. How could he allow a restaurant right in Heublein's backyard to not stock the brand?

Waldron says, "A couple of times, I went to restaurants and there was no Heublein wine and so I got up and left. We said the hell with it. Why should we give the business to the competition. In consumer products, the 'call' is very important. I would never order anything but Heublein wine. If I ever found an employee drinking anything but Smirnoff vodka or Heublein wine, they'd be fired. First of all, it's the 'call'. If you ask for a product, then the place has to stock it. So it's not only product loyalty, it's promotion."

When he was running things, he says, the policy at Heublein was that if an employee went to a bar and wanted a vodka drink and didn't specify Smirnoff, he would be slapped with a fifty-cent fine.

Waldron says that even after he's moved on he remains loyal to companies he's worked at. He remarks that the Farmington house, for instance, is equipped with GE appliances.

"Yeah," Mrs. Waldron says. "We had major problems. The door fell off the refrigerator. I'd say, 'Why did you buy these junky products?' "

"Do you use Avon cosmetics?" I ask Mrs. Waldron.

"Oh yes," she says. "Hicks made me throw away all my old cosmetics and replace them with Avon."

Then, when he excuses himself to use the restroom, she confides that she does in fact keep a secret drawer of several of her old favorites that she uses sometimes for special occasions.

The waiter arrives for our order. Mrs. Waldron says that Waldron's favorite dish is spaghetti and meatballs, though here he always orders linguine and meatballs. His wife has the same.

When the food is served, Waldron falls to with a hearty appetite.

We talk a bit about how Avon fell on hard times and whether there are enough signs to alert a CEO to trouble before it gets dire. Can you just walk in one day and the wheels come off?

Waldron says that the financial numbers are the warning and that, like a bloodhound, a good CEO should be able to sniff trouble. A company shouldn't suffer a couple of years of down earnings before action is taken.

Then he says that he thinks David Mitchell, his predecessor, is a "great CEO," because he owned up to the fact that he had no more ideas and knew his company was in trouble and so he went to the outside and hired a replacement for himself. A lesser CEO, Waldron says, would have hung on to the spoils of the job. He says there are various ways you can be creative with the numbers without doing anything illegal, to keep things looking good until you retire. "You change the way you depreciate things," Waldron says; "you cut back on advertising. There are a lot of gimmicks to postpone the inevitable." But Mitchell, he says, was great because he didn't do that.

I write all that down, though it occurs to me that a great chief executive would never have run out of ideas in the first place and have had to replace himself.

Waldron cleans his plate, but Mrs. Waldron can't polish off all of her linguine. When the waiter comes, she asks to take the rest home in a doggie bag.

When we get back to the house, Waldron says, "How about a game of pool before we turn in?"

Waldron and I play some eight-ball. The chief executive is at best a fair pool player, though next to me he is Minnesota Fats. Nevertheless, fate shines on the underdog and I unceremoniously win when he sends the eight ball into the pocket after having built up a seemingly insurmountable lead. Then Mrs. Waldron joins us for some "cutthroat," a game in which a player picks either the five lowest, five middle, or five highest balls as his own. The winner is whoever has balls left on the table. Even playing pool, Waldron is emphatically the boss. He notices that the closet doors don't close properly, and he says, "Evelyn, you've got to get your doors fixed." Every shot his wife lines up, he peruses carefully, frowns on those he deems unmakable. Easy shots he refers to as "no-brainers." Unlike at the office, though, where his say is final, Mrs. Waldron frequently overrules him and attempts improbable shots anyway, occasionally making them.

His wife, after a slow start, turns sizzling hot and captures the first game. The second is closely contested, but Waldron squeaks out a victory. Each of us has now won one game, so Waldron suggests a final decisive contest. He creams us.

Before turning in, Waldron meanders into the adjoining den and clicks on the Panasonic big-screen TV, playing with the channels until the end of an old Jack Benny rerun comes on. Benny is shopping in a supermarket. He stops at the butcher and asks for a pound of sausage. The butcher weighs a string of sausages and says that it's 1.3 pounds. No, no, Benny says, he wants only one pound. All right, the butcher says, and he bites off a chunk out of one of the sausages, reweighs it and says there's your pound. Benny, thinking he will fix him for that indelicacy, then asks for a pound of raw liver. The butcher weights a hunk of raw liver and says, 1.4 pounds. "I said exactly one pound," Benny says. "Okay," the butcher says, and turning toward the back room calls out, "Here Fido, here Fido."

Waldron lets out a rollicking laugh.

□ □ □

SATURDAY STARTS EARLY for Waldron. He has agreed to put in an appearance at a breakfast meeting of the Conference of Black Mayors of the World, since part of his job is to massage as many constituencies as possible and this constituency is at least geographically convenient, since the breakfast is being held at the Hilton in Hartford. Avon has also chipped in twenty-five hundred dollars to be identified as a sponsor of the breakfast. The timing is something else again. The breakfast starts at seven-thirty.

Seven-ten, and Waldron and I are in his big Lincoln, heading for Hartford. The roads are empty.

I ask Waldron why he's doing this when he could be sleeping?

"We as a company have a huge stake in the black community and the cities," he says. "So this presented an opportunity. Plus, if there is a legislative issue that we might want to support, the black mayors could be an ally."

I asked Waldron how often he lobbied legislators.

"Well, you know, I once asked Reg Jones at GE

how many days a month he spent in Washington. He said, 'It isn't a question of how many days a month, it's a question of how many days a week.' He would spend about a day a week there. I've spent none in the last year and a half. Frankly, I'm too low. I think the upcoming tax reform bill will have some things we'll want to take a strong stand on. Countervailing measures with foreign markets is something to watch. At Avon, we really have only a few issues—the FDA occasionally with color agents and such things. But we haven't established contacts in Washington. We do have a pretty good relationship with the mayor of New York. The mayor used to give away a key to the city to visiting dignitaries. So last year Avon presented him with thousands of little lapel buttons to give out. They're Big Apple buttons with greetings from the mayor on one side. The other side says, 'Avon, the creator of the most beautiful women in New York,' and it's signed by me."

Waldron deftly squeezes his car into a tight spot in the Hilton garage. We stroll through the lobby. Deserted.

"Look at that," Waldron says. "Nobody gives a shit that we're here."

When we get to the room where the breakfast is being held, Waldron marches up to a woman who seems to be in charge and says, "Hi, I'm Hicks Waldron. I'm the chairman of Avon Products. We're sponsoring this breakfast."

"Yes, just a minute," the woman says. "I'll see."

She returns in a few minutes and says, "What company did you say you were with?"

"Avon," Waldron says.

Tony Carter, a young member of Avon's public relations staff, spies Waldron and hurries over. He gives the boss a quick briefing. He says that last year Avon contributed five thousand dollars to the black mayors. This year, they asked for ten thousand. Avon said no. "This may come up for discussion," Carter says. "Now, you're supposed to offer some greetings. It can be short. We thought you might say something like, 'These are mostly mayors of small towns and Avon is doing a similar thing, trying to improve life in small towns.'"

"Right," Waldron says.

"So you say something short like that," Carter says.

"Right," Waldron says. "Now a very important question: Are there going to be twenty-one speeches, as the memo I got said?"

"There could be more," Carter says. "Now, I don't know if you want to sit through twenty-one speeches."

"Well, I know," Waldron says. "I sure as hell don't."

"Well, whatever you want," Carter says. "We can get you out."

"I hate like hell to leave an empty seat," Waldron says. "I don't want to do anything that would embarrass Avon."

"We told them that your schedule is very tight," Carter says. "Someone went to this last year in St. Louis and it went till almost noon."

"Without a break?" Waldron asks.

"Yeah," Carter says.

"I don't see how even mayors can go four hours without a break," Waldron says.

"Well," Carter says. "Some of them are Baptist ministers."

Johnny Ford, the mayor of Tuskegee, Alabama, and the president of the group, now comes over and greets Waldron. Three photographers trail him and snap a bunch of pictures of the two men.

Ford tells Waldron how glad he is that he was able to come, then he says, "You know, Avon gave the first five thousand dollars seed money last year."

"Yes," Waldron says, "and I understand we couldn't do the same this year, but we may revisit that issue."

Waldron then asks Ford, "What is the most important thing that the organization has achieved?"

Ford says, "Well, the collective trying to make the world better."

The breakfast starts at seven-fifty with some opening remarks, a prayer, and then a series of speeches. Waldron sits on the dais, his arms folded, looking monumentally bored. For some reason, a Chinese delegation is also in attendance at the breakfast and has been seated at the dais.

There is a pause in the speech giving for Rhonda Lee Love and the Love Sisters to perform some musical selections.

Speech after speech.

After about a dozen speeches, Waldron's turn comes. He is introduced as "Hicks Wallburn."

Waldron tells the audience that he's greatly impressed by the Chinese delegation and says he thinks of all the women there who could use Avon products. Then he says that Avon does best in the small cities of the country and that the company has a mission similar to that of the black mayors, trying to improve life in the small cities.

More speeches. More songs from Rhonda Lee Love and the Love Sisters. They sing, "We Are the World." The audience is asked to stand and join hands and sing along. The breakfast has by now taken on the feeling of a revival meeting.

It seems to me that there is something to make of Waldron being here, but I am unsure of what it is.

There he is, the only white man on a dais of fifteen black men and five Chinese. He is holding hands with them and, even though not exactly gifted with the best voice there, is singing, "We Are the World."

Finally, Johnny Ford gives the keynote address. He talks about uniting and communications and the importance of mayors. He says that there are more mayors in the world than any other type of elected official. He is a magnetic speaker. As he talks, there is soft singing by the Love Sisters in the background. People shout out from the audience: "Yeah, tell 'em, Johnny"; "That's right, Johnny"; "Yessir, now you're rolling, Johnny."

At nearly eleven, everyone stands again for one more rousing rendition of "We Are the World," and the breakfast finally breaks in time for people to start giving some serious thought to lunch.

Waldron finds me and we speed out of the room as if we were wanted criminals. "That Johnny Ford is some speaker, isn't he?" he says. "I told Johnny that I wanted him to lead our annual meeting."

12 □ NUMBERS WILL ALWAYS GET YOU

"**I** HAVE THE advantage of just having read this this morning, so it's a fresh perspective," Waldron says, sinking into a chair. He's talking about the draft of the press release that Avon will be issuing a week hence, in late April, reporting the company's first-quarter earnings.

Jules Zimmerman is in the room, as are John Cox, Margro Long, and a couple of others.

Every three months, to judge by the zeal of those working on it, a project goes on that seems to be on the order of a NASA moon mission. Dozens of men labor over spreadsheets and computer printouts, enough paper to start a paper mill. The goal is a single orderly sheet of numbers, among which one figure will loom above all others. It will define, starkly, the fruits of the labor of Avon's thirty-eight thousand employees. This is the bottom line, the net income figure, or profit, that Avon and every other company work to fashion.

Earnings releases are a corporation's report card; it is just as accurate to say that they are a chief executive's report card. Poor earnings for more than a few years, and a CEO will find himself an ex-CEO. In the unlikely event he ever forgets that, the CEO of Pillsbury keeps a sign on the wall of his office that says, "Bad numbers will get you every time." Also, CEOs run into each other all the time.

They read the agate in the newspapers the way horseplayers read race results. They know whose numbers are up, whose are down. When I asked Waldron about how the earnings affected his moods after Avon had reported a tough quarter, he said, "When someone says, 'How's business?' and you just turned in a quarter that's up twenty percent and the stock is up and your sister-in-law from Florida just called and said, 'Gee, I'm happy, because I just bought eleven shares of your stock,' I would feel much better about life in general than I would as things are now at Avon. This morning at the CIGNA board meeting, someone asked me, 'How's business?' and I caught myself and said, well, our health care is booming and Mallinckrodt is doing well, but, gee, our Avon beauty business is having trouble. I found myself giving a long answer that was almost an excuse or a rationalization. Now, I'm told that I'm expert at not reflecting my moods outside. But we all have pride in what we do. And I take pride in my work and my work is measured in part by earnings per share—that bottom right-hand corner. So the numbers are on your mind."

The latest news is not particularly wonderful, though at the same time it's not wretched. Earnings have fallen by 17 percent from the first quarter of last year to $23.1 million, or 29 cents a share. Avon, though, had been budgeting a shortfall, because of continued weakness in the domestic beauty business. The budgeted figure was 33 cents a share, compared with last year's 35 cents. Still, the company hopes to pick up steam and compensate for the first quarter later in the year.

Waldron has some quibbles with the two-page release. "I had to read this twice," he says, "to realize that it was U.S. only that was down and not the whole beauty products division. One way to solve that is capitalize 'Beauty Products' in the first paragraph and decapitalize it in the second. I read it stone cold and I had to go over it again before I was clear on what we were saying. The other thing, Jules, didn't we budget the first quarter to be down?"

"Yes, we did," Zimmerman says.

"Then we ought to say here somewhere that we expect to make up for the first quarter later in the year. Because I think it's important to announce to the world that we didn't budget a big increase and then had a 17 percent decrease."

Cox says, "I think that's what we're trying to do in the second graph, where we say 'we expected . . .' "

"Yeah," Waldron interrupts, "but expected isn't the same as budgeted. We could have added up the numbers yesterday and it was down and so we expected it. I don't know. How do you others feel?"

Zimmerman says, "I think you may be overemphasizing it. You said it several times in your speeches."

"Uh-huh," Waldron says. "Okay."

Then he looks at Long and asks, "What do you think the reaction is going to be to the twenty-nine cents, Margro?"

"I don't think there will be much reaction," she says. "The estimates on the Street have been between twenty-five and thirty cents. So this is at the upper end."

Waldron skims over the release again and comes to a sentence that notes that the first quarter usually produces 15 percent of the company's annual earnings. "Didn't I say in my last speech that it was 12 percent?"

One of the group says, "We took a long-term look and it seems that 15 percent is right."

"Well, we should be consistent."

"Why don't we say less than 15 percent?" Cox suggests.

"That's good," Waldron says.

Then Waldron says, "I haven't seen the word 'dividend' once in any of this."

"We're leaving that for you to talk about at the annual meeting," Zimmerman says.

"Well, the thing is, we're a yield stock," Waldron says. "The shareholders really don't give a damn about anything we tell them. All they want to know is am I going to get my two dollars a share. Should we throw in anything on this, Margro?"

Long says, "Well, the sell analysts know this. We've said it will be October before we judge the effectiveness of our program and so there shouldn't be any change in the dividend until then. So I don't see any reason."

"Okay," Waldron says. "Fine."

□　　□　　□

IT IS OFTEN SAID that most top executives share an inbred preoccupation with short-term considerations. In its most common form, the malady has the symptoms of a refusal to be distracted by anything beyond what the bottom line will show three to six months in the future, coupled with an unquenchable desire to make those quarterly numbers bigger and bigger, at any cost. If the preoccupation happens to end up putting the corporation on the ropes ten years hence, well, that's the next guy's problem.

"There is a fixation," Waldron told me one day in his office. "And I think it's terribly unhealthy. I have the sickness, too. I don't break out in goose pimples. But I have the sickness. I'll give you a theory on why it's true, which may not be worth anything at all. Seated in your chair ten to fifteen times a year is a securities analyst quizzing me on the company and trying to make a judgment on the company and whether to recommend the stock. And you can't get these people to think ahead more than six months. Some you can't get past the present quarter. Now, why is that the case? It just seems to be that companies like our own have money managers in and put them through terrible torture once or twice a year. How's our money doing? And if they say it's gone phsssst, we say, okay, you've got one more quarter or we replace you with someone else. And they scamper out and say we've got to find some stocks that are going to go up. So I think that what's driving American business and causing this fixation on quarterly profits is American business itself. So part of it is brought on ourselves."

"What's the effect of the fixation?" I asked.

"Well, you make some pretty stupid judgments," Waldron said. "Clearly, it's highly possible to manage earnings. Example: Run a quarter-end promotion that will steal money out of the next quarter. You need the money now because the Street is looking for fifty-three cents for the quarter. Or you raise prices. Or you cut prices. Or you were going to have a nice advertising campaign in the third quarter and you move it to the fourth quarter. Cut out a research-and-development item. Say you're planning to put on a first-class scientist in April. Gee, earnings look bad. Let's put him in in October. You lose six months of his talents. These are not things that are necessarily good for the long-term health of the company, but you need the short-term profits."

"Have you done these kinds of things?"

"Yup."

"Done things that you felt weren't in the best interests of the company?"

"Yup. I probably do this with [Ray] Bentele when I say to him we have a profit problem, and he says we'll see what we can do and I get a half-million or a million dollars in cuts. I don't know that those cuts were so wise. It may have been robbing Peter to pay Paul. It really gets to be a pressure pot."

"Have you ever done anything you dreaded?"

Waldron thought that question over for a moment, then he said, "Yes. I can remember in the liquor business. You would have a hell of a campaign at the end of the month to load up your distributors. You'd book those sales then and have profits and they end up with a hell of a lot of inventory of your product that they better move. So there's the theory that they'd work harder on your brands. I'm not sure it works that way. I think we just burned up money and ended up having to cut back on production later."

"What can you do about this sickness?" I said.

"If one can achieve credibility, like we're trying to achieve and that GE has achieved and maintained forever, with the investment community that there will be no surprises and the results can be rationalized and they can be perceived positively even if the short-term results are bad, then I think you could have a flat or down quarter without a ripple on the stock price. Then a rational manager could manage according to the rhythm of the stock market. A good example of that is the poultry business. You will find hardly a single public company in the poultry business, because you have wild rhythms. You make a lot of money part of the year and then you lose a lot of money. Even though you have a good fifteen percent a year return, it makes for bad tales."

□ □ □

WALDRON HAS LOOKED at the slides once, and now he gives them a second glance. His dark hair gleams. The phone trills in the next room and gets rapidly intercepted, disposed of, by Maureen Ivory. Sitting at his desk, on a Monday morning, a few weeks later, Waldron is studying some pictures of his wife and him scuba diving off the coast of Florida. During a lull in his CEO demands, he had managed to escape for a six-day vacation to the ocean. Waldron is entitled to five weeks vacation, but he generally uses only four. He takes three days around Easter to go diving at the Grand Cayman Island off the Miami coast, a week in August that Mrs. Waldron plans and doesn't tell him about until the last minute, a week in November to go scuba diving, the week before Christmas to ski in Vermont, and a week's worth of Fridays in January and February to ski.

The diving was great, he says. He tells me about a 103-foot "pornographic" dive, during which he observed two sponges copulating. "Did you know that sponges have sex?" he asks me. I said I had no idea. He gives the slides a final look of approbation and then hands them to me. "It's kind of ridiculous taking pictures underwater," he comments. "With all that gear on, everyone looks the same."

Waldron signs a letter, glances at a couple of memorandums before throwing them into the wastebasket, then looks at his calendar. Now he is scheduled to conduct one of his informal coffee sessions with employees he doesn't often encounter.

Checking his watch, he rises slowly out of his chair. He is a few minutes late. When he saunters in, everyone is already halfway through their first cup. He clears his throat and brings the meeting to order.

"So what's new?" he asks a manager from the Avon beauty division.

"Well, there's pressure on the average order," she says, and then she goes on to give some specifics of "campaign ten."

"What's campaign ten again?" Waldron asks. "I have to get my numbers right."

"That's May."

She talks about how gift books did well in campaign eight, but not in nine, and they may do well in ten.

"Well, the name of the game is to get that average order up in campaign ten," Waldron says.

"That's right," the woman says.

"I see where day one was very good. When was one—Friday?"

"Yes."

"Of course, one day doesn't make a chicken," Waldron says. "But we're encouraged."

Waldron asks the group if anyone knows someone by the name of ———. No one does.

"We were shopping this weekend in Stratton in the Jelly Mill," Waldron says. "This big red barn where you can buy everything from great art to junky ashtrays. Unfortunately, my wife is buying the art. And this woman yells out, Mrs. Hicks Waldron, where's your husband? And I'm brought over and she throws her arms around me and says, 'I love you.' She says she was a district manager for Avon in Washington for eight hundred and eleven years or something. She said that getting up every morning and going to work for Avon was like going on a vacation. There's a line for my next speech. And she went on, ta da, ta da, ta da. That sure is better than someone yelling, you goddamn so-and-so."

Everyone murmurs agreement.

"Well," Waldron says. "Who's got the idea of the week? It's Monday. There should be an idea of the week."

No one has one.

"Any impact from our analyst meeting?" Waldron asks someone from investor relations.

She says, "People are definitely feeling that you are less sure of a turnaround in the Avon division. The anxiety of getting on with it. They want to see some action. They're a little bit nervous about the dividend."

Waldron says, "Boy, when that bastard Meade, if you'll pardon the expression, comes out with his report."

"Yeah," the investor relations woman says.

"This is the First Boston analyst," Waldron says. "He's going to bring us down to earnings of two dollars a share and a dollar dividend. He's not only reducing our dividend but defining it. Remember the last time he did a report? Our stock went down one and a half points in a day. Then we made our statement and it went back up. So we'll get out the same statement, dust it off, and get it back up there."

There's some talk about who are the largest holders of Avon stock. Waldron says, "United Bank of Colorado is our largest. A real warm group of people. We like to go out and visit our biggest shareholders and they don't want anything to do with us. They couldn't care less if I existed or all the rest of you existed. I once had it arranged that I would call their chief executive at twelve-ten, and they said, don't even waste your time, we won't answer the phone. All they want is for us to keep that dividend up."

Nobody else has anything to say, and so Waldron concludes the session by getting up and saying, "Now remember, hold on to those Confederate dollars. The South will rise again."

Later on, Waldron walks across the hall to the board room, where the top executives of the Avon Beauty division are seated to conduct a meeting about its competitive situation.

The primary speaker is a man named Maury Dewhurst. He isn't an Avon employee, but a consultant with the firm Strategic Planning Associates out of Washington. For the last year, he has been working for Avon, studying its strengths and weaknesses against the competition and trying to help formulate a strategy. He is young, lean, very corporate-looking, very poised, very sure of himself, or at least very able to appear as if he is very sure of himself.

He begins with a slide presentation. It's entitled "Strategy Development Summary. Part II." The main topic is what has been learned about Avon's competitors. Dewhurst says, "Some people out there play very tough and are going to be tough to beat and have certain advantages."

Since this is a continuation of an earlier meeting, Dewhurst gives a wrap-up of what was said at that last session. Various charts, boxes, axes, arrows appear on the screen. They show, among other things, that HDS (home direct selling) will in the future represent a shrinking portion of the division's profit pie.

Waldron interrupts to ask if the division has given up on the idea that it can grow home direct selling.

Jim Preston says, "We don't know if we can grow it. But my view is the home direct system as we know it today can't grow."

"Okay, I buy that," Waldron says. "But I see a yellow flag here. You start talking about something in these meetings—using a certain type of terminology, and you can't shake it. I guess that's how Edsel got named Edsel. In a secret warm room someplace somebody said, 'Let's call it Edsel,' and sure enough it got named Edsel. You're going to get the organization thinking the heat is off home direct selling, because it's going to decline, and I'm a little concerned about the mind-set getting fixed in the corporation. So I encourage you to come up with some other way of thinking about it."

There is a bit more discussion, then it's decided that the chart will be redrawn so that the HDS segment (what Waldron refers to as the doorbell department) in the chart will be shown getting bigger at a slow rate—maybe 2 to 3 percent a year—so people don't think it's shrinking, even if it is. Reality and charts don't always coincide in business.

"Okay, that's better," Waldron says. "Because if word gets out that the heat is off direct selling it could be all over."

A chart is put up that shows that the "competitor module" consists of makeup, fragrances, and skin care and jewelry.

Then another chart breaks down the makeup category into brands. The high end is Estée Lauder. The middle has Avon, Max Factor, Revlon, and L'Oréal. The low end is Maybelline and Noxell.

Dewhurst says that the middle group has lost twenty-four share points between 1973 and 1983. He says ten have come from Avon and ten from Revlon. The big winner, he says, was Estée Lauder, which gained five share points.

"In summary," he says, "very good overall growth, but the high end overtaking the middle end."

Dewhurst turns now to specifics of several individual competitors. Noxell, he says, was one of the big winners of the 1970's. "We believe the linchpin of their success," he says, "was their choice of distribution channel. They focused heavily on the discount channel [supermarkets and bargain drugstore chains]. The deep-discount channels have been the growth areas. So they backed or helped create a winning distribution system."

An extremely complex chart shows that Noxell also picked the right customer for the channel—the younger customer. Dewhurst says, "They also pushed products correct for the channel and customer—eyeshadow, nail enamel, and mascara. Then they backed them with heavy advertising, twice the industry average."

Then Dewhurst says, "Noxell has a big problem now called what do I do for an encore."

Now he turns to the other big success story: Estée Lauder. It concentrated on department stores as a distribution channel and targeted the affluent woman. It also picked growing products—mascara, eyeshadow, and enamel.

"Appropriate to the channel," Dewhurst says, "Lauder used relatively little advertising, but it does very targeted ads, heavy in-store promotions, and print ads."

"Well, who's after Lauder's ass?" Waldron asks.

Preston answers, "Pretty much everybody."

Dewhurst concludes by saying that Avon is severely hampered in competing with either Noxell or Lauder in their chosen segments, so it should steer a middle ground between the two.

The meeting has gone on an hour now, and a coffee break is called. Waldron has an important phone call to take.

After the break, Dewhurst resumes by exploring

the "fragrance module." It's entirely different, with 1.3 percent annual real growth, compared to 6.2 percent for makeup.

Dewhurst says that in the 1970's two success stories stood out: Charlie (a Revlon product) and Chloë. Distribution got tougher in the eighties, as a crush of products hit the market, and the big winners were Vanderbilt and Giorgio.

"Vanderbilt's aim was to quickly build a mass brand and so it picked a multiple distribution channel," Dewhurst says. "It was the first time a designer image was taken to mass market. What Vanderbilt was prepared to do was spend its way to success by spending unheard-of sums to get share. They were blowing a lot of bucks. The upshot was they lost money in the first few years. But by 1984 they were making a healthy amount of money."

He goes on, "Giorgio's secret was they created a new channel of distribution. They went to direct mail with the trick of scent strips. They had to do that because they couldn't get into department stores, because they were all full up. Once the scent strips worked, they got into the department stores. Also, they spent unprecedented amounts—double what anyone had done—for a prestige brand."

"These stories suggest," Dewhurst says, "that as competition has increased, the formulas for success have become increasingly complex."

Dewhurst now begins to recite the lessons he feels can be learned from the investigation.

Lesson one: Strategies for current channel must reflect the characteristics of that channel.

Lesson two: Makeup is now, and fragrance is rapidly becoming, a distribution game.

Lesson three: Big successes usually occur when distribution play, customer opportunity, product, and support all come together in an integrated strategy.

"The implications," Dewhurst says, "are that the Avon division must look beyond current channels. What the Avon division has to do, we feel, is to figure out what the hell is coming next."

Dewhurst flips through a succession of charts. Waldron, who has been listening quietly, clearly seems to be getting exasperated by the length of the presentation.

"Our hypothesis," Dewhurst says, "is that the next distribution wave will be a hybrid system."

He goes into each type of distribution channel and rates them on various factors. Endless. Waldron, at various points, makes some criticisms. At one juncture, he calls everything on one line "a bunch of horseshit."

Dewhurst expounds a bit on "follow-up"—people calling up after a customer has bought a product to see if she likes it and is using it—and says that it is an important criterion.

Waldron interrupts to say that follow-up is practically meaningless. "Hell, they call you, Maury, probably while you're watching a basketball game and you say you hate the product, because you're watching the game. So it's not important at all."

"All right," Dewhurst says.

Dewhurst then concludes by saying that Avon is in a good position to develop that hybrid system, because it has windows into a number of systems.

Dewhurst's colleague then gets up and finishes the presentation with a summation consisting entirely of platitudes and jargon:

"Improve productivity."

"Rebuild image."

"Optimize market."

"Segment."

Someone then says, "It's important to keep in mind what you're hoping to do while you develop the new hybrid channel."

"That's absolutely right," Waldron says. "The name of the book is how to live through the operation. Because we're right on the knife's edge."

13 □ MONEY

FOR WORKING a total of 336 days a year, Hicks Waldron was paid $500,000 in 1984 in straight salary, a gross weekly paycheck of nearly $10,000. On top of that, he received a bonus of $297,105. Waldron's bonus is allocated according to a sliding scale—ranging up to 130 percent of his salary—tied to how Avon's earnings per share for the year compare with what they were budgeted to be at the start of the year. If the earnings exactly match the budget, then Waldron gets a bonus equal to 65 percent of his salary. If they surpass expectations, the bonus keeps growing to a maximum of 130 percent. On top of that, Waldron is part of a "performance unit plan," offering long-term incentives if the company's profits grow. Cash distributions are made every three years. If, for instance, the increase in the earnings per share of Avon exceeds $1.04 from 1984 to 1986, bonuses will be paid. From 1985 to 1987, cash will be apportioned if earnings grow more than $1.09.

There are a number of perquisites of the job that add to the financial benefits. A $2-million life insurance policy is fully paid for by Avon. When Waldron took the job, he was living in Farmington and Avon wanted him to move to New York so that he would be more readily accessible to handle the demands on his time. He bought the Trump Plaza cooperative apartment himself for $2,217,000, but Avon pays the maintenance costs, which are $6,420.34 a month. Also, since Waldron didn't want to risk losing any money in the Manhattan real estate market, Avon agreed to buy back the apartment from him when he retires at his original purchase price plus his interim costs, including interest. These costs are reckoned at $240,000 a year.

Waldron belongs to the company's retirement plan, which pays benefits according to the average of the five highest years' compensation during the ten years prior to retirement and the number of years of service. There is also a complicated supplemental plan for top executives. Since Waldron joined Avon late in his career, he also negotiated an additional pension that will equal a percentage of his final Avon compensation. He has been granted stock options that could be converted to ninety thousand shares of Avon stock. The ten most senior officers of the company have executive contracts, the so-called "golden parachutes" that have been lambasted by many critics of executive pay. If a majority of Avon's outstanding shares are acquired by one person or group, or if, as the result of a business combination, the majority of the board changes and Waldron is discharged without cause during the succeeding three years, he will get a payment equal to the value of the last three years' compensation prior to termination of employment and the present value of three years' benefits under all company plans, along with a payment to cover taxes due on the money. In short, if somebody took over Avon and fired Waldron, he would lick his wounds by taking away a mighty pretty sum of money.

Every chief executive thinks he is worth the kind of sum princes dream about in fairy tales. And these days he usually gets it. Only five executives earned

more than $1 million in 1977. By 1983, at least
thirty-eight exceeded that amount, with eighteen
topping the $2 million mark. At the hundred largest
industrials, the median salary (not including sweets
like stock options) for chief executive officers was
$655,000. Salary, however, is only a portion of the
rewards; there is always a compensation package
plump with stock options, bonuses, perquisites,
and "golden parachutes."

Why do executives make such seemingly scan-
dalous sums of money? Easy. They are the ones
who decide how they should be compensated.
Boards of directors do no more than offer pro forma
blessings (and directors pretty much serve at the
pleasure of the chief executive). A study done by
researchers at Brigham Young University, for example, found no relationship whatsoever between
stockholder return and executive compensation.

Clarence Randall, the late chief executive at In-
land Steel, once described how a top executive gets
himself a large paycheck: "True, the board of directors must give pro forma approval to his recommendations, but it almost never challenges them. In
actual fact, therefore, he himself is the one who
decides what compensation he shall receive."

More publicity has been given to the considerable salaries of chief executives and other top corporate managers in recent years, and a fair amount
of controversy has been stirred up by the sums dis-
closed. A report issued in 1984 by the Democracy
Project, a New York-based research institute
headed by Mark Green, former aide to the consumer activist Ralph Nader, said, "If waste is de-
fined as something for nothing, the current
corporate pay system is one of the clearest examples." The institute recommended that companies
establish compensation committees composed

solely of outside directors. The panels would have their own budgets and retain their own consultants, lawyers, and other professionals independent of management. Management guru Peter Drucker suggested in 1977 that the maximum compensation of all executives should be a multiple of the lowest-paid regular full-time employee. He went on to propose a ratio of fifteen-to-one for small business and twenty-five-to-one for large ones—which would have worked out to a top compensation, in 1977, of some $433,000 a year.

Graef S. Crystal, a vice-president of the New York management consulting firm Towers, Perrin, Forster & Crosby, has written that one company "offers its executives huge amounts of cash if they remain with the company for a number of years. To earn the money requires only that the executive demonstrate his or her ability to breathe in and out 17 times a minute and keep his or her other vital signs within normal tolerances. In fairness, however, the executive does have to accomplish these demanding tasks while on the company's payroll."

The big pay has its army of defenders. Many management-compensation specialists argue that the high numbers are a result of inflation and that executives have been justly rewarded for guiding companies through recession or saving them from bankruptcy, as did Lee Iacocca with Chrysler. Some experts say that the salaries result from the scarcity of people of senior stature to lead American business.

Michael Jensen, professor of finance and business administration, and Kevin Murphy, assistant professor, both at the University of Rochester's Graduate School of Management, wrote in an article that appeared in 1984 in *The New York Times*: "If executives set their own salaries, then the marvel is why salaries are so low. On average, star executives have been unable to 'set' their salaries higher than those for rock stars, sports stars or even for television anchormen (who four years ago earned an average of $650,000). Dan Rather's 1980 contract was reportedly valued at $8 million, with first-year pay of $1.6 million. In 1983, only nine top-level executives received salary plus bonus exceeding this level, and none exceeded NBC anchorman Tom Brokaw's reported $2.2 million."

But, of course, many untalented people are at the helms of companies and their poor performance seems to have no relation to their fat salaries. It is more a matter of the members of the club taking care of one another.

I talked to Waldron one day about compensation. Was he paid too much? How did he justify clearing $800,000 a year?

"When I was at GE in the management-training program," Waldron said, "my boss said to me, 'What do you think you'll ever make in your lifetime?' And I said I think I'm going to make nine thousand dollars some day, and he said, 'You're a dreamer.' The numbers sound big, but it's a big world out there when you pay thirty-five dollars an hour for a guy to plug up a hole in your sink. It's a big world."

Hadn't things gotten a little out of hand? I said.

Waldron cleared his throat. "Salaries for some have escalated in my opinion more than they should have. Then there are some abusers who get the headlines. What about an article about the ten lowest-paid CEOs? That would be a big ho-hum and nobody would read it. The press always has a ball when you put big numbers next to anybody's name."

Waldron explained that everything was relative.

At Avon, he said, every year he looks at twenty-seven other companies comparable to Avon and examines the salaries of the CEO, the president, the chief financial officer, on down into the divisions. Then he tries to set pay around the averages. "Every company says it wants its people to be in the top twenty-five percent of pay," he said. "Well, if everyone wants to be in the top twenty-five percent, there won't be any bottom twenty-five percent."

"What about your pay?" I said. "Is it fair?"

"I think my compensation is about right," he said. "It's about average for those twenty-seven companies. And the bonus was a little higher—we hit plan last year and I got a full bonus. Whether all of us making more than five hundred thousand dollars are getting the right amount, I have some trouble. I don't know. I have a sense that some of this money has gotten out of hand. But I guess we all look like this [Waldron points his index fingers at each other]. If he'll pare back, then so will I."

Waldron was quiet for a moment or two, rolling numbers in his mind. "The responsibilities of being the chief executive. The risk involved in being the chief executive. If we hit the budget this year, I'll get, say, eight hundred and fifty thousand dollars. As I look around at the world out there, I'd have trouble being critical of that compensation. Comparing myself with a lawyer or an entertainer or a baseball player. With thirty-eight thousand employees and a million women depending on this company. Then you compare yourself to thirty-five bucks an hour for a carpenter. If he puts in the hours I put in—and I figured it out once—it comes out to a hundred and twenty thousand dollars. There are a lot of risks. The risks today are enormous. The CEO can be hit with product liability

suits, and a CEO can even go to jail—and some
have. We have products that go on the body and
with Mallinckrodt that go into the body. Because of
one's visibility and the simplicity with which CEOs
are measured—earnings per share—frequently if
the earnings aren't there you're fired. If the company's performance lags below a not necessarily
well-defined standard, it's bon voyage. Then you
live in a goldfish bowl. Because of the visibility, we
all live in fear of theft and kidnapping. You'll notice
that the names of all my neighbors are out on the
driveway at my home in Connecticut. But no Waldron. I'd like to have the name out, but there's a risk.
And you give up something of yourself. It's difficult
for us, because of the visibility, because of all the
responsibilities, to let the guard down, to relax, be
yourself."

□   □   □

JIM PRESTON LOOKS TERRIBLE. He rises to the thirty-
sixth floor, strides briskly down the hallway, and
makes an abrupt left into Waldron's office. It is his
first stop since returning from the Circle of Excellence get-together in Vienna. He is not a happy
man. What he found in Vienna has caused his plans
for his division to come to a standstill. Several
months ago, a convention of all the sales managers
had been held in Atlanta, and one of the important
messages delivered by Preston and Waldron was
that, unlike in the past, when all the shots would be
called in New York and everyone would live under
"cookie-cutter conformity," district managers were
going to be given new latitude. They'd be handed
a budget and then allowed to spend their dollars as
they saw fit. They would truly be their own bosses.

"Contrary to what we expected to happen," Preston said of what he heard in Vienna, "these people were telling me that not only didn't they have more latitude, they had less. I realized I had a very serious problem on my hands. The credibility of management, in my opinion, was at an all-time low. A few months ago, Hicks and I had stood up and talked about decentralization and they had gone back to their districts and found out that wasn't the case."

Part of the problem has been that, after the Atlanta conference, when the managers were given their budgets, it was made clear that this would be a tight year. Everyone had to watch their costs. The leadership in New York, though, had apparently put too much emphasis on clamping down on expenses and not enough on the decentralization. In Preston's words: "There was a leadership problem. People here botched things."

Preston explained the crux of what he had found out in this way: "A district manager in Vienna said to me, 'I wouldn't mind it if you told me we have to button down and cut some expenses. Fine. I'll cut out my refreshments at sales meetings and cut down classified advertising, which wasn't working anyway. I can live with that.' Instead, what happened is here's a manager with maybe a twelve percent increase last year and his boss tells him, 'You spent forty dollars on postage. I want you to cut that in half. How much are you paying for gas? Have you tried pumping your own?' They were nickeled and dimed to death."

And so the district managers were miffed and they were depressed. "In my twenty-one years at this company," Preston said, "I had never seen my sales managers as dispirited as they were at that moment. They were people who loved this company. They would kill for you. To see them as hurt and angry as they were was incredible."

Waldron, being told this, is astonished. "So the problem was things weren't getting through the trough," he says.

With their crowded schedules, CEOs are often forced to rely on what they are told. Communicating in a big corporation often is like playing the old party game where people sit end to end and one person whispers a message into the next person's ear, and then he whispers it to the next person. By the time it reaches the last participant, the message is grossly distorted and everyone has a good laugh. By the time Waldron hears things, they are often garbled, too. The national sales manager had been telling Preston that things were going swimmingly, and Preston had whispered that on to Waldron.

Waldron is visibly shaken now by what he has learned from Preston. He grills Preston for some time about his findings, grills him about what he plans to do. Preston wants to make some immediate management changes that he had sketched out on the plane ride back from Vienna. He wants to strip the national manager of sales and distribution of his position, the person directly in charge of communicating the new way to the field. He wants to add a few other people to the division to shore up things. Waldron concurs. "I decided we had to shake at the top," he would later tell me. "If shaking at the top didn't do it, then we'd shake further down."

Go do it, he tells Preston. And do it fast.

Preston himself was becoming a lonely man. His world was coming down on him. He tells me later, "I've had to sit here and approve the termination of close to one thousand district managers, four hundred people in Kansas City, a couple of hundred others, seven hundred people in the home office, probably close to twenty-five hundred people altogether. It's not fun to do. At the same time, you know in the heart and you know in your gut that the business has so much potential if we can get it turned around. Obviously, you feel the pressure. Shareholders aren't happy. The board of directors can't be excited. No, I haven't been having much fun. Not much fun at all."

14 □ ALONE AT THE TOP

A CHIEF EXECUTIVE, it's often been said, has a "love" relationship with the company that he runs. And so when his company is wounded he feels wounded. Most corporate leaders feed off pressure the way a shark hunter feeds off danger. They're like firemen. The bell rings, they jump into their boots, and slide down the pole. Who knows why. Did Armand Hammer, Occidental's chairman, benefit from being trained as a physician, taught to make hypotheses, get data, think things through? Was Harold Geneen, the former ITT leader, helped in riding out stressful episodes by doing the Canadian Air Force exercises every day?

The annals of business, nevertheless, are filled with instances of kettles exploding. What happens to the chief executive when the pressure builds up? He races his motor fast. He drinks. He becomes abusive. He commits crimes. He kills himself.

There is the famous case of Sewell Avery, the head of Montgomery Ward, who, in 1944, refused to comply with an order of Franklin Roosevelt's War Labor Board and was carted, arms collapsed across his chest, from his Chicago office by two soldiers. Others, when they cracked, went further. On an August Sunday in 1982 Alvin Feldman, president of Continental Air Lines, who had been fighting—and losing—a takeover battle against Texas

International, lay down on a couch in his office and put a bullet through his brain.

Unfortunately, one could go on and on naming such examples. It's become a cliche by now—the loneliness at the top. But as with many cliches, it has the ring of truth. Psychiatrists agree that a pivotal reason why undue stress may cause chief executives to buckle is the icy isolation. They have no one to talk to. They fear appearing mortal. Where they are, the buck stops. One psychoanalyst who sees a good many chief executives supine on the couch told me, "I have a theory that in a hierarchical situation, there is a tendency to feel inside of you that the person above you is something like a parent figure and the person below you is something like a child figure. It comes out in such things as 'The boss needs no praise.' He's like a god. He's omnipotent. So, looking upward, people always overestimate the power of the boss. Downward, the boss always underestimates his subordinates. People attribute all sorts of power to the chief executive. And many chief executives want to buy into that belief. And that's a very serious situation. They can't stand to lose face, to admit any weakness. They can't share with anyone how frightened they are. I always think of the Wizard of Oz. You know the booming voice of the person whom you never see? Everyone fears him. Then you look and it's this little old man. In other words, keep up appearances."

So the chief executive is very powerful but, at the same time, he is very lonely. I have sensed some of this loneliness when I have watched Waldron, alone at his desk, reading papers and reports, no one to talk to, most of his advisors no doubt in meetings, left only with his own thoughts.

When I asked Waldron once whom he confided

in, he said, "I find that on a lot of issues, Evelyn's perspective is very helpful. She was in business and she managed other people. And she's quick. I have developed a great relationship with Spencer Stuart. We've become very close friends. So he frequently is someone's judgment I would trust. Third, directors. Within the company, there are people I have a more confidante relationship with than others. I would think every CEO would have a different relationship with the chief financial officer than anyone else, because he has a pulse on every part of the company. And the CEO would have a very different relationship with the human resources director. So you pick your shots. You discuss different notes with different people. But you don't have somebody you can just sit down and kick the whole gong around with."

The most stressful period in Waldron's life was in the early part of 1977. He had not yet fully gotten over losing his son. He was recently married and adjusting to a new wife. Kentucky Fried Chicken started sliding downhill at the same time that the bottom fell out of the wine business. Waldron began drinking more than he should have. It was more than that. He had lost a lot of weight and looked dreadful. He was tired all the time. He was having fifteen cups of coffee a day. He was smoking seven cigars a day. He would accept a cocktail before dinner, several glasses of wine with dinner, a nightcap afterward. He was devouring a great deal of fatty food.

So what happened in May 1977 was perhaps inevitable as a rather pernicious manifestation of the pressure of his world.

"He came home one day from the office and he had fallen asleep at the board meeting," Evelyn Waldron recalled. "He said he had to go to bed, he couldn't stay awake. I asked him what was the matter? He said he had this pain. I thought he was having a heart attack. Typical Hicks, he said, 'If I go to bed, I'll be all right.' The next day, he wasn't all right. I insisted he go to the hospital. He was diagnosed as having pancreatitis."

The pancreas emits enzymes that digest fats, protein, and carbohydrates. When pancreatitis strikes, the pancreas swells and closes off the duct that the enzymes flow out of and so they are blocked and begin to eat the pancreas itself. It is extraordinarily painful. As Waldron described it to me: "It feels like someone is chewing on your ass."

Diet and rest are the only cure for this ailment. From May 24 on, Waldron would never have another pat of butter. He would never have another drink except for occasional glasses of wine. Waldron was confined to a hospital for a month and spent another month at home in bed. Unable to fulfill his myriad duties, he found it necessary to resign his position as chief executive officer of Heublein. Though he kept the title of president, he did not work at all for months. "I had no role," he says, "no role at all." He wondered if he would ever run a company again. He wondered in particular how he could run this corporation. "Here I was the CEO of a major liquor company and I didn't drink."

The doctor ordered Waldron to totally extricate himself from his pressure-cooker world. So his wife and he went down to a house in Madison, Connecticut, along the shore. He was put on a zero-fat diet. He ate Jell-o, fruits, vegetables without butter, chicken broth, and noodles. He couldn't have caffeine, hard liquor, or tobacco. He would get up at nine or ten, not six or seven, stay up for an hour, go to bed, get up, turn in early. Mrs. Waldron and he played cards or games. Occasionally, some friends would visit. He couldn't open the mail, not even from friends. Slowly, he regained his strength.

After a few months, he started doing a half day of work, then scaled up to a full routine. He wanted to be the boss again, but the board of directors was far from convinced that he should be. The business had worsened. Plus there was the question of his health. One member in particular thought someone else ought to be hired for the job. So Waldron bargained for his future.

"I told them that I didn't buy Kentucky Fried Chicken. But I let it go down the tube, because like everybody else here I didn't understand the business. So I made a deal. I'll go down there and turn the franchises around. The deal was one year. Either turn it around or bon voyage. That's a short version of it. But that was the deal."

"I set up an office in Louisville and took responsibility for Kentucky Fried Chicken and tried to turn it around," he went on. "Evelyn and I were in that company plane five days a week traveling around the country visiting franchises." He engineered a total upheaval of the business. Outlets were remodeled, the menu was revamped. Business perked up. One year after he had struck his bargain, Waldron was reelected chief executive officer.

Waldron's inner equilibrium these days, he told me, is such that he leaves the office pretty much behind when he goes home. "In the six blocks between the office and the apartment, I can shut on and off," he told me. He says he always "sleeps like a rock."

15 □ FACING THE PRESS

THE CEO's car moves slowly through the crush of traffic, into a gritty area amid rubble and decay way over on the West Side, where it jerks to a stop outside a television studio. In the early evening, squeezed in before dinner out with his wife and the play *Brighton Beach Memoirs,* Waldron has agreed to do an interview on a cable TV show called *Business Times.* The interviewer is a young woman who had relinquished a career as a librarian for TV glitter.

Like many CEOs, Waldron mistrusts the press. He describes interviews as "pressure situations for me." When a reporter comes calling, it is his habit to keep a tape recorder running and he compares quotes afterward (though he chose not to in any of the sessions I had with him). He often complains to editors when he dislikes a story. In fact, he has permanently barred representatives of one major magazine from Avon's premises, because he feels he was duped by one of its reporters about what she intended to write.

"I am much more negative on the press than positive," Waldron told me once. "I think journalists develop an antibusiness bias when they're in journalism school. I think it's a case of someone starting on course A and not being deflected onto B or C or any other course. Certainly the owners of media properties don't exert any effort to change this. I think the move against Dan Rather is right on. [His reference is to efforts to buy CBS stock to reverse the alleged liberal leanings of its news reports.] It's a stupid way to do it, but the goals of the move are right on."

I mentioned to Waldron the other side: that reporters all too often are misled by CEOs, that too many companies open their doors when there is good news to trumpet and close them when there's bad.

"Yes, it's not all a one-way street," he agreed. "This was a company that if there was good news, let's get it out quick and if there's bad news, let's not talk. So a company that won't be candid does itself a gross disservice. Ultimately the truth will out."

The interviewer starts off by asking Waldron to assess the progress at Avon in the last year and a half.

Waldron says that there has been brightness in earnings and in strategic planning, but "we've lost a little bit of ground as we've done the turnaround. We lost some representatives as we restructured. We didn't anticipate the negative impact of the turnaround."

Interviewer: "What about last year's fourth-quarter earnings decline? That wasn't anticipated."

Waldron: "I would call that shooting oneself in one's foot." He goes on to say that Avon overpriced its products in its gift and decorative line, and that it was hindered by the deterioration in the size of its selling force.

Interviewer: "So are more heads going to roll?"

Waldron: "Well, heads don't roll very often. I'd say there were some smarting behinds."

There is some discussion of Avon's direct selling

method, the fact that it still sells none of its products in retail stores.

Interviewer: "Aren't you fighting a losing battle? Why do you have to sell direct? Why aren't you in stores?"

Waldron: "If I had it all to do over again, I would put in the exact distribution system we have."

He mentions that Avon is testing other means of distribution: In Hartford and Raleigh, it's testing electronic kiosks. It's testing catalogue sales. It's testing an employed representative called a personal beauty advisor.

Interviewer: "The thing you haven't mentioned is the retail store."

Waldron: "We can sit here for an hour and you won't hear me mention a retail store . . . We will do nothing to jeopardize our direct selling system."

The interviewer asks about the sluggishness of the beauty business.

Waldron admits that the whole cosmetics business is not what you would call dynamic; in fact, it has a growth rate of perhaps 2 to 3 percent a year. Then he says, "But there are some hot growth areas within cosmetics. Skin care is the fastest-growing area. Within that are skin-care regimens, with even more growth opportunities."

Interviewer: "What are you doing new?"

Waldron: "Avon in the new product area has been a follower by design. In our new strategic plan we don't intend to be a leader. But we do intend to be a high-tech close follower. That's the new strategic plan lingo."

Then he mentions a new "breakthrough" product being introduced this week. Called "BioAdvance," it is designed to treat skin and create the appearance of younger skin. Waldron says, "The crow's feet begin to disappear and the lines we experience as we get older begin to disappear." He says that BioAdvance will be the most expensive product in the Avon line, with a three-month supply costing $49.95.

The interview winds down after roughly an hour of questioning. Mary Tavon, an account executive from Michael Klepper Associates, asks John Cox whether Waldron has had training in dealing with the press. She says that her outfit specializes in what she calls "crisis communications—how to handle tough questions." She says Waldron did very well.

Cox says, "Yeah, I think he had some training when he was at Heublein."

Executive image and communications counseling is an odd little industry that was spawned in the early 1960's, when plastics and oil companies started to be berated by Ralph Nader and the rising consumerism movement. Chief executives had never showed up on the nightly network news, for the simple reason that they were never asked. Now that they were in the news—and news that the man on the street cared about—they found themselves under the hot lights and they typically didn't fare very well in this unfamiliar world. Wherever there is a need, or even an apparent need, there is a consultant to step in and fill it, and fill it consultants did. In an article about one of these enterprises, the managing partner suggested that the difference between a good executive and a great one is 20 percent competence and 80 percent style. So she was prepared to improve your style. Some of her tips were to use gestures when speaking, because then people will think you're smarter, and talk louder than normal, because then people will not only think you're smarter but also more witty and interesting.

After he has his makeup scrubbed off, Waldron and his wife hop into a waiting car, a rental limousine from London Towncars Limousine Service, and speed off to dinner. Waldron tells the driver to give me a lift home and then to deposit his briefcase and his wife's purse with the concierge at his apartment building.

"Will do," the driver says.

Once we are alone, the driver tells me, "We do a lot of Avon business. The car costs thirty dollars an hour. I had Mr. Waldron once before. We got stuck in pretty heavy traffic and he finally leapt out and walked the rest of the way to where he was going. I take a high Merrill Lynch official back and forth to work every morning. The other day, I got hired by the heir to the Coca-Cola fortune. She had to go to this party, I think a charity ball, that's what these rich people usually go to, you know. She had to pick up her daughter and go to Kenneth's to have her hair done. Then home and beddy-bye. That was six hours at thirty an hour—a hundred and eighty dollars plus tip, so figure two hundred. Funny how people get around this city."

□ □ □

JOHN COX IS TALL (a six-footer), rangy, with graying temples and a stolid face. He has a taciturn, professorial air—rather a strange demeanor for a public relations chief.

Cox's office is down the hall and past the receptionist from Waldron's. Aside from the desk and an adjacent table with a computer on it, there's an area with a small couch and two cozy chairs where Cox likes to sit when he's meeting with someone. A white telescope of good quality stands pointed out the window.

Cox, among his motley chores as Avon's public relations oracle, is the words behind Waldron. Years ago, chief executives had relatively infrequent contact with the public relations people. But these days, the top PR man usually has an office right on the executive floor, and, like the President of the United States and his press attaché, the CEO is constantly huddling with him.

"I was down at Kentucky Fried Chicken when he came to Heublein as president and chief operating officer," Cox says. "I was in charge of franchising and public relations, and the first speech I did for him was when he appeared before the franchisees. I knew the franchisees better than he did, and so I drafted a speech for him. Coincidentally, my writing style and his speaking style were pretty much the same, and so there weren't that many changes. Then I went up to Heublein and did most of his speeches there. Now, when we do a speech, we'll sit down and talk a little about what he wants to say. Since I'm part of corporate management, we don't have to spend much time on background. Then I'll go at it and he'll either buy it or not buy it. Sometimes, he'll send me back to the drawing board to have a go at it all the way from the beginning. That's rare. But he does work them over pretty hard. Most of the speeches then go around to the members of the corporate management committee for suggestions. Sometimes it's word suggestions, or sometimes substantive. You send out a piece of paper—everyone's going to scribble something on it to show that they read it. He likes the twenty-minute body, because he thinks that's about the attention span of most people. It varies month to month how many speeches I write. Lately it's been like a speech a week. More typically, it's like one a month.

"The style we shoot for is very conversational—so it hopefully comes out just the way he's speaking. He likes—self-deprecating is too strong a word—but he likes to poke fun at himself. He likes some humor but he doesn't do jokes. He's not in competition with Bob Hope. Some people try that, and it usually doesn't work."

I ask about press interviews, another chore of Cox's.

"He will take almost every interview he is asked for. He's comfortable with the style. But he also realizes Avon needs more visibility. Avon was a very low-profile company. We are now fairly high visibility. We are in New York, so we are very accessible. There's quite a bit of press demand. It's everything from *Gallagher Reports,* which is a trade sheet, to *Business Week* to *Wall Street Journal* to *Women's Wear Daily.* The subject matter is everything imaginable. A woman is coming in in a few weeks who's writing a book about the role of women in business. A guy from *Gallagher Reports* wants an overview of the company. I try to find out something about where they want to go so we can do our homework. For the woman doing the book, I dropped a note to Phil Davis and asked him to put together some statistics on where we are and any kind of comparisons to see how we stand relative to other companies. I try to get information for him to prepare ahead of time. Sometimes it can be quite a bit. I'm trying to arrange an interview with a publication on health care, and I prepared a white paper of about three thousand or four thousand words."

16 □ WATERLOO

WALDRON IS the last to arrive. Dutiful greetings and effortless smiles come from executives all around the table. From the devotional looks in their eyes, one might think that Marlon Brando has just walked into a junior high school drama class.

Nine o'clock. The first Wednesday in May. What is taking place is what takes place at this time on the first Wednesday of each month. Avon's corporate management committee meets. The milieu is the stately boardroom, with the paneled walls and the big oblong table.

All the big guns are here: the president, the four division heads, the chief financial officer, the vice-president of planning, the vice-president of communications, the vice-president of human resources, the legal counsel. They wear sober ties and have stripped off their jackets, as if they had gathered for an early-morning poker game. White coffee mugs sit on the table in front of each chair, and a coffeemaker gurgles against the wall.

The CMC, as it is always called on the Avon executive floor, is the inner sanctum of power at Avon, the top management body under Waldron. It has no decision-making authority. Its purpose is to convey information and opinions important to Waldron in order to make decisions. Some chief executives cultivate what are referred to as "kitchen cabinets," a

165

handful of high-level officers whom the chief confides in and solicits help from when tough decisions have to be made. Waldron doesn't like to have a kitchen cabinet. He thinks of the CMC in its totality as his confidante.

There is a routine to CMC meetings. Jules Zimmerman, the chief financial officer, is always first to speak. He gives an update on how the all-important quarterly numbers look. The month just gone by is examined. After he's done, Waldron, as he puts it, "goes around the horn," calling on each member to summarize the doings in his area of specialization. The other members are free to interrupt with questions when they see fit. Waldron himself tends to be the most tenacious questioner. At some point well into the meeting, a guest speaker generally shows up to talk to the dignitaries about a topical matter. This month's meeting will be graced by a discussion about health-care costs by someone from personnel.

A matter of some urgency currently facing the CMC is that business, particularly domestic beauty product sales, is not living up to earlier projections. Consequently, the company is in real danger of suffering rather poor earnings in the second quarter. So every member of the CMC has been implored to cut expenses, in the hope of knocking off a total of $15 million of expenses. A confidential memorandum went out to the CMC members last month pressing for the reductions. Even though the problem area was Avon's domestic beauty business, the memorandum said, "The total amount cannot be obtained from Avon U.S., without seriously damaging programs essential to current strategy. Any change in the Corporation's general strategic direction at this time will have a serious negative impact on API [Avon Products Incorporated] management credibility. We must stay on course."

Some "running rules" on how to make the cuts were then suggested, including:

"All use of consultants should be given particularly close attention. Expenses in this area have shown enormous growth."

"Close attention should be given to the consequences of not filling positions that are currently open."

"Be as creative and far-reaching as possible. This is an appropriate time to 'think the unthinkable.' "

"Preference must be given to required support for API's seven key businesses."

Corporations dread reporting disappointing earnings, especially if they are below what the investment community has been expecting. Any CEO, therefore, will go to imaginative lengths to wring out the right numbers before he will report a down quarter. When I once asked Waldron if it was fair to say that he does everything he can to avoid releasing numbers that are below plan, he replied, "Do everything is an understatement. 'Kill' is the word. You have to have the killer instinct for the bottom line."

Waldron starts off the meeting by reporting some radical high-level managerial shuffling in the domestic Avon beauty division, the aftermath of Preston's Vienna trip. Preston had lowered the boom and replaced the national sales manager with a rather surprising choice—Phyllis Davis, a petite, cheery woman of fifty-four, who had been in charge of communications and advertising for the division and had never had any sales experience. The sales manager was offered a different position but turned it down and chose to leave. It was announced, as the charade usually goes at big corporations, that he had resigned "because of his desire to pursue other interests." What's more, Paul Markovits, a lanky, dark-haired man of forty-two who had been in charge of the international side of the business, was put in a new post of executive vice-president, in which role he would be expected to help engineer a turnaround in domestic beauty. Bob Pratt, the corporate planning officer, was also being assigned to the division to direct its planning.

They were bold strokes. The chanciest one was Phyllis Davis. As Waldron told me, "It's gutsy. She didn't have that much management experience. What she had was great enthusiasm and she was a bright, bright person. And it doesn't hurt a bit that she's a woman." Waldron, though, had already given Davis orders that couldn't have been blunter. "I told her that Waldron would be all over you like a blanket. I told Phyllis that you don't have all week. If you can't get the job done, we'll put somebody else in there. If you fizzle, we'll bring you right back and put you where you were."

After Waldron gets done reporting the news, he says, "We're going to spend most of our time this morning on what we're not doing—which is meeting our budget, and Jules will cover that in a minute. First, I'd like to make a few remarks."

Waldron says that at the last meeting everyone was asked to come up with profit protection cuts. "You have been asked to deliver and you did deliver and that's positive and I commend you for it."

Jules Zimmerman is now given the floor. He hands out sheets of paper with reams of numbers on them. Then he runs through them, referring to charts on an easel. He reveals that profits for the next quarter seem to be above 1984 but below plan. He points out what everyone already knows—that most of the problem lies in the domestic beauty business, which is well below last year. He goes into the details of "cranking in this" and "factoring in that."

"Not a good picture from a plan perspective," he says in summation, "but if we come in in that range I think we'll be well perceived by the financial community."

"Any comments on that before we go around the horn?" Waldron asks.

Zimmerman puts in that Avon has fairly high levels of commercial paper outstanding and it should avoid any capital expenditures without considering carefully the need and the timing.

"Let's have everyone drag their bureaucratic feet," Waldron says.

"Review, review, review." Zimmerman says.

The ritual now is for each division head to report on his business. Waldron asks Preston to lead off.

Preston troops up to the easel and shows a chart of representative staff count. A green line stands for the planned number of representatives. A red line is reality. Reality looks a lot worse than the hypothetical.

"Unfortunately," Preston says, "in the last few weeks the trend has gone the other way.

"What we have here," Preston goes on, "is a management problem. What we don't have is a recruitment problem. People aren't executing properly. We're doing several things. We're making some management changes and we're doing some more training. Obviously these results have implications for our annual results. Our projections are no shoo-in with these trendlines. We have to reverse those trendlines or those profit projections are in jeopardy. We have nowhere else to go in cutting expenses. We are cut to the bone at this point in time.

We'll watch this on a day-to-day basis and look for every buck we can get, but we've got to get some sales improvement."

Jack Chamberlin, Avon's recently appointed president, asks, "Do you have any things that are showing improvement?"

"Yes, Jack," Preston says. "We have some managers who are doing very well. We have some divisions that are running at a par with a year ago, if not ahead. So it can be done."

"You're really convinced it's managerial?" Chamberlin says.

"Let me put this in perspective," Preston says. "There's no question there's an industry-wide recruiting problem. But take five percent of the shortfall and attribute it to that. Take seventy-five or eighty-five percent of that and I say it's our problem —a managerial problem."

"Which is the best thing," Waldron says. "An industry problem is hard to fix."

Preston turns to the international beauty business, where the picture is much brighter, helped by the weakening of the dollar. Then he talks about four new business opportunities that are off the record.

"Ray?" Waldron says, and Ray Bentele, the head of Mallinckrodt, starts his presentation. He spews out his latest numbers. He says he's pleased with operating profits but not sales. The hospital business is very good, he says, but flavors, fragrances, and cosmetic chemicals are very weak. He tells Preston that if it's any consolation, he sees very weak orders from all the cosmetic companies, even in sunscreen, a hot product category.

"Hmm," Preston says. "That's surprising."

"I just saw a report on this the other day," Bentele says. "Sunscreens are very weak."

Then he says, "I don't know if you've been following earnings releases in our related industry.
The chemical industry has been absolutely horrible
—terrible results. I can't think of a company that
has had an up quarter. So that's a concern. Imports
are blamed a lot. The dollar is blamed a lot. The
drug business, though, is holding up well."

Waldron asks if the Mallinckrodt ingredient that
goes into Tylenol is "still going gangbusters."

"That's slowed down," Bentele says. "The flu
season is pretty much past. We need Typhoid Mary
to walk around."

The morning passes slowly, though there is no
sense of impatience on the part of the participants,
except for some occasional wiggling in the cush-
ioned chairs. A silver coffee pot has been arranged
on a table against the wall, and the CMC members
periodically collect their mugs and quietly go over
for a refill. During the protracted course of the
meeting, I entertain myself by trying to derive a
correlation between the speaker, or subject matter,
and the number of visits for coffee made by the
listeners, thinking that this will identify the pre-
mier eye-glazing speakers within the Avon top ech-
elon. Diligent as I am, I can make no sense of my
informal study. No matter who is speaking, several
people fetch coffee.

Steve Nagy, the head of the Foster home-health-
care division and Avon's young lion, gets the nod
from Waldron. The numbers. Pretty much on plan.
To make the second-quarter targets, he says, he has
created what he calls a "May scare." He says he
plans to crowd more acquisitions into the month.
All managers, he adds, "have been thoroughly sen-
sitized to May needs and are to bring in buckets of
good news."

"We've got to get it done," Nagy says. "It's not

easy. Every month is a struggle. I think the third quarter is the key. If we get the third quarter, I think we'll get the year."

"Thank you, Stephen," Waldron says. "Mr. Fashion Plate."

Bill Willett, the head of the Direct Response division, stands up and runs through his numbers, which are okay. Then he says that he is rolling out a sweepstakes—the $1 Million Great American Dream Sweepstakes—with the Avon Fashions catalogue. "In testing this last year," he says, "we found it gave us a seventeen percent increase in response."

"Any concern about the effects on the image of using a sweepstakes?" Preston asks.

"I had the argument a year ago at *Time*. All of the editors were against sweepstakes. But we found it had zero effect on image. What it does is give the customer another reason to buy. It creates a sense of urgency. Gets them inside."

"You're not doing that with James River Traders, are you?" Waldron says.

"I wouldn't rule it out," Willett says.

"Well, I think you should think about it," Waldron says. "Mrs. Sixpack wouldn't care. The Avon Fashion person wouldn't care. But the James River Traders customer is a little different and might care about image . . . So let's put that in your think-it-over department."

"Is it going to be some screaming gold label on the catalogue or what?" Bentele asks.

"No, sir," Willett says. "It's very tastefully done. It's still a sweepstakes. But it's well presented. I think you'll all have a copy of it within the week. I think it's an appealing thing. Besides, I need the seventeen percent increase in response."

A short break is called by Waldron to "take care of Mother Nature."

During the break, Waldron tells me that, in addition to the ritualized proceedings, the CMC may mull over any number of unscheduled questions. For example, Avon has a set of guiding principles that were conceived by David McConnell. They smack of motherhood and love. ("To render service to customers that is outstanding in its helpfulness and courtesy." "To maintain and cherish the friendly spirit of Avon.") Waldron questions whether the principles make much sense in the modern world and has asked the CMC to think about whether they ought to change them. Also, now that Avon is in the home-health-care and critical-care businesses, he has been thinking about changing the name of the corporation from Avon Products to something that better reflects its diversity. The CMC has been asked about that.

After the break, Bob Duff, the director of benefits, comes on to give the guest address on health-care-cost management. He uses a slide show. He says that Avon's health-care costs are $27 million and he thinks that conservatively 10 percent could be carved from that. He says that a preliminary study was done of twenty-two people to get a feel for their attitudes about health care. They were found to be confused and worried. He says seven different brochures have been worked up to give out to employees.

The last revelation draws some groans from the CMC participants, who say they are not eager to hand out brochures. Waldron says that each division has a different culture and different needs.

Waldron's voice is a little bit pugnacious now, almost as if he were inviting someone to a duel.

"I think what you're hearing here is a deep interest in your subject," Waldron says. "What you're also hearing here is some criticism of your methods and maybe you need to go back to the drawing board on that. So maybe you're hearing more than you wanted to hear."

"Absolutely not," Duff says sagely.

Waldron thanks Duff. Duff in turn thanks the group, then collects his things and hastens out, doubtlessly making a mental note to himself that the next time he is invited to appear before the CMC to be sure that he has an all-day dental appointment for root-canal work.

Waldron now goes around the horn to the staff people, asking for any "goodies" they may have.

Bob Pratt: "Nothing."

John Cox: "Nothing."

Don Moss: "Nothing."

Zimmerman mentions that insurance costs are creeping up and need to be looked at. He says that officers' and directors' insurance is coming up for renewal and the rates are way up.

"Seven to eight times premium, and you can't get it," Waldron says.

"Wow!" Cox says.

"We may have to self-insure," Waldron says.

Thomas Knight, the legal counsel, says, "I don't normally bring before this august body little nasty suits, but there's been a lot of press on this one. We terminated a general manager in Iowa for dismal performance and she sued for age discrimination and there's been a lot of nasty press in Iowa. You will read something in *USA Today* about this."

"No, you will not," Cox says.

"Did we squelch that?" Knight asks.

"After talking to us, she decided there was no story," Cox says.

"Well, I guarantee you there is no case," Knight says. "We will win this."

Then Knight says that the company has cancelled a contract on a new projection system for district manager meetings because the product is of poor quality.

"It was a five-million-dollar order," Waldron says.

"You're talking big bucks," Knight says. "The short version is it didn't work. It wasn't on time and we didn't get what we paid for. Whether that is going to amount to a lawsuit is a damned good question. I think it might."

That concludes the business of the meeting. It is twelve-thirty now, and so the CMC members shrug into their suit jackets and head down the elevators to the twenty-seventh floor, where the executive dining rooms are located. Another ritual mandates that all of the members take lunch together following their monthly meeting.

Once they are seated, the talk turns to baseball. Everyone agrees that George Steinbrenner is bad for baseball.

Waldron says, "I met Yogi Berra at a party, and he was a very nice, very short guy."

"Yeah, he is short," someone says.

"When is the UFL going to fold?" Waldron asks. "I saw in the papers where some team in the NFL drafted Herschel Walker, figuring he'd be free soon."

Bill Willett tells a faintly amusing story about his too-short tuxedo pants. It seems that he was attending a black-tie dinner with other Avon officers last night and found himself at his office with the pants to the tuxedo of his sixteen-year-old son. He lived in the suburbs and had no time to retrieve his own. So he borrowed pants that were about four inches short from a friend.

"At least four inches short," Knight says.

"So I wore them as low as I could and they were still above my socks," Willett says. "Thank God I had clean socks on."

Then the talk turns to how the public's image of business seems to be so poor.

Chamberlin says that he thinks CEOs need to tell their story better.

Waldron says that once at Heublein he got so mad at the University of Connecticut that he took a week off and went and lectured there in the English and economics classes. "It was the hardest week I ever had," he says. "I came home and all my muscles ached."

Pratt says that there's a real problem at the big schools. "Half of the professors are antibusiness."

Everyone has finished eating. Waldron wraps up by saying, "Anybody have any other business? New business? Old business? Monkey business?"

Nobody does.

Closeted in his office some time afterward, Waldron alludes to the shake-up in Avon beauty almost as if it is his Waterloo. He feels the strategic plan is right. Now he has trundled up his big guns to execute it. It has to work.

Kicking around in some of the paperwork that is so much a part of big corporations is a sort of last-ditch, if-nothing-else-works-this-is-it alternative for the beauty business. And that is to forget about being a beauty company altogether and plow into distribution of everything and anything. Hand the representatives a Sears, Roebuck-like catalogue and have them peddle grass seed and chain saws and billiard tables as well as cream rinse. Waldron's basic view of that plan is that if matters ever boiled down to that, "You might as well sell the damn company. Who the hell wants to be just a distribution company!"

"What, then, if these management changes don't work?" I ask Waldron.

"If these changes don't do it, then we have a much deeper problem than anyone knows," he says. "A much deeper problem." Then, gazing across his office as if lost in a river of thought, he says, "If they don't work, we'll have to make another move. But I don't know what it will be."

17 □ VISITING THE TROOPS

HOME FOR the Avon corporate jet happens to be Teterboro Airport in New Jersey, and that is where, a bit groggily, I board it at seven o'clock one May morning. The place is virtually deserted. The only conversation seems to be among a cluster of sparrows gathered for some apparent convention on one of the runways. I am to spend a couple of days on the go with Waldron. The first leg of the trip will take us to the largest Avon beauty products facility, located in Springdale, Ohio, on the outskirts of Cincinnati; the next day we're due to fly to Glens Falls in upstate New York to visit the Mallinckrodt plant that makes health-care products.

Waldron, as it happens, is in Connecticut, where he was billeted for the weekend. No problem. We'll head over to Hartford, pick him up, then continue on to Ohio. When you're the CEO, one of the little delights of the job is that you get to use the corporate jet in much the same way that mere mortals use a taxi.

Nice plane. A Falcon 20. Seats six. A capacious couch in the rear to sprawl in once you're in the air. A phone adjacent to the seat that Waldron customarily occupies. Oatmeal carpeting on the floor and the walls. The plane sort of came with Waldron from Heublein. Once R. J. Reynolds had swallowed up Heublein, Waldron put the corporate jet on the

block, since Reynolds had a perfectly adequate
fleet of wings to service its new child. When Waldron took charge at Avon, he discovered that there
was no plane for the executives, so he checked with
Heublein to see if the Falcon had been sold. Not
yet. A new Falcon 20 would command two and a
half to three million dollars. Waldron offered
roughly seven hundred thousand dollars and got his
plane back.

As I slip into a seat and buckle in, the pilot hands
me a cup of coffee without my having to wait for
seventy-two aisles ahead of me to be served. Within
a matter of minutes, we take off.

En route to Bradley Field, I have a choice of
diversions. Spread out on the seat in front of me are
copies of this morning's *New York Times, Wall
Street Journal,* New York *Post, Daily News,* and
USA Today. A deck of playing cards is stashed in a
pouch before me, as is a copy of the book *Isaac
Asimov Presents Super Quiz II.* I rummage through
the quiz book and randomly glance at some of the
questions: "Plato was his tutor." "He portrayed
Messala in *Ben Hur.*" "Who was nicknamed 'Win-
nie'?" "His favorite expression is 'Dy-no-mite.' " I
try to envision Waldron sitting aboard the plane, on
his way to some vital strategic meeting having to do
with mounting a hostile takeover of Revlon, search-
ing his brain for the person whose favorite expression is "Dy-no-mite."

We descend and land at Bradley's Executive
Terminal. Since Waldron isn't scheduled to show
up for another fifteen minutes or so, I deplane
and stretch my legs. I sit and watch some TV, then
visit the men's room. I notice that it's outfitted
with an automatic shoe-shine machine and patrons
are invited to have a free shine. I figure, why
not.

A limousine arrives bearing Waldron. He is in an exceptionally good mood. The morning is sunny, the sky CinemaScope blue. The pilot greets the boss with a certain amount of overly obvious deference and takes his suitcase. We board, the engines are fired up, and we quickly take off.

"This tour will be mostly for visibility," Waldron tells me once we're aloft. "I'll be walking around and shaking hands with people on the line. Frankly, I'd rather spend more time with division managers. When you go out on one of these things, though, everyone wants a piece of the action."

He goes on. "I have an objective of being out in the field three days every two months—either in the U.S. or out of the country. The first purpose is visibility—the notion that the CEO is alive and a human being and cares and is interested enough to be here. This is especially important right now, when we've made some changes again in the beauty business. The second purpose is to gain knowledge. To learn firsthand what the hell is going on out here and what our problems are. That's how Preston found out about how we were screwing up the decentralization."

One of the ways that Waldron fills up his time in the air, he tells me, is by catching up on the requisite reading of his job. I ask him what he reads, and I get an answer with almost the same sort of numerical precision that I have routinely witnessed in so many of his meetings.

"I read *The New York Times* and *The Wall Street Journal*," he says. "I read *Business Week* with a seventy percent success rate. I read *Forbes* with a seventy percent success rate. *Fortune* with a forty percent success rate. I skim *Advertising Age*. That's one-third of my reading. The rest is things like economic reports from the Conference Board."

He opens the tray that folds out from in front of his seat and plops his briefcase on it. "Let's see what I have in here," he says, and he unlocks the case and pokes around inside it. I notice that there is a small headshot of his wife packed away, as well as a nail clipper, a small scissors, and a plastic name tag with his name embossed on it.

"Here's one that I never miss," he says. He holds up the Sunday *Times* crossword puzzle, pretty well filled in. "I usually finish it," he tells me. "When they get nasty, though, I have to get nasty and use the dictionary."

He does a bit more exploring, then hands me something that he identifies as a good example of his reading material. It's a fairly lengthy proposal from a law firm on an antitakeover technique that the firm thought Avon might want to learn more about—for a fee, of course. It had arrived, I see from the date, more than a month ago.

"I usually read this," Waldron says, and he shows me a copy of a deadly report put out by CIGNA entitled *Monthly Economic Perspective*. Then he extricates a report on consumer lifestyles done by Grey Advertising. Then a proposition from Xerox soliciting a contribution to the John F. Kennedy Center for the Performing Arts. "That's about a five-minute reading job. Do I want to contribute or don't I?"

Waldron slams shut his briefcase and says, "There is probably enough reading material coming through literally to spend a day a week. That doesn't count books, which I usually don't get a chance to read. On vacation I sometimes get to open a book. I like spy stories. *Eye of the Needle* is one of the last ones I read. I read *In Search of Excellence*. I read part of *Megatrends*. Frankly, I don't get a hell of a lot out of those books."

Waldron is momentarily distracted by a thread that he discovers dangling from his pants. He inspects it carefully and doesn't like what he finds. He declares, "What a way to start a trip! That son of a bitch is ripped." He fishes the scissors out of his briefcase, trims the tear as best he can, then pats it down. The rip has unnerved him about as much as any faltering sales figures I've seen him review.

I ask if there are any general magazines he looks at. "Oh yeah," he says. "I read *Time, National Geographic, Skin Diver.* I browse through *Architectural Digest, Town and Country, People.* We get every magazine known to man at the home."

Wheels thump, and we set down in Lunken Airport, Cincinnati, slightly behind schedule. CEOs never have to worry about hailing cabs or schlepping their luggage aboard one of those stubby rental-car buses and then giving a clerk their license and credit card and deciding whether to accept or decline the supplementary insurance. They are always met. And they are always met by someone of suitably vertiginous stature. An élan vital grips underlings. The division manager doesn't ring his secretary on the intercom and tell her, "Hey, Dolores, you want to hop in your car and shoot on down to the airport and ride the CEO back here?" The division manager gets his own car washed and waxed, makes sure his son's plastic tommy gun isn't still lying on the back seat, puts on his best suit, and goes and picks up The Man himself.

Thomas Murtach, area vice-president of the central sales organization, and Thonas Jensch, the head of manufacturing for the Springdale plant, greet Waldron warmly and with ear-to-ear smiles. They take our luggage and put it in the trunk of Murtach's shiny Oldsmobile. We're told not to worry about our accommodations for tonight, for some functionary from Springdale has already been directed to check us in and deliver our luggage to our respective rooms. Murtach tells us about how, the last time Waldron came to town for a visit, he got stopped for speeding on the way to pick up Waldron and he just about died because he thought he'd be late.

Riding out to the Springdale facility, Waldron asks Murtach how things are going, and he says that business is sort of slow, though he says that he talks to people and everyone agrees that the business itself is basically sound.

"Just need a few more representatives," Waldron says.

"That's right," Murtach says. "A few more of them."

Waldron then asks Jensch how manufacturing is doing, and he says that things are a little slow.

"These guys can't get enough orders for you?" Waldron says.

"Yeah," Jensch says. "We have about a hundred people on layoffs, either voluntary or involuntary."

Murtach hands Waldron a copy of the business section from the Cincinnati *Enquirer,* which features a lead piece on Avon. "This was in yesterday, in case anyone asks you," Murtach says.

Waldron glances at it and says, "Here's a lead for you. 'To sum it up, Ding-dong, Avon's falling.' Have I read the whole piece, Tom?"

Murtach says, "You've pretty much read it. That's the tone."

Waldron skips through the article quickly, seeming to read something like every other paragraph, and then he looks up and says, "Well, nothing there I can quarrel with."

The Springdale facility is a huge, low, sprawling building, encircled by an enormous parking lot. Before we park, Murtach drives Waldron around back to take a look at one of the delivery trucks, which, at Waldron's insistence, has been newly painted with the Avon name on its sides. Apparently, the trucks before had no identification at all on them, and Waldron thought every opportunity should be taken for some free advertising.

"The people out here love it," Murtach says.

"Some companies have abandoned railroad cars parked with their names on it," Waldron says. "We had the damned trucks."

Murtach pulls alongside one of the idle trucks and we admire it.

"Nothing wrong with that," Waldron says.

Murtach says, "There sure isn't. A real morale booster."

Next, Waldron is taken on a tour of the plant by a young woman manager.

A woman processing orders at one of the computer terminals sees Waldron and says, "Nice to see you in person."

"Well, thank you," Waldron says.

Another woman says, "We see you in the videos all the time."

We look at machines that automatically read order slips. We look at the data-processing center. We look at a "hold order" area, where orders are held from reps who haven't paid for their previous orders. We look at the cash sales area, where employees can buy their own Avon products right off the shelves.

Waldron's guide says to him, "I have to tell you, I had to go out yesterday and buy a can of Clairol hair spray. It was the most heartbreaking thing I ever did."

"Because we're not there anymore?" Waldron says.

"Right," she says.

We look at the order fulfillment line, where "pickers" snatch products out of bins and dump them into boxes to be shipped out to representatives. It's explained that items are grouped by parts of the body: hair, eyes, jaws, neck.

"Jaws?" Waldron says. "What the hell are jaws?"

He fishes a product out of the "jaws" bin and looks at it.

"Mother's Day candy," he says. "That's a stretch, but I'll buy that."

Waldron says to one of the women on the line, "Hello. If this woman messes up, we close down the whole company. That's why we haven't had to close down the whole company."

The woman beams.

Next, we take a tour of the manufacturing area. Waldron waves amd smiles at the workers. The feel is of a politician up for reelection out barnstorming with his constituents. The tour moves at a cracking pace. Several functionaries lag behind, checking their watches roughly every half-second to make sure Waldron doesn't fall behind the tightly arranged schedule.

"Hi, Hicks Waldron," Waldron says to a man who has something to do with making heavy lotions.

"Hi," the man says. "You look well."

"I feel well," Waldron says. "You're doing a great job here."

"Thanks," the man says.

"Well, nice meeting you," Waldron says.

"Okay," the man says. "Good luck."

Then Waldron encounters a group of workers milling about talking. They are big and rather tough looking.

Waldron says to them, "Boy, if I ever get into a fight in Cincinnati, I'd want you guys on my side."

One of the guys retorts, "Well, we're looking for that son of a bitch from the Cincinnati *Enquirer*."

(I am glad here that Waldron neglects to introduce me to the guys as a journalist.)

Waldron climbs up a ladder and peeks into a machine that's making soap. He scoops up some in his hands and feels it. Then he's introduced to a young man named Eddie.

"How are you?" Waldron says. "How are things going?"

"Okay," Eddie says. "I'm trying to make soap for you."

"Well, we're going to try to do a better job of selling it for you," Waldron says.

"I'm sure you'll work it out," Eddie says.

As it happens, a bunch of Avon representatives from Michigan are taking a tour of the facility today, and the manager asks Waldron if he would just say a word or two to them.

Waldron tells them that he'd like to say that he came all the way from New York just to see them, but that would be a lie. Then he thanks them and congratulates them for all their hard work. He says that changes are being made in the company that will make their careers even more exciting. He gets a healthy round of applause.

As we take our leave, Waldron says to me, "Well, you were just surrounded by a bevy of real live Avon ladies. It's a little scary."

Lunchtime. Our dining companions will be seven Avon district managers from surrounding towns. Waldron, when he ventures out of New York, likes to periodically dine with sales managers in order to hear what's on their minds. What he

usually hears are complaints. (I once asked Waldron if it bothered him to be criticized, and he said,
"Of course it bothers me. It bothers me when my
wife criticizes me, and she's always fair. I'm like
anybody else. I just got a note that we've done a
terrific job of improving the morale of Avon representatives, but they could use more stroking.
'Stroke' is the new buzzword these days. I like to
be stroked, too.")

All seven managers—no surprise—are women.
They're all smiles as Waldron greets them individually. It's pretty obvious that they have put on their
best clothes and maybe a touch too much Avon
makeup.

It's a buffet lunch. Waldron falls into the rear of
the line, gets a good helping of everything, and arranges himself at the head of the table. After some
perfunctory small talk, he implores the managers to
be frank and tell him what sort of problems they're
experiencing.

A woman from Michigan clears her throat and
says that she finds that the representatives are quite
frustrated by "Findings," an Avon test of a direct
mail line of cosmetics. "They see Findings," she
says, "and they want to sell it. They also want more
jewelry. Trendy jewelry. Not expensive jewelry.
Cheapy jewelry. The reps don't like too much to
sell skin care. But they like jewelry. It's quick. It's
high profit."

"That's interesting," Waldron says. "Do we need
a different commission structure for the two lines?
Because the future is clearly skin care. We can't
ignore it. It would be like the auto industry saying
we're not going to build small cars."

Another woman says, "The thing they don't like
about skin care is having to sell against other com-

panies. Women say, 'We're using this brand, why should we switch?' They don't want to have to argue with them."

"I think it's product knowledge," another manager chips in. "The more knowledge they have, the better they can sell it."

Several managers point out that the newer reps eagerly go to skin-care classes and like the product line, but the established reps are very much set in their ways and are resisting the line.

Waldron scribbles some notes on a sheet of paper.

"What can we do about recruiting?" Waldron asks, looking around the table.

One woman says that some new incentives that have been introduced, prizes from Avon for bringing in new blood, should help. "I really think you will see the names come in when a rep can say, 'I won this vacuum cleaner or this toaster from Avon.' That really matters. The money is an abstract thing with them."

"I'm really happy to see the one brochure being brought back," someone else says. "It's very difficult working with a new rep and telling her there are two brochures, plus there's a catalogue to deal with."

"Are we back for good with one?" another manager asks Waldron.

"Well, if we aren't, I think we are now," he says. "I don't know for sure, but I'll check it."

Someone else asks, "Do you know if you're thinking of a guarantee for our Honor Society members. Maybe forty-five percent earnings. President's Club members are guaranteed forty percent."

"I don't know," Waldron says. "What do you think will happen?"

"I think it would be an incentive for reps to make Honor Society," the manager says.

"I worry about giving money away if we don't get more back," Waldron says.

Someone else asks, "Can you tell me, is the fifty-dollar order unprofitable? Is that why we went to seventy-five dollars?"

"I don't know," Waldron says. "I would think it's profitable. But it's less profitable."

"Because I had less volume this year. I had less reps, but I also had fewer of the fifty-dollar orders. They may be less profitable, but they give me volume."

"But that's a volume, not a recruiting issue," Waldron says. "We have a recruiting problem."

"This is a recruiting issue," the manager says. "There are women who work in a doctor's office or something and they can make maybe thirty dollars. They'll take the other twenty dollars themselves and get the fifty dollars. But they can't do seventy-five dollars."

"I have one woman who's going to write to you about this," another manager says.

"Great," Waldron says. "Another letter."

"She was a schoolteacher and she could make the fifty dollars, but when it went to the seventy-five-dollar minimum it blew her mind. She said, what's the matter, doesn't Avon want the little people anymore? So she quit."

A few more less-than-dynamite ideas are tossed out, and then Waldron says, "I want to go back to New York with a trillion-dollar idea on recruiting. We really are in terrible shape. We need to recruit."

A manager named Barbara says, "I think we did very well with an 800 number in Louisville. We had an 800 number on TV for call-ins. We got quite a good response from people who were sitting at home with nothing to do. The thing is we're not getting much TV advertising."

"Yes you are," Waldron says. "You're getting three times more. You're not watching it, I'm glad to see. If I catch you at home watching those goddamn soap operas . . ."

"Before, we used to get a mix of recruitment advertising and image advertising," someone says. "Now we don't get many recruitment ads. Could we get more of a mix?"

"The answer is no," Waldron says. "You can't do too many things with advertising. When I came to Avon, I asked how much we spent in advertising. Eighteen million dollars. We spent more than eighteen million dollars at Heublein on A-1 steak sauce. That's not very much. So now we're spending much more—thirty million in the last nine months. But you can't do too much. Our research showed that our image was crappy. Is crappy. So we're trying to build our image, and that will benefit everything."

One manager says that she is surprised by how many women call out of the blue and want service.

"Well," Waldron says, "our consumer research identifies at least ten million women who would buy Avon products as we sit here if they knew how. That's one billion dollars. That's why I keep coming back to how are we going to get more people to sell our products."

"We have to spread the word," one woman says. "I'm going to give a speech before about a hundred people at some lodge. We need to have more reps do that."

"Let's get back to telephone recruiting," Waldron interrupts. "I'm old-fashioned enough that I still say my prayers every night before I go to bed. In the morning when I wake up I sometimes throw up one and say thank you that I'm still alive. Some days I'm not sure that I want to be thankful. The one thing I go to bed with every night, though, is how are we going to get more representatives. It's the one thing that's keeping us from moving ahead. Everything else is working. So I wake up every morning and wonder what all those women are doing. Is this telephone recruiting thing something that might work?"

There are some murmurs of optimism, then one of the managers says, "You know, I always wear my name badge that says 'Avon District Manager,' and I wear it even when I go to the post office or when I run into Wendy's for a hamburger. And you'd be surprised. Last week, I got two or three different people for customer service and one lead for a rep. I didn't hire her, but I got the lead."

"Yes, we don't have enough badges," another manager says. "And the ones we have don't say Avon."

"What should they say?" Waldron asks.

"I like 'Avon Beauty Manager,' " one woman says.

"I like 'district manager,' " is another opinion.

"How about 'chairman of the board'?" says another manager.

"You don't want the damned job," Waldron says.

Another manager says, "I had one woman who had an Avon bumper sticker, and she went to a mall and when she came out there was a note on her windshield that said, 'I looked in your car and saw from the products that you were associated with Avon. I'd like to order Avon.' "

"You use the key trick?" Waldron says. "I was at one of these clinics and a woman told me about the key trick. You have this ring with Avon on it for your keys. If you're in line to check out at the store and there are four or five people behind you, you drop the keys on the floor."

"I love it," one of the women says. "Love it."

"We have five minutes more," Waldron says. "What is the one thing you would do if you were chairman of the board?"

"Meet more district managers," one of the managers says. "We are the key link to the business."

Another: "My people are concerned about the product line. They're concerned about the pricing. We have so many competitors out there. They are concerned that the prices are getting a little high. They are concerned whether they can compete. So I want products to sell."

"One more," Waldron says.

"I think the company has always been a people company," someone says. "I think every time a decision is made, it should be realized that it affects people and thus morale. The morale was definitely affected by the seventy-five-dollar decision. We should be concerned about people."

"Definitely," Waldron says. "We keep that in mind."

Waldron then gets up and walks around the table and shakes each of the women's hands and then strolls out of the room.

Later on, I ask Waldron about the value of the advice he got at the luncheon.

He says, "It's what I call mother-in-law research. You know, some guy says, 'I talked to my mother-in-law over the weekend and she said da-da-da-da-dee-dum,' as opposed to professional research. You listen to it, but you don't really look for solutions to act on. For example, when I ran the audio products division at GE, whenever we were coming out with a new line we would sit down with the cabinet-maker. I quickly learned that what I liked in cabinet design had nothing to do with what sold. What I liked, what my wife liked, what my mother-in-law liked was not important. But mother-in-law research is a good indication of what the problem is and it helps you in trying to come up with a solution."

I tell him that I wondered how sincere he was when he told the women that he went to bed every night practically frantic about the dilemma of how to recruit more representatives.

"Well, I was being a little dramatic there," Waldron says. "When I brought God in, I was stretching it a bit. But the number of representatives has a direct effect on our bottom line. Everyone is worried about the dividend, and so I have to be worried about the dividend, and if we have to cut our dividend and thus our stock price in the middle of our strategy, then we have to reexamine that strategy."

□   □   □

KAREN MILLER'S HOME is a modest, well-kept place in a neighborhood encircled by a ruff of trees. It appears to be somewhat more upscale than is customarily associated with Avon country. There are a few kids' bikes lying on front lawns, some backyard pools, lawns that have been exquisitely manicured.

Karen Miller is an Avon lady. Her mother was an Avon lady. Her mother, in fact, had the same route of a hundred homes that her daughter has patrolled for the past six years. Pitching Avon is a part-time occupation, though, for Mrs. Miller also works as a beautician.

Waldron, when he's on the road, likes to drop in on some of the sales force and occasionally shadow one or two of them on an actual housecall. Time is running short, but Waldron nevertheless feels that he can cram in one visit with Karen Miller.

Mrs. Miller is an appealing, friendly young woman, with alert eyes. Her house, she points out, has pretty much been furnished with bonus gifts from Avon. "Let me show you what Avon gave me," she says to Waldron. She directs his attention to a veritable army of knickknacks, two television sets, a sewing machine. She says she redid her daughter's room with the material she got with the sewing machine. She points out the clock in the kitchen, the percolator. "Even my front porch I owe to Avon," she says.

"I never saw an Avon porch before," Waldron says.

"Well," Mrs. Miller says assuredly, "there's going to be another side porch and a Jacuzzi next year."

Mrs. Miller gathers up her sample case and a bag of Avon products that the customer she's visiting had ordered last time, and we climb into her car and take off. She tells Waldron that what she could really use from Avon is a product that would cut her weight in half. Waldron tells her he'd be the first to try it. The way it works at Avon, selling takes place in two-week "campaigns." The rep visits a customer, gets her order, then pays a return visit two weeks later, at which time the order is fulfilled and a new one taken. I notice that this customer will be getting $23.40 worth of goods. Mrs. Miller says that last year she racked up $17,000 worth of commissions, selling Avon.

We pull up to a split-level on a tree-dappled street. The lawn could belong to a golf course. A perky middle-aged woman in a pink sweater and gray slacks answers the door and invites us to make ourselves comfortable in the living room. A dog is barking in the other room, and the woman says not to mind him. Waldron tells her what a lovely house she has.

Mrs. Miller gives the customer her order and collects the $23.40 in cash. Then she starts extracting sample goods and pitching them. She shows her a belt buckle intended as a Father's Day gift.

"Best day of the year," Waldron chimes in.

She shows her some cologne, then a manicure set.

"With a ten-dollar order, you can get this nice zipper case for two dollars and fifty cents," Mrs. Miller says.

"That is nice," the woman says.

Mrs. Miller shows her a tie tack with a miniature car on it. "This one's the Cadillac," she says. "So the man can say he's got a Cadillac."

She shows her a ceramic bowl in the form of strawberries. Then she shows her some foot products.

"And the new mascara," she says. "I use this myself. When I go out in the daytime, I don't want to have too much makeup, so I use the brush from the top part. In the evening, I unscrew the bottom and there's a thicker brush so I can put a little more on."

She shows the woman some perfume. "You know how much perfume you buy from me," she says.

Waldron says to the woman, "I don't know how you can resist all that. If we had a few more like her, we'd be a bigger company."

The woman now pages through the catalogue and calls off her order as Mrs. Miller scribbles it down on her pad.

Mrs. Miller reminds her that the eyeshadows that she likes are on sale for $2.50.

"What's that color I like?" the woman says. "That blue one."

"That used to be the frosty amethyst."

"Okay. And I'd like the bamboo earrings."

"Do you have any of the talc on sale?" the woman asks.

"Talc? Let's see. Yes, we have some talc on sale. A good special."

The woman orders enough that she goes and takes the bonus zipper case, too.

"All righty," Mrs. Miller says, and she totes up the order, hands the woman a receipt, and tells her that she'll see her again in two weeks. Waldron thanks her for her indulgence and we leave.

Back in the car, Mrs. Miller tells Waldron, "Normally, I'll stay there for about a half-hour. She orders more when we sit there and talk. So we talk, she orders, we talk, she orders."

Waldron, who seems to like Mrs. Miller's spunky style, suggests that she take on some more homes, perhaps another full territory, and then she'll make even more money.

"No," she says. "I stay pretty busy."

"Instead of just that Jacuzzi," Waldron persists, "you could put in a whole swimming pool with another territory."

"No," she says again. "I don't think so."

☐   ☐   ☐

SOON THEREAFTER, a limousine, raising dust, whisks Waldron to his next appointment over at Fries & Fries. Fries & Fries is a small but prospering company buried deep under Avon's corporate umbrella. It's technically part of the Mallinckrodt division, but its business is the arcane one of making artificial flavors for foods and beverages.

Raymond Bentele, the head of Mallinckrodt, had asked Waldron a while ago if he would pay a visit

to Fries & Fries next time he was in the area. He
was somewhat troubled that the company's executives were discontent with the bureaucracy of the
corporation and that some of them were not really
behaving as if they were part of the team. The presence of Waldron, he felt, might provide a boost in
morale and bring them into line.

Waldron tells me in the car, "Here, you're probably going to hear some bitching about expense
controls. Because they're off in their plan, but not
that much off. Yet we've had to put a tight lid on
everything."

Jon Fries, a young man whose grandfather
founded the company back in 1919 and who now
runs it (later in the year, he would resign), greets
Waldron warmly and directs him into the company's conference room. Also on hand is Jack Ufheil,
the chief operating officer of Mallinckrodt, who's
come in from Saint Louis to be here while Waldron's around.

Jon Fries starts off with a slide show and spiel in
the conference room, covering the company history, its strategy for future growth, its position relative to its competition.

As he follows along, Waldron occasionally mut-
ters a word or two of approval:

"Great!"

"Terrific!"

"That's just wonderful!"

A vast assortment of sample products has been
assembled in the room, and they get passed around
for our pleasure. Fries carefully explains to me that
I mustn't identify any of the products that Fries &
Fries creates flavors for, because the food companies are extremely skittish and many don't like it
known that there are any artificial flavors in their
products or at least that someone other than their

own scientists concocted the flavor. I agree to keep the secrets under wraps and, like everyone else, I dig in and gorge myself with tasty————cookies, crunchy————crackers, then wash it all down with some delicious————soda.

Waldron has four or five cookies and a bunch of crackers. He says, "Boy, I better not come here too often."

Next, Fries takes Waldron on a meteorlike tour of the plant so he can get a feel for how flavors are made. At one point, Waldron says to me, "You've been to one food-processing plant, you've been to them all. If you went to one of Heublein's plants, it would look exactly alike."

"I imagine it would smell different," I say.

"Yeah," Waldron says. "I'm not sure if it would smell better. But different."

Back into the limousine and on in comfort to the Westin Hotel in downtown Cincinnati, where Waldron will have a chance to briefly freshen up. Then Jon Fries is feting him at a dinner party at his farm on the perimeter of the city. Cocktails at seven. Dinner at eight.

Ufheil rides with Waldron to the Westin, and he mentions that Jon Fries has been a bit of a problem lately. He's been grumbling about the thick layers of corporate bureaucracy.

Waldron says that he imagines that Fries made himself a few million dollars when he sold the company to Mallinckrodt.

"He sure did," Ufheil says.

Waldron says, "When you get to a late-night drinking session with someone like that, you say, 'Okay, we'll give you all your authority back and you give us all our money back.' That sobers them up pretty fast."

Our keys had already been delivered to us when

we left Springdale, so we don't need to bother stopping at the registration desk of the Westin. I had noticed from Waldron's itinerary that he was booked into a two-room suite, while I'm ensconced in a single. I also notice that some nuts and wine were ordered for his room (not even a Coke for mine), though he had scribbled on the itinerary, "Thanks, but no thanks."

When I go into my bathroom to wash up, I see that the room has been stocked with an array of Avon products. There's some Avon Aloe Vera Conditioner, Avon's Musk for Men, Avon One-Step Conditioning Creme Rinse, Avon Care Deeply Extra Creamy Lotion for Dry Skin, Avon Moisture Therapy Body Lotion, Avon Aloe Vera Shampoo, Avon Keep Clean Anti-Dandruff Shampoo—all of which will be essential if I elect to spend the rest of the night devoting myself to washing and re-washing my hair.

□   □   □

JON FRIES trundles down the stairs, his hair still soaking wet from the shower. He says his wife is going to give it to him, everyone is there early and she isn't even dressed yet.

"Want to take a walk around the grounds?" he asks Waldron.

"Sure, you bet," Waldron says.

Walking around the grounds can occupy much of a lifetime. The place is so huge that it's unclear where it ends, or if the boundaries are even visible without the aid of a powerful telescope. The main house has white pillars and resembles a southern plantation. There's a swimming pool with a pool house. There's a house for a caretaker. There's a long, low barn that Fries says used to house turkeys. There's a regular barn and a silo. There's an interesting-looking tree that Fries says is the only cucumber magnolia tree in Ohio.

When we troop back to the house, we are introduced to Fries's wife whose name is Jan. Fries, however, calls her "Blue," because that's her favorite color. She then takes Waldron and me on a tour of the house. It's got countless rooms, all beautifully decorated. Everything seems to have been cleaned and straightened up for the occasion, most notably the two children's room, which are spotless. Later on, Waldron tells me he can't believe that young kids live there; he says there must be a closet somewhere in the house that is packed to the bursting point with thousands of kids' toys.

Cocktails are served. Waldron accepts red wine. Shrimp and cheese have been laid out. Several other Fries & Fries executives are here in addition to Waldron and Ufheil. Conversation runs to fairly trivial subjects. Waldron tells a story about scuba diving when he lost his tank in a cave. He says he was taught not to panic and he didn't. He calmly retrieved it and put it back on. Presumably this says something about why he is the CEO and nobody else in the room is. One of the Fries & Fries executives tells about a skiing episode when he lost control and flattened another skier, just about killing him. He gets kidded about the incident for the rest of the evening.

It's about this time that things begin to go poorly for Jon Fries. The cook, it seems, is a bit forgetful. Among the things she has recently forgotten is to start the dinner. Waldron had made it clear that he had had a long day and would like to make it an early evening. Eight o'clock comes and goes. Eight-thirty. The cocktail hours drone on. The cheese and shrimp are being devoured.

One of the executives is due to catch a flight tonight and had arranged for a cab to pick him up at
eight-thirty, when he thought he would be finished
eating. The cab pulls up outside. He has to excuse
himself, even though he is doubtlessly famished.
Jan Fries thoughtfully rustles together a plate of
some food from the kitchen and gives it to him to
take along in the cab. Jon Fries, meanwhile, has the
look of death on his face.

Waldron tries to be reassuring. Reaching for comforting words, he says, "It's no problem at all. Not
even worth mentioning."

At nine-fifteen, we finally sit down to dinner.
Fries makes sure that Waldron sits at the head of
the table. Once we are all in place, Waldron proposes a toast to Jan Fries and then to Jon Fries.
After the hours of drinking, everyone is in a rather
jovial mood. The belated food is delicious—prime
ribs, fresh spinach, baked potato, salad. Dessert is a
delectable mousse and strawberries.

Waldron tells various anecdotes. One is about a
Kentucky Fried Chicken franchisee meeting in Las
Vegas. A franchisee left his wife at the blackjack
table and said he was going up to bed. She had five
dollars left and said she'd be right up. He never
saw her again, Waldron says. She went to the craps
table, made eight thousand dollars, and vanished.
Waldron then says that on another night he had
been cleaned out of his hundred-dollar limit and
went to buy some cigars. He got several silver dollars in change, so he repaired to the slot machines.
He had been trying to avoid a particularly nettle-
some franchisee. Just as he was about to plunk his
last silver dollar into the slot machine, the franchisee tapped Waldron on the shoulder. As he turned
around to deal with him, a woman happened by,
dropped a dollar into the slot, and watched seven

thousand dollars rain out. "I'll tell you this," Waldron says. "The man wasn't a franchisee the next week."

At one point, someone asks Waldron what he thinks of President Reagan. Waldron says he thinks he's done quite a good job, and everyone nods in ready agreement. Speaking of his politics, Waldron motions with his hands and says, "If Republican is here and Genghis Khan is here, I'm to the right of Genghis Khan."

Someone mentions that Mario Cuomo, the New York Governor, could be the next Democratic candidate for President, and Waldron says, "I can't even associate the word 'vote' with him."

(Later, Waldron tells me that he wasn't entirely joking. He says he is a registered Republican and generally supports the most conservative candidates for public office. He favors minimal regulation of business by government. He opposes such intrusions as laws requiring motorists to wear seat belts, even though he says his son wasn't wearing a seat belt when he was killed. He says he firmly supports permitting prayer in schools, "but I don't come down hard on requiring it." He is a staunch crime-and punishment man and supports the death penalty. He favors American intervention in Nicaragua, as well as in any foreign country that poses a threat to this country. The subject on which he tilts to the liberal side is abortion. He thinks women should have free choice.)

Things have been going too well, and so when the bar-tender comes around with after-dinner cordials, he spills two of them. One nearly splashes Waldron. The Oriental rug on the floor beneath Waldron gets a good dose. Waldron tells Blue that the best thing is soda. Somebody once spilled red wine all over the white pile rug in his apartment,

he says, and his wife poured Seven-Up on it and it
vanished. Taking his advice, Blue gets some club
soda and starts dripping it on the rug.

"Put some more," Waldron says. "Really pour it
on."

Blue really pours it on, and the stain vanishes.
Once everyone has a glass, Fries proposes a toast,
thanking Waldron for coming and telling him what
an honor it is to have him in his home.

We retreat into the next room so the table can be
cleared. Waldron says he probably ought to be getting on, he's got an early day again tomorrow. Jon
Fries mentions that the heavyweight championship
fight between Larry Holmes and Carl "Truth" Williams is about to start. Waldron speculates that the
fight won't last more than a round or two, why not
catch the beginning of it. So Fries clicks on his big-
screen TV in the den and everyone groups around
the set.

Williams is a heavy underdog, yet Waldron says
he'll bet a dollar on him against anyone who will
give him odds.

Nobody wants to give the odds.

"All right," Waldron says grudgingly. "A dollar
even."

One of the Fries & Fries executives takes the bet.

The fight is good and close. Everyone seems to
think Williams is winning it, though he takes a bat-
tering in the latter rounds. In a close decision,
Holmes is declared the winner. Waldron says he's
been robbed. He gets up, pulls out his wallet, peels
out a dollar, and hands it over. It's past midnight
now, so Waldron says he had better be going. Jack
Ufheil, who is also staying at the Westin, rides back
with us.

In the car, Ufheil and Waldron talk about boxing.
Then Ufheil thanks Waldron for making the visit.

"It really has an effect on the people," he says. "You could see it in their enthusiasm tonight."

"Yes," Waldron says. "They're quite a bunch of guys."

Then Waldron says, "I haven't had a chance to ask you the big question. How's business?"

"It's mixed," Ufheil says. He mentions that he's been annoyed by two recent product recalls that he fears could leave a blemish on the company's reputation. Waldron expresses surprise when Ufheil tells him that one of the recalls involved a tracheal tube, sold to a hospital, that came apart in its package.

"How the hell do you let that get out if it falls apart in the package?" he says.

"I don't know," Ufheil says. "That's what I'm trying to find out. I'm not letting the product out again until I find out what the quality-control problem was."

"You sure as hell better not," Waldron says.

"I know, Hicks. I know."

□   □   □

A LIMOUSINE is outside the Westin at seven-forty-five the next morning to take us back to Lunken Airport for our flight to Glens Falls. In the car, Waldron reads *The New York Times*. Silently, he clips out a story reporting that Governor Cuomo is pulling New York State investments out of companies operating in South Africa and ordering the state not to do business with those companies. Waldron says that he's going to write a letter to Cuomo arguing against that stance.

"Some Brim, Mr. Waldron?" the pilot asks brightly, once Waldron has settled into his seat.

"Jesus, I thought you'd never ask," Waldron says.

There is a tray of pastries aboard sufficient for a dozen hearty eaters. Waldron and I split one. Then he gets up and moves the tray to the back couch so he won't see it and be tempted to have another.

Waldron flips leisurely through *The Wall Street Journal*. He spies *Life* magazine and picks it up. "This is something I never see," he says.

Then he makes a phone call to his office to see if anything's doing and to report that the trip seems to be going fine. Nothing much is doing.

Waldron and I chat aimlessly. I ask him whether he's taken any instruction courses to help him in his job. Management seminars, I've been made aware, are quite popular in corporate circles, though I've been dubious that they are all that informative.

"At Heublein I did take a course in public speaking," Waldron says, "and we ended up giving it to all our people at Kentucky Fried Chicken. I think that's important. I think you can teach people the art and skills of public speaking. I have trouble with teaching the average person the skills of management late in life. But I think a guy who's running a business who has trouble speaking would be well advised to learn that skill."

"What did you get out of the course?" I ask.

"Not an awful lot. I like to speak. I think I'm relatively good at it. The theory of the guy I took my lessons from was that you should never start or end a sentence looking at your notes, nor should you look at your notes when you're making the point."

Waldron then demonstrates for me how you're supposed to do it. He grabs *The Wall Street Journal* and starts randomly reading an article. He looks down and memorizes five words, looks up and says them, looks down and picks up five more words, and so forth.

"It feels so strange doing it," Waldron says, "but when you it on videotape, it's really better."

As we talk, I notice that Waldron's eye keeps being attracted to something outside my window. I look and spot a small aircraft hovering some distance away.

"I want to keep an eye on that plane," Waldron says. "That son of a bitch is getting closer to us."

Finally, Waldron unbuckles himself and troops up to the cockpit to consult with the pilot. After a few minutes, he returns and says a little sheepishly, "He told me it's four thousand feet above us."

Waldron downs a Life Saver. Of all the things he swallows, one of the ones he likes the most is Life Savers. "I eat these things like peanuts," he says.

At ten, the Falcon sets down in Warren County Airport in Glens Falls, a bucolic community of about twenty-five thousand people sandwiched amid rolling hills in upstate New York. Once we deplane, there is no car waiting, and Waldron gets a chance to pace around with his hands sunk in his pockets. He asks me to guard his briefcase while he ducks into the men's room. The pilot, sizing up the situation, says to me, "Boy, if I was supposed to meet him, no way I'd be late. I mean, no way in the world. I'd be here the day before to make sure."

Approximately six minutes late, three executives from Mallinckrodt, including Ray Holman, the group vice-president who works out of corporate headquarters in Saint Louis and who has come out just to be sure things go properly with the Waldron visit, scream up to the terminal.

We drive to the critical-care facility, which is actually in the town of Argyle. It makes products like endotracheal tubes, esophageal stethoscopes, and suction catheters—the sort of things, as Waldron puts it, that you don't want to ever have to use.

Waldron is ushered into a small, plain conference room and the inevitable briefing starts. It's delivered by one of the executives, a man named Fred Giardinello. He begins by reciting the division's mission statement: "MCC will, on a worldwide basis, manufacture and market specialty medical products, primarily disposable, which monitor or maintain vital signs and functions for the critical-care patient."

"You know," Waldron interrupts, "you guys are so high flying, would you mind adding to your mission statement high margins. You could get into all sorts of exciting new things and watch the margins go down."

"Well, some of these are commodity businesses," Giardinello says.

"Depends on your perspective," Waldron says. "When I was at Heublein, refried beans were our commodity business. When I took charge of Del Monte, refried beans were a specialty product for them. So what was a dog commodity product for us was a specialty item for them. This is so exciting a business that, maybe not in your mission statement, but tattooed on your underwear, should be high-margin business."

Nods of agreement around the table.

There's some talk about a small company that the division recently acquired.

"How's that been?" Waldron asks. "What were the surprises?"

Ray Holman answers: "Well, the earnings were not as good as we had expected. Certainly not in the first quarter. But we're convinced that they're good products. Really good products."

"And the high margins are there?" Waldron says. "I forget what they were, but they were reflecting really high margins. Now that you've gone over the rocks, are they still there?"

"Yes, we think so," Holman responds. "They're good—forty percent or so."

"They're not in jeopardy?" Waldron asks.

"No, we don't think so."

Then there's a discussion of critical issues affecting health-care products—new alternative-care facilities, health maintenance organizations, and so forth.

"And you're tracking that very carefully?" Waldron says.

"Yes," Holman says.

Mark Throdahl then reviews the organization structure and some of the key issues facing the business. Waldron, meanwhile, clips his fingernails.

Then Noel Harmon, the plant manager, takes Waldron and the others on a plant tour. Everyone is outfitted in a white lab coat (Waldron asks for a 44 long), a woman's hair net, and plastic goggles. Everyone looks utterly absurd.

"The good thing," Waldron says, "is we all look equally ridiculous."

Throdahl says, "The women get so used to all this that they wear it out to the supermarket."

Waldron is shown how an endotracheal tube, the heart of the division's business, is made. As he moves along the assembly line, he is introduced to the workers.

"How are you?"

"Take care."

"Have a good day."

One woman stops Waldron and says that her brother, a doctor, played football with Waldron at Green Mountain College. Waldron shows polite interest. She says perhaps he might want to get in touch, and gives Waldron a scrap of paper with his address on it. Waldron thanks her.

Being that Waldron had been informed the day before by Ufheil about a recent recall at the facility because a tracheal tube had a design flaw and the end of it came apart in several doctors' hands (though fortunately not inside a patient), when Waldron reaches the end of the assembly point of the tube, he asks what the problem had been. He's shown how the design has been changed. One of the executives remarks that the flawed design was the work of another company that the division acquired. "It wasn't our design," he says.

Waldron at once undercuts the lame excuse: "That and a dime will get you a cup of coffee."

Waldron is taken into the company cafeteria for a quick look and for him to give a wave to the dining employees, and then we get rid of our getups and prepare to leave.

Waldron now has time for a quick lunch and then has to get back aboard the plane. I ride to lunch with Noel Harmon, while Waldron goes with Holman, Giardinello, and Throdahl.

I ask Harmon if field visits like this have much effect on employee morale.

"Oh yeah," he says. "The people on the line are thankful just to shake the man's hand. That's why I thought it was important to walk into the cafeteria so anyone we missed could just see the man. You know, just gaze at him."

Lunch is at the Red Coach Grill, not much of a place, but the best in the immediate vicinity. The stock market has been strong the last couple of days, and Waldron is asked if he thinks the upward trend will continue. He says that interest rates have come down, and so what normally happens is people start moving their money into equities. There's some talk about the fight last night, and how everyone thought Larry Holmes had lost. Someone asks Waldron if he's been skiing much. He says not as much as he'd like. He says that he bought season ski lift tickets this past winter for $735, rather than paying $25 each time out. He put the tickets on the bulletin board at home so Mrs. Waldron and he could check off each time they skied to see if they made the wise choice. "We went five times," he says. "Five times twenty-five is a hundred and twenty-five dollars."

Waldron is buckled into his plane seat by two-thirty-five. He has a board meeting of the Connecticut Bank and Trust Company in Hartford at four o'clock. Then he has to fly to Philadelphia for a dinner session with a committee of the CIGNA Corporation board in preparation for a CIGNA directors' meeting tomorrow. At the time Waldron also sits on the boards of Sea-Land, Allegheny International, and Hewlett-Packard.

I ask him what he gets out of them.

"Quite frequently I pick up things of use for Avon," he says. "Financing deals for the company. What's new in shareholder rights issues. What's happening in the South Africa issue. Compensation programs. Tax laws. Quite often I come back with one idea per meeting. The whole area of what's going on in health care. CIGNA, for instance, has been helpful to our people in that area."

The trip has been a frenzied one for me, with no opportunity for some private relaxation. I am on the edge of exhaustion. I ask Waldron how he feels.

"I get tired," he says. "I was tired like you last night. But I enjoy it. I enjoy the hard life. I work hard and I play hard. And I relax like a professional. I have the ability to completely relax at any time when I have to. I have the the ability to not let the business get to me too much. I tell myself that worrying about it not only won't do any good, it will do some harm. I can go home even after I find out the quarter will be down thirty percent or something and totally relax. The thing that gets me the most stressed is uncertainty. If someone says I have to talk to you tomorrow about something important, I have to know what it's about right then. I'm a firm believer that worrying about the uncertainty is worse than the facts. The only exception was when the doctor told me my wife had cancer. Then I wished I didn't know the facts."

18 □ ONLY DOGS
GET MAD

HURRY, HURRY. Waldron must get to the boardroom. Ten people have arranged themselves
around the table, mountainous stacks of paper in
front of them, legal pads and felt-tip pens at the
ready. This is a meeting being held in early May, to
run over potential questions at the annual shareholder meeting to be conducted three days hence.
The investor relations department has put together
a book of questions and answers for Waldron to use
at the meeting, as if he were preparing for a final
exam. If all the questions were asked, the meeting
would run for the rest of the month. The booklet is
seventy-five pages long.

Once he's seated, Waldron says, "What I want to
know is who put the holes in the corner of the
sheets? I could shoot that person. Because the hole
is different in every single piece of paper. I tried to
feed that son of a bitch through there about four
times this weekend."

Nobody admits to the transgression, and so Waldron allows the session to proceed. Margro Long, the
head of investor relations, runs the meeting. She
calls out page numbers, and if anyone has a problem, he or she is to stop her.

"Okay, one," Long says. "Two."

Companies are, in effect, run on trust, and most
of that trust is put in the chief executive officer. The

stockholders, the actual owners of a company, have relatively little power. In theory, the shareowners are invested with all the power; they elect the directors, on the basis of one share, one vote. The directors in turn appoint the top managers. But the stockholders are deprived of their real power, mainly because of their awesome numbers and also because of their studied indifference to what is going on at the company they own shares in as long as the company keeps fattening them with dividends. In practice, the CEO generally selects board members and proposes them to the shareholders for approval. They consistently vote the mangement slate. About the only time that shareholders—or at least a small minority of shareholders—raise their voices and are heard is at the annual meeting.

These affairs are often noisy and sometimes downright unruly. Guards sometimes have to eject heckling shareowners. Many of the major meetings often are attended by one or several of the so-called professional shareholders or gadflies, people who make an occupation of buying stock in companies or obtaining the proxies of other shareholders, then attending annual meetings to raise questions or propose resolutions. They tend to add the few stinging questions that get aired at stockholder meetings, but often in such a boorish or silly manner that they have no real effect. They, rather than management, frequently find themselves the target of thunderous boos and stamping.

Just about all CEOs, whether they'll admit it or not, detest annual meetings. They hate the exposure to insulting questions. They hate all the preparation they have to do for something that seems to them to be trite. Chief executives are entirely comfortable within their kingdom, where underlings know their place and know better than to suggest to the boss's face that perhaps he could get by on something less than a million dollars a year. But they are decidedly ill at ease when they venture beyond the moats.

When I once asked Waldron what his sentiments were about annual meetings, he didn't need to reflect for more than a microsecond before he said, "Annual meetings in my opinion are worthless. Let me describe what would be an ideal annual meeting. It would last a couple of hours. It would be preceded by a product display. We would have all our officers and directors there. We would encourage a big turnout and invite all our employees. We'd invite high school classes to attend. We'd have maybe a forty-minute presentation on the state of the business. We'd showcase a new product the way Dr. Land always had a new camera or something at the Kodak meeting. We'd answer all the questions that legitimate shareholders had—meaning that some guy with one share couldn't get into the meeting. That could make all the preparation and expense and time that goes into an annual meeting worthwhile. That would be a mature meeting.

"What's happened today is these meetings have become showcases for the gadflies interested almost totally in self-publicity and self-aggrandizement. They come with a list of questions and while you're answering one question they're looking at the next one. They couldn't care less what the hell the answer is. These aren't legitimate questions. They ask about the company planes and compensation and limousines and all the horseshit, not the critical problems of running a twenty-billion dollar or three-billion dollar company. It's all a waste of time. J. D. Fuqua is said to have had the shortest annual meeting of all time—one and a half minutes.

I'm with him. I find these meetings annoying. You get irritated when someone who doesn't know anything at all starts acting like a compensation expert and asking about my apartment. At Heublein, the meetings were a lot rowdier than at Avon. There were some local gadflies who would go over the expense accounts and how much business you did with each director. They'd want to know if the wives went with the directors to board meetings. You always tell them yes, and explain that when the wives go you spend less money and that's good for the shareholders. That always gets a laugh. But those meetings were something. They were so bad that one year I started the meeting with *The Star-Spangled Banner* to get people's attention. It was barely over before the first gadfly was up."

"Page two," Waldron says. "What we have to do is find out what other companies are spending in charitable contributions. Is it one percent, John, or whatever?"

"I'll check it," Cox says.

"Three," Long says. "Four. Five . . ."

Cox stops Long at page twelve and says he doesn't want to use the word "verbatim" and have to give the whole thing.

"I wouldn't say 'verbatim' anyway," Waldron says, "because I don't know what the hell it means."

Long calls out pages: "Thirteen, fourteen."

"Page twenty-eight," Waldron says. "Dilution from acquisitions. We say the actual dilution in 1982 was eleven percent. What about 1983, 1984, 1985? I don't want to just let that eleven percent sit there, because it got better."

"Okay," Long says.

"Twenty-nine, thirty . . ."

"Jim," Waldron says, looking over at Preston, "on

thirty-five, all this waltzing around market share. The numbers have been taken away. It seems to me this is actually a no-brainer. When someone asks us what our market share is, we can say we think it's twenty-two or whatever it is."

"The actual numbers are sixteen, twelve, eight," Preston says. "What we're saying is, overall cosmetics we're number one. In fragrance, we're number one, makeup we are number four, skin care we are number four, in bath we're number one, in jewelry we're number one."

Waldron scribbles the information down. "Okay, and in overall we're number one."

"Yes," Preston says.

"Okay," Waldron says, "those are good numbers."

Everyone is writing like crazy.

Long calls out more page numbers: "Thirty-six, thirty-seven, thirty-eight, thirty-nine."

Preston says, "On pages thirty-nine and forty, I don't want to get into this hundred million coming by 1990 and all."

"No," Waldron says, "that's back-of-the-hand stuff. Forget it."

"Fifty-nine."

"I guess I have to embarrass myself here," Waldron says. "What is the difference between Racof and Esop?"

The human rescources chief says, "Esop is the employee plan. Racof happens to be the particular one being used now. It's based on payroll."

"Sixty."

"We really have to discuss this," Waldron says. "We have to make sure what the five top-paid people were paid last year and what they are paid this year. We have to get the actual numbers and make sure they're right . . . There certainly isn't enough in that little thing there. I'll need a two- or three-pager that I can spread out before me on compensation. This is going to come up every year. This is one I can't duck. I can't get my little gun out and have a thing that comes and says 'bang.' "

"You need real bullets," someone says.

"Right," Waldron says.

"Sixty-four."

Preston says, "On animal testing, you use the word aesthetic rather than anaesthetic."

Everyone laughs.

"This is one we'll always get," Waldron says. "Compensation and animals."

Cox says that he's made another attempt at answering animal-testing questions and hands out a sheet of paper for everyone to look at. The response notes that the beauty division went through about 5,000 animals last year, mainly rodents, a third of what it used five years ago. It also mentions that Mallinckrodt, for its medical research, exhausted 11,157 animals—10,801 rodents, 317 rabbits, and 39 dogs.

Waldron begins reading, and when he gets to the reference to rodents, says, poker faced, "Mostly rodents from the Chinese restaurants in town."

After he finishes, he says, "One of the notes I made is to never talk quantities in animals."

"You can't win," Preston says.

"Now, these characters didn't show up last year," Waldron says. "They did the year before. Did they give advance notice of their coming?"

"I think they did," Preston says.

"They didn't give advance notice when they picketed us the other day," Cox says.

"What I'm afraid of are the nuts who will kidnap animals and all that," Waldron says.

Then he says, "Well, there won't be any picketing at the meeting. We're not letting anyone in with anything bigger than a briefcase."

"Do you want to answer questions on animals, or Jim?" Cox asks.

"I'll answer them," Waldron says. "If it turns into a contest and I'm losing, I'll turn it over to Jim and let him lose it."

Laughs.

"Jim," Waldron says, "I have a question that I think would be a nifty one if I were coming to the meeting. Who has the authority to decide to use animals and how many? You probably don't know."

"I sure don't," Preston says.

"If I had a cosmetic," Waldron says, "and I wanted to squirt it onto a rabbit and put it under a sunlamp and maybe I wanted to be sure so I'd try three, who can do that?"

"I sure don't know," Preston says.

"We should have a statement on that," Waldron says.

"Well, I'll get a statement and get it to Margro," Preston says.

"Seventy-two."

"On seventy-two, this is grossly out of date," Waldron says, referring to a question on charitable contributions made to organizations that board members are involved in. "So we have to dress this one up. The answer has got to be something like three hundred thousand dollars or six hundred thousand dollars. Maybe a better answer is, I don't know."

Now there is a supplementary list of issues that Long has put together and everyone turns to them.

She mentions that a man who is threatening to sue about the sale of some land in Rye may show up. He's been making a stink lately, and Waldron should be prepared for him.

"Okay," Waldron says.

"Dividend," Long says. "The questions are getting more specific here. They're getting around to would we cut it in August if the second quarter is weak, or how soft does the business have to be to cut it?"

Waldron says, "I think the answer here is we are not going to rick and muck our dividend up and down depending on a given quarter's results. The dividend is a long-term thing and if we see a long-term deterioration then we might take proper action on the dividend. All the other questions are so hypothetical that we really can't comment on them. But I think I have to keep the door ajar, as I always do."

Then Waldron says to the group, "Does anyone else have any guesses as to the major issues?"

Nobody does.

"I think that they'll be compensation and animals," Waldron says. "And I would say probably first-quarter performance and dividend, even in a nonsophisticated audience."

Next, the group turns to the speech to be delivered by Waldron to the shareholders.

"Page three," Waldron says. "At the top, I talk about the audience, the hostesses wearing our beautiful fashions, and the office tour. It seems to me that that's the only sex we have in the speech. I think we should flower that up. I want to describe what the hostesses are wearing, ta da, ta da, ta da."

"Okay," Cox says.

"Then, the other thing is, let's not give gifts," Waldron says. "Why ever give gifts to a shareholder?"

Peter Thauer, the assistant secretary, says, "Well, we weren't having a product display this year, so you said let's give gifts."

"Am I supposed to remember that?" Waldron says.

"It was agreed to," Thauer says.

"Well, I have a ten-year history of saying no gifts to shareholders," Waldron says. "I can't believe you got me in a weak moment and got me to agree to that."

Then he says, "How expensive are they?"

"About four dollars a shareholder," Thauer says. The intended gifts for the attending stockholders, which have already been assembled, consist of bags of samples of various beauty products.

"Well, that's a terrible procedure," Waldron says. "I apologize for leading you down the primrose path. But I'm going to make you a hero. We're not going to give gifts."

Thauer says, "Well, we have four hundred white bags to throw away."

"Are they paper bags?" Waldron says.

"Yes."

"Well, we can use them somehow, I hope."

"The only time I found that giving gifts was helpful," Waldron says, "was when one year at Heublein we were under attack for some damn thing. Stuart Watson was chairing the meeting. Some stockholder submitted a resignation paper to Watson and told him he ought to resign right then and sign the letter of resignation. So Stuart looked at his watch and said, boy, it's getting late and we'd planned on giving out gifts and I hope we have enough for everybody here—and vrooom, they all took off."

A good bit of laughter.

"So I'm sorry," Waldron says, "but let's not give out gifts."

Some other possible questions are thrown out.

"South Africa?" Cox says. "We're not in there, but it might come up."

"I can handle that," Waldron says. "Famous last words as I run off the podium and out of the Plaza."

Preston says, "There could be something on product discontinuation or something."

"I can handle that," Waldron says.

That exhausts the issues. A rustle of paper as everyone straightens up their notes.

Then somebody suggests that the executives have a pool to guess what time the annual meeting will end. Everyone throws in five bucks. The meeting will start at ten and the range of times chosen stretches from ten-fifty-two, the pick of Ray Bentele, to eleven-forty-two, which Steve Nagy bets on. Waldron puts his money on eleven-eleven.

Before the meeting breaks up, Waldron announces that there will be a little celebration in the waiting room in honor of Jim Preston's birthday today. He is fifty-two.

Everyone is given a glass of Inglenook Chablis and Waldron proposes a respectful toast. As the group stands around and polishes off the wine, Waldron mentions that he attended a charity dinner last night at which the comic Rich Little gave an absolutely hilarious one-hour performance.

"The one joke I remember," Waldron says, "is he was talking about this woman and he says that she was so ugly that we sat her in the corner and fed her with a slingshot."

Everyone seems to think the joke is extremely funny.

□　□　□

IN THE MONTHS OF MEETINGS that I sat in on, I never saw Waldron stirred to anger. Though there were occasions when he clearly was a little testy, a little short with someone, I never heard him raise his voice or saw his face flush. Afterward, I say to him just that, that I never saw him mad.

"And you won't," he quickly replies. "Sometimes I get mad as a son of a bitch. Then I remember what my Dad told me. 'Only dogs get mad. People get angry.' I have a little homily that I try to abide by, and that is that a leader cannot display emotion. A leader cannot chastise a person in a crowd—and a crowd is three or more. I have a short fuse when it comes to people doing work at a lower quality than they are capable of doing. When a bad piece of work comes in or when I see a bad piece of work or it's late, it irritates me as much as anything else. Another thing that would irritate me is someone who has welched on a handshake. My style is participatory management. I don't say to Preston, 'Go forth and get those numbers or I'll have your head.' I'll call a guy in and chew his ass. But you don't try to scold or spank someone. You show him what he did wrong and how he should have foreseen the problem. I'll give you an example. Preparations for a board committee meeting and a member of my staff was supposed to do some homework. The meeting comes up and there are some questions and it's clear we don't have the answers. I was visibly irritated at that session and there was a dressing-down later. I'll give you another example. We were to be picked up by a limousine to go down to have lunch with the head of Morgan Guaranty on Wall Street. We went down to the street and waited and waited. We came back in and called. He's out there, we're told. We went out and waited and waited. And he was parked way down the block. Now, in a world with the atom bomb and Ethiopia, missing this building by three hundred feet is not so terrible. But we were twenty minutes late. Then he drove us all the way down on the avenues. We couldn't get him to go on the highway. So I really told him what I thought."

Business doings, Waldron says, never bother him for long. "I love the life," he goes on. "I love the job. And I know that that means you have to take it all, not just the good parts. It's like the relationship with your wife. You can't have sex with one woman, eat with another, and play tennis with another. You take it all."

I ask Waldron then if there weren't ever times when he got depressed, figuring that he will tell me about some night after he discovered that third-quarter earnings plummeted 302 percent or after a revolutionary new shampoo that would cut pounds from your figure as it cleaned your scalp bombed in the marketplace. Instead, he gives a curious answer.

"Yes, I'll tell you something that depressed me almost more than anything since my son died," he says. "After my first wife died, I bought a cemetery lot. You always buy a cemetery lot under great pressure. So my daughter, son, and I went to a cemetery and I said that my wife just died and I need a lot. The guy took us out on a tour of the cemetery. I wasn't really all that goddamn interested. He said, how big did you want it? And I said, well, big enough for her and myself and I guess my son and daughter. It was like making a long-term forecast in two minutes. How do they come, I asked, in twos and fours? And he said they were in fours and eights. And I said, okay, we'll take that one for eight, figuring for grandchildren and all. It had four spaces above and four below. I wrote out a check. The next year, my son died, and so back I went to the plot. Last Sunday, Evelyn and I went to the cemetery, as we do almost every other Sunday. We water the flowers and say a prayer. There's a little garden there. My wife loved flowers. So we went there and watered and did some weeding and we looked down and two of the other top graves were used, and had been used for some time. I was grossly disturbed. I played golf that afternoon and my stomach was in knots. I know I bought those eight lots. My emotions really grabbed me on that."

☐ ☐ ☐

"GEE, I DIDN'T KNOW that there were windows in this room," Waldron says. "The wall was always closed."

He was in room 28A now, down on the twenty-eighth floor, a bit early for a meeting concerning the latest proposed acquisitions by the Foster Medical subsidiary.

The folding wall that usually blocks out the windows is only partly open. Waldron wonders if the entire wall can be parted to allow some light in. Jules Zimmerman tries to accommodate Waldron by pushing some remote controls. Nothing.

"Wait," Waldron says. "You push it and maybe I can help by shoving it."

The wall opens perhaps an additional half-inch.

Waldron glances at Jack Chamberlin and says, "Well, Jack, that's your responsibility—operations."

Steve Nagy, the head of Foster Medical, begins the meeting. Foster is probably the most entrepreneurial corner of Avon. I can see that from the style of the three Foster people gathered here with Nagy. One of them is wearing a less-than-conservative sport coat, an open-necked shirt, no tie, a gold chain around his neck. He could be sitting down with

some retirees to see if they'd be interested in buying a new lawn mower from him.

Nagy talks about the subsidiary's strategy. "We
have an ambition to be national," he says. "In order
to be a major player large-scale, we have to have
national replicas of branches. Second, we want to
try to grab a presence in what we call the top fifteen
geriatric states [these are states with the largest
numbers of people over the age of sixty-five]. Third,
we want to expand in fifteen states we have identified as important."

Nagy mentions that it's important for Foster to
maintain the "deal flow," to keep buying more and
more small companies. Foster has been growing
like Topsy, in large part by buying three or so companies a month. This meeting, a regular monthly
session, is for Waldron to hear about this month's
prospects and, if he sees fit, to authorize Nagy to go
ahead and buy them. Two final deals are on the
table.

"How many offers all together do you have?"
Waldron asks one of the Foster executives.

"We have twenty or thirty offers outstanding and
forty companies under review," the man says.

"How's that compare with last year?"

"More," the man says. "That's twenty or twenty-
five percent more."

"Okay," Waldron says.

Nagy turns the meeting over to one of his subordinates, who proceeds to review this month's candidates. He says, "Convalescent Aid got my
number one pick this month, just because of size."
He mentions that the company has some two
hundred million dollars in cash.

Waldron says, "Isn't this the one that has the two
hundred and fifty million dollars in payroll or something? Or is that the other one?"

"Well, they all have debt," the subordinate says.

"The one note I have on this one," Waldron says, "is that isn't that a little high? Or is my observation not valid?"

"Not entirely. Most companies we buy have no cash, and this is a much better deal than most."

The subordinate now hands out a map that shows the acquisition flow in April. There is talk about where Foster is the "whole show" and where there is room to buy more properties. Pages of numbers are reviewed.

Nagy mentions that he and Waldron recently had a debate on whether Foster should be a slowly growing company with a high operating profit or continue to grow very fast with a lower operating profit.

"As I recall, it was a fairly short debate," Waldron says.

"It was a short debate," Nagy agrees.

"How many people have you been able to keep when you make an acquisition on the average?" Chamberlin asks.

"Three or four people have left in the thirty-nine acquisitions we have made," one of the Foster people says.

There is some discussion about how, when people leave after an acquisition, it becomes difficult to enforce agreements that they won't compete against Foster in any future venture.

A Foster man says that there's been only one case where an executive decided to start another health-care company. However, he went to another state.

Waldron asks, "Can't you expand the noncompete to include the world?"

"Well, we're told the bigger it is the less enforceable it is."

"It's not enforceable within a town," Zimmerman

says. "If someone wants to compete, how do you stop them?"

"Well, we have the resources to fight them better than they have the resources to defend," a Foster man says.

Nagy says, "We're getting a lot tougher on this."

"You should be," Chamberlin says.

"The minute they leave," Nagy says, "out goes the noncompete letter."

"And there's that five-year note out there," Waldron says, alluding to the money they are being paid for the company. "If they compete, screw you, Charlie."

"I'm not sure Mr. Knight [the legal counsel] would agree to that," Zimmerman says.

"That's why he's not invited to these meetings," Waldron says.

The Nagy subordinate now gets back to the second acquisition under discussion this month—a company I'll call Supreme Care. "The price was right," he says. "Exactly three times trailing earnings. Earnings have been a little disappointing, which we attribute to poor management. He's a clinician [the president], he's not a businessman."

Waldron says, "So you're going to keep him as a branch manager and give him to———?" He's referring to a highly regarded Foster executive who is known as a businessman, not a clinician.

"We're going to take him out of day-to-day operations of the plant," the Foster man says.

"The one question I had on this one," Waldron says, "is how the hell does he come off spending eight percent of sales on advertising?"

"Well, he's a bit erratic. He gives out prizes at clinics. He gives out T-shirts. He gives out suits."

"Suits?" Zimmerman says.

"Full men's suits."

"With the person's name on the back?" Zimmerman says.

"And probably something on the label," the Foster man says.

"Is that what your label says?" Waldron asks. "Was that part of the deal?"

Laughter.

"The guy is a well-known terrible businessman," the Foster man says.

"Oh yeah?" Waldron says. "Well-known?"

"Several people have told me he spends money like a drunken sailor."

It is now money-authorization time. Normally, acquisitions follow a long, somewhat circuitous route through the upper management levels of Avon for requisite approvals. With Foster, however, since the Avon top executives don't know the business well, Waldron has arranged things so that he signs the front sheet of a package of papers that authorizes Nagy to make his purchases. Nagy now shoves the package in front of Waldron.

"Hey," Waldron says. "I don't see your initials on the bottom of this."

"Oh," Nagy says. "You want me to put my ass on the line first. Well, one more time I'll do it."

"That seems fair to me," Waldron says.

Nagy signs the sheet. Then Waldron signs it. Eighteen million dollars can now be spent.

□　　□　　□

NEARLY EVERY WEEK some outside commitment intrudes on Waldron's time. This week he has been invited to give a speech before the ninety-eighth annual meeting of the Church Club of New York, a social organization of fairly elderly, fairly liberal Episcopalian laymen. The setting is the somber

Union Club on East Sixty-ninth Street. The title of Waldron's speech is "Christian Values and the Corporation." Recently, Waldron has gotten a bit exercised over the protests against American corporations doing business in South Africa. Avon is not in South Africa, though internal debates have been going on over possibly entering that market. In any event, Waldron thinks the companies there should be cheered, not booed. He has decided to broach that idea, among some others, at the Church Club, which one would think might not be the most receptive audience.

"When I was preparing for this evening," Waldron tells the group, "I talked with a number of people, asking what they thought a lay church group might be interested in. The first fellow I asked said, in effect, that he thought corporate Christian values was a contradiction, or an oxymoron—like jumbo shrimp, death benefits, and military intelligence.

"His belief was—maybe it still is—that profit is the sole factor in all corporate decisions. That may have been true in the days of the robber barons, when Commodore Vanderbilt said 'the public be damned,' when industrialists broke union strikes, and when the only thing corporations contributed to their communities was pollution from their smokestacks. The Golden Rule in those days may have been 'He who has the gold makes the rules.' . . .

"I'm not proposing all corporate leaders for immediate canonization. While I believe that there's a broad streak of decency in most people, I don't believe that all corporate executives are guaranteed first-class seats in heaven. Some undoubtedly are going to have a heck of a time in the next life, and they will deserve all the heat they get . . .

"In fact, it's been my experience that business

people are at least as moral and ethical as the general population. And, as surprising as it may sound, my guess is that the higher an executive rises, the more Christian virtue he or she may exhibit . . .

"I suspect—because business is competitive—that those not in business believe it is un-Christian. In fact, business people often use terms and techniques drawn from war. We talk about objectives, strategies, tactics, market-share battles, and winning and losing. This could lead people to believe that business is a white-collar war, and what could be less Christian than war.

"Business is not war, but economic democracy. Every time a consumer buys a product, he or she is voting. I am not in business to kill my competition or drive them out of business.

"I am in business to satisfy the consumer better than our competitors can. Sometimes I do. And this joy is not that I've hurt my competitor. The joy is that I've won the hearts and acceptance of more customers, including some that used to buy from someone else.

"People who try to make analogies between business and war are missing several important points. The first is that in business there's never a final victory. The game is never over. Occasionally I'll hear a manager say, 'We own that market,' and he's wrong.

"Leadership positions are transitory. Take something as prosaic—but critically important, if you have a baby—as diapers. Not too many years ago, diapers were made of cloth. Then someone invented a disposable diaper, which stole the market from the cloth variety. Then Procter and Gamble came along with Pampers, which owned the market. Then Kimberly Clark came out with a better product, Huggies. Now P & G is reported to have

an even better new disposable diaper. The beneficiaries are the babies, who are drier and no longer
get stuck by pins, and the parents, who no longer
stick themselves . . .

"I would not put on my list of bad guys the companies who do business in South Africa. In fact,
quite to the contrary, I can say this with some objec-
tivity, since Avon doesn't operate in South Africa
. . . Far from agreeing with apartheid, I absolutely
abhor it. I think it's morally repugnant. And I think
that it's beginning to self-destruct . . . But the companies that operate there are not condoning the pol-
icies of the government of South Africa any more
than you women wearing diamond rings or gold
jewelry endorse the Botha regime. To the contrary,
American companies there are a force from within
for changing and improving conditions for the op-
pressed.

"Maybe not that much of a force, because there
aren't that many American-owned businesses there.
Maybe protestors would better serve the cause of
freedom if they tried to force Columbia to invest
only in companies that did operate in South Africa.
Those companies are freedom's fifth column in that
country.

"American businesses bring many South Africans
—black, white, Asian, and colored—their first taste
of equality. They work alongside each other. There
are black supervisors with white subordinates . . .

"My view is that change in South Africa would
come more quickly if there were more—not less—
American business involvement there. Having said
that, I'm afraid I'm not prepared to take Avon into
South Africa right now. The benefits that Avon
would bring to South Africa could be more than
offset by the damage that misguided people in this
country might do to Avon."

Then he says, "Business is not perfect. Far from it. But its imperfections, I believe, stem from the fallibility of man, not from a lack of Christian virtue.

"Yes, Christian virtue is alive and well in our corporations."

There are only a handful of questions. One man wants to know if Waldron thinks the corporate income tax should be done away with. Waldron says no, but that "the tax today on income and dividends is a double tax and is too much." Someone else wants to know if he can get a copy of the talk.

As the crowd disperses, John Cox's wife mentions that there were some pretty strange people here. She tells me about a man at the head table who was talking about his pet rabbit. "He said that the rabbit didn't show love in the normal way, but by sitting there you would absorb his affection."

19 □ STOCKHOLDERS IN THE RAIN

IT IS pouring down rain. Every so often, there is an explosive crack of thunder. There's also a heavy enough wind that not even an umbrella keeps you dry for long. Never has Waldron been happier to see the rattle of rain. Today, the first Friday in May, is annual-meeting morning. Waldron knows that the downpour is going to keep a lot of people at home and that means far fewer embarrassing questions fired at him.

Waldron has his raincoat on and his speech protected by one of his wife's satchels, which boasts a unicorn on a gaily colored background. John Cox needles him that he better not let the shareholders see him lugging that around. He walks with Cox and me across the street to the Plaza Hotel, where the session will be held. We wend our way through the Plaza labyrinth and find the meeting room, deserted now except for a sprinkling of Avon functionaries. A dozen hostesses are scattered just outside to greet the shareholders. They are actually Avon secretaries, outfitted in clothing from Avon Fashions that they get to keep in exchange for their labors today.

"You look lovely, ladies," Waldron says to no one in particular.

A portable coatrack has been installed near the door, reserved for the directors so that they can

233

quickly grab their raincoats after the meeting and hasten back to Avon, where the monthly board of directors meeting is to be conducted.

Waldron snatches a hanger and loops the end through the hook under the collar of his coat. He says to me, "I always put the hanger through this loop, so if anyone tries to run off with my coat they're going to have to work for it."

An executives arrives, smiling, and says, referring to the sloppy weather, "Chairman's dream!"

Several of the functionaries converge on Waldron and give him a last-minute rundown on the schedule. Then Waldron drifts outside and sizes up the opposition. He warmly greets Avon employees, securities analysts, and various shareholders who recognize him. The crowd is small, just as the unpropitious weather promised. Maybe a hundred people have checked in. Men who look like Ed Asner and Buddy Hackett are shaking off their umbrellas and looking around, perhaps for Avon executives. There are cigars in evidence, also teased hair and bleached hair and a few too many examples of how not to wear Avon makeup. I deliberately look around for old ladies in tennis sneakers with funny hats. I don't spot any tennis sneakers, though I do see a couple of distinctly plump middle-aged women in floppy headgear. I suspect that they will be trouble. After a while, Mrs. Waldron arrives with a woman friend. She gives Waldron a kiss and then they settle into seats in the middle of the room.

It's nearly ten, so Waldron positions himself before the podium, raps the gavel, and calls the meeting to order. About 150 people have spread themselves out in the audience. Waldron thanks the stockholders on hand for braving the elements. He introduces each of the directors, who stand up, then he segues into his prepared speech, expatiating on the future glories of Avon. There is no mention of the ongoing representative recruitment problems. The speech lasts about fifteen minutes and draws polite applause.

Then voting by written ballot is done on the three items on the agenda: the election of the management-sponsored slate of directors for the coming year; the election of the outside auditing firm; and the amendment of the stock option incentive plan to add five million shares. All pass by landslides.

Then Waldron throws the meeting open to questions from the floor. Annual meetings are not known for high intellectual content. It quickly becomes clear that this one will be no exception.

A beetle-browed man, his eyes very wide, stands up and says that he owns a thousand shares of Avon. He says that he would like to suggest that, in addition to stock options and all the other corporate perks, there be "stockholder appreciation rights for all shareholders who have suffered with the company for three years and through various upheavals and seen our investments dwindle."

"Thank you very much for the comment," Waldron says evenly. "We will consider it. Let me point out that all our compensation plans are competitive. But I appreciate your comment."

A middle-aged woman with a German accent says that she is an Avon representative. She says that she hears that the company is looking for other businesses and recommends the travel business. "I don't know what the return is in the travel business," she says, "but maybe it would be good."

"Thank you," Waldron says. He points out that the company has investigated the travel business, tested it, and had no luck.

The first questioner gets up again, saying, "I'm sorry I'm not in a more positive mood."

"It's the weather," Waldron says.

Then the man asks if the figure in the proxy for Waldron's compensation includes his apartment. If so, he says, does it include both the maintenance and the interest expense?

Waldron wets his lips and replies that it includes the former but not the latter. He explains that the arrangement is that the company will eventually buy back the apartment, and Waldron will make no money on it.

"It's still a tremendous expense for the company," the man says.

"I'm afraid living in New York is a great expense for everyone," Waldron replies.

"Well, yes," the man says. "But a lot of people manage to travel in by train for forty-five minutes or so. I did it for years and my company was making money."

"And so is Avon, I may point out," Waldron says.

"This reminds me of the federal Government in the way it tries to contain costs," the man says.

"Boy, you really hurt me there," Waldron says, giving the man a killer glance.

"Well, I don't mean to pick on you," the man goes on. "But someone should ask the tough questions."

"And I must say you do it very well," Waldron says. "Very well."

After years of chairing annual meetings, Waldron is by now quite adept at deflecting questions. One of the executives had told me that at last year's meeting a shareholder got up and said, "I have a civil suit filed against the company. Do you want to hear about it?" "No," Waldron replied, and that was that.

The questions today are actually quite mild by

the standards of many big corporate gatherings. Waldron, for instance, had told me about a gadfly who had stood up at one meeting and brazenly asked the chairman why a good-looking man like him was married to such an ugly woman. The chairman's wife, as it happened, was sitting in the audience. The infuriated chairman glowered at the questioner and told him that that was a disgusting comment. "I thought he should have thrown the clown out," Waldron said to me.

A woman with cherubic cheeks gets up and introduces herself as a shareholder and a customer. She asks if it's possible to get products delivered to customers faster. "I become very annoyed," she says, "waiting two or three weeks for a product that I could pick up at my corner drugstore, though it's not as good quality."

"Boy that question is loaded," Waldron replies. "Yes, I have stopped beating my wife." He says that the company will take a look at speeding up delivery.

The Avon representative returns with another comment. She complains that the long delivery time is costing the company business. "We have Mother's Day coming up and a lot of people wait till the last minute to pick out their gifts," she says. "We lose that business."

"Thank you again," Waldron says. "Any time we can do anything to enhance our relationship with our customers, we work hard at it."

Preston answers the final question. The meeting is adjourned by Waldron, mightily relieved at having gotten only one question on compensation and none at all dealing with animals. The time is eleven o'clock sharp. That happens to be the precise time that Preston picked in the pool. Later on, he gets razzed by the losers, who protest that he glanced at his watch while he was answering that final question and speeded up his response.

□   □   □

AFTERWARD, THE DIRECTORS STRAGGLE into the anteroom outside the boardroom. Coffee and a plentiful supply of pastry and cookies have been arranged there for them. Once Waldron arrives, the directors parade into the board room and take seats around the table. I have been allowed to sit in on the meeting, though everything that is said is to be off the record.

There is nothing terribly mysterious about the meetings. They follow a format similar to CMC sessions. After some introductory remarks by Waldron, which generally consist of birthday greetings (in this case he also awards Preston the annual-meeting pool money), each division head reports on his finances and fields questions from directors. The presentations tend to be abbreviated versions of what the CMC hears.

Directors sip coffee, shift in their seats, move their chins from the right hand to the left hand and then back to the right hand. Waldron, of course, is presenting a posture here, too. For one thing, he doesn't seem to be exhibiting the depth of worry I imagine he feels over the earnings problem at Avon beauty.

Directors I have talked to admit what everyone knows, that a board can't possibly be as informed as management itself, so that, as long as the numbers point in the right direction, directors must trust and approve what management proposes. None of the Avon directors could think of any matter that they opposed Waldron on. When I spoke with Spencer Stuart about Waldron's leadership style, he re-

counted the famous story about Arthur Vining
Davis, the former Alcoa chairman. Once, when he
presented a real estate deal to his board, only he
and one other member voted for it. Davis said,
"Okay, motion passed." One of the board members
told Davis afterward, "Arthur, I don't think you
heard the vote." Davis looked at him and said,
"Sometimes you count the votes and sometimes
you weigh them." "Hicks," Stuart said, "tends to
have his vote carry a bit more weight."

Among the things that get done at this meeting,
as it does four times a year, is that the quarterly
dividend is voted on. The directors, I have been
told, are not fully in agreement on the future of the
dividend. Some feel it ought to be cut soon, because it's draining too much of the corporation's
cash. Waldron disagrees. In any event, it gets
passed once again.

The meeting over, the directors gather for lunch
in one of the twenty-seventh-floor dining rooms.
Everyone eats heartily.

□   □   □

A FEW WEEKS AFTER the stockholders meeting, Paul
Markovits and Phyllis Davis come into a conference
room, joking and feeling a little nervous. Waiting
for them are the brass: Waldron, Chamberlin, Preston. They have mapped out a plan to resuscitate the
beauty business, and now they need papal blessing
to put it into action.

Listening intently, Waldron is told about the gen-
esis of the plan. It has not been hastily designed.
Last month, they had hired an outside consultant,
the Futures Group, to study the last five years of
recruitment history in the division. It looked at
what sort of programs were tried to lure represen-

tatives and how influential they were. Then a model was drawn up. The model is unveiled, Markovits and Davis talk. The gist of their argument is that the domestic beauty business will end the year down 15 percent in representatives unless Waldron allows them to spend several million dollars to do four broad things: improve morale, add people to do recruiting, cut from twenty-five dollars to five dollars the fee required of representatives signing up, and sweeten the incentives for the district managers who produce good orders.

Markovits and Davis had come to a number of conclusions. Recruiting Avon representatives is a name game. So-and-so knows so-and-so, who might be good. The more bodies you have, the more names you get. So they want to add "more arms and legs." They want to make representatives feel better. It has been forgotten, they believe, that this is a loving, hugging type of business. Waldron himself, Markovits believes, has grossly underestimated the emotion of the business. One thing they intend to do is send out a letter and gift to all the representatives telling them how much New York loves them. The gift will be a Christmas ornament. (Representatives will not be told that the ornament is an excess item from last year that Avon no longer has any use for.) To get a better handle on the marketplace, Markovits and Davis want to introduce a planning process that will embrace four campaigns, or eight weeks, to replace a quarterly schedule. "People were sending in numbers almost from the point of view of pleasing people and making sure the numbers looked okay," Davis says. "And then they would be frustrated when they didn't meet those numbers." Then there is a problem with the product line. It has gotten boring. There is trouble in particular with the gift and decorative line,

which accounts for some 20 percent of sales. The
Avon gift from a student to her teacher is an institution in the country. So is the Avon Mother's Day
gift, the Avon Christmas gift. There was talk,
though, of Avon having "gone uptown." There was
talk, for instance, of the seventy-five-dollar duck.
Avon's core customers aren't rich. Thirty thousand
dollars a year is good money in Avon country. Yet,
to get more revenues, the marketing people had been
inserting higher- and higher-priced gifts into the
line—including a hand-carved wooden duck that
sold for seventy-five dollars. Markovits and Davis
want to dump a good portion of the all-important
Christmas gift line and substitute cheaper products.

Waldron's gaze skips over the chart. It shows the
road to the promised land. It shows that, if the millions are spent, the representative count will at
once stabilize and start to climb upward. "So go
spend the money," he tells them. But he also makes
one thing clear: His patience is running out. He has
shareholders and directors and Wall Street to fend
off. He says he'll be waiting in their office if this
doesn't pan out. He has had his fill of empty
dreams.

20 □ PROBLEMS AND MORE PROBLEMS

WALDRON'S DAYS wear on, unremitting processions of meetings. A few weeks later, Jim Preston arrives with several other Avon beauty executives to talk about a cost analysis of printing a regional Avon beauty product brochure. Waldron has been unhappy that Avon has one brochure for the entire country. The entire country is not the same. The example Waldron likes to cite about the shortcomings of one brochure is the fact that sunscreen can't be bought in Florida during the winter, because it's not a winter product in the northern households that Avon ladies knock on. So Avon plans to introduce regional brochures at some point in the future. As part of that effort, the beauty products division has been asked to work out what the additional cost would be.

One of the marketing specialists, a smiling, dapper young man named Ken, begins the presentation. He mentions that right now Avon prints 420 million brochures.

"What happened to the eight hundred million figure I've been using?" Waldron asks.

"We've never printed more than five hundred million," the marketing man says.

"I used to say we were between *TV Guide* and *Reader's Digest*," Waldron says.

"We are ahead of *Reader's Digest*," Preston says.

242

"Maybe it's worldwide," Waldron says.

"That could be," the marketing man says.

He goes on now and points out that, to capitalize on regional interests, *Time* magazine prints three hundred weekly editions.

"Three hundred editions!" Waldron says. "That blows my mind."

"It blew my mind when I saw that," Preston says.

"Okay, page five," the marketing man says. "The big numbers are on this. Three hundred and sixty-four thousand dollars is the estimated cost per campaign. Nine and a half million is the bill per year."

Waldron's eyes widen. He immediately asks why the cost is so high.

Preston picks up Waldron's coffee mug to illustrate how the printing gets done. He says that on one round cylinder are all the pages of the catalogue. "You can't simply take a piece of this cylinder and change it. You have to go to a whole new cylinder."

Waldron says, "This plan as proposed has a new cylinder for each brochure, even though only a few pages are changed from brochure to brochure. It's estimated that this will add five million dollars in loss of volume efficiencies for doing it with new cylinders." He then suggests that the brochures be printed as two sections; the few pages that change from region to region can be done on one cylinder and the other pages on another. Then it won't be necessary to have a different cylinder for each region.

"Soon as I saw this number," Waldron says, "I started thinking of other ways to get it done. I don't like that much."

Preston concedes that that might be a solution.

The marketing man now mentions that creative production costs will come to $4.5 million.

"I suppose my idea would do nothing to that?" Waldron says.

"No," the marketing man says.

"Ken and I have a little war here," Preston says. "I would scale that cost down significantly."

"I'm glad to hear that," Waldron says.

"Page seven," Ken says. "Suggestions to reduce costs."

"Increase sales," Waldron says.

"Yes, right," Ken laughs.

One suggestion is to accept ads.

"Interesting idea," Waldron says. "It doesn't grab me, but it's an interesting idea."

Ken says there would be some conflicts and problems with representatives if they ran ads.

"You're being kind," Preston says. "The reps would rip the pages right out of the brochure."

Starting to sum up, Preston says, "We've moved from can we do this to we're doing it. How should we do it?"

"Well, the notion here is so exciting," Waldron says. "This is our retail store. We should do it the best we can. Theoretically, we should have one for each customer. That's the ultimate. Now, what's the next step?"

"We'll have to look at the data in our computer base as it comes in and see what the geographical differences are."

"The one thing we can't get is competitor information?" Waldron asks.

"No," Preston says, "but we can overlay competitor information to what we have. We could never do that before."

"Okay," Waldron says. "We are coming. We are coming."

Waldron brings the subject back to cutting the expense of the brochures.

One of the men says, "If I were guessing, I think we could cut that nine and a half million in half."

"What you're talking about is twenty million dollars in incremental sales," Waldron says. "The easiest way to get that is through margin—through pricing. That's the hardest thing to do."

Then it's mentioned that if prices vary from region to region, the representatives will run into customers saying that they're getting ripped off.

"We had that problem in a St. Louis test," Preston says.

"Well, the Revlons of the world have that problem," Waldron says. "You go into a different store and the prices are different right on one block."

"That's right," Preston says.

"The only thing is they don't have all those goddamn representatives screaming at them and reminding them of this," Waldron says.

"You know," Waldron goes on, "at Heublein we did some research and found that thirty-five percent of all the brands were consumed in Wisconsin. You could sit here until you're a hundred-and-four years old and not come up with that fact. We said, screw the rest of the country. So we put all our advertising into Wisconsin and increased our shares there fifteen points. The rest of the country didn't matter."

"That's amazing," Preston says. "Well, you know in the first run of this product-tracking system we looked at sunscreen by geographical area. And we found that in Texas sunscreen sales were like five times greater penetration than anywhere else."

"Well, this all sounds great," Waldron says.

☐　　☐　　☐

"I MUST FEEL a very close relationship to my product to do a good job," Waldron is saying. "I must like it. I must stand up in church and talk about it, so if I were running a brothel I would have a lot of trouble in a mixed congregation."

We are discussing, after Preston and the others have left, how important it is for a CEO to care about what his company sells. Despite all the attention he seemed to devote to product details, Waldron obviously didn't meet a lot of Avon customers in his circles.

"I had a lot of trouble at Reynolds," he goes on. "To me, you have two heroes. Your customer is a hero and your product is a hero. I couldn't look at a pack of cigarettes as a hero. I can feel good about a GE refrigerator or a piece of chicken. I can feel good about A-1 steak sauce or even some Smirnoff. Well, you could say, oh you're rationalizing the booze area, and maybe I am. But I'm talking about rational use of booze. It doesn't make a damned bit of difference that I don't use the hair spray or the shampoo. I have to feel good about the product and comfortable about my product."

I say that I imagine that most of the offerings in the Avon catalogue would not be of exceptional interest to someone of his grand income. Isn't it difficult to run a company that sells to a much lower-income consumer?

"No, I wouldn't buy most of the things in the catalogue," Waldron says. "I don't like red glass, or whatever color that cranberry glass is." He picks up a catalogue and flips through it, until he gets to a page featuring all sorts of dishes and plates in an ugly reddish color. "We sell millions and millions of dollars of this. I don't like it. It doesn't appeal to me. But I have no trouble selling it."

He picks up the Avon Fashions catalogue and

starts paging through it. "Here's a green dress. Have you bought a green dress lately? What would you guess it costs?"

I guess around seventy dollars.

"Eighteen ninety-nine."

He puts the catalogue down. "Now, these are not the kind of clothes my wife would buy or Maureen would buy, because they can afford more. But it's good stuff. We resist the temptation all the time to upgrade the products. We say we don't want anything in there over forty dollars. I have to resist my tastes and ego. Now, I will say that it was a lot more fun for me to go to a cocktail party and talk about the Tiffany line when we owned Tiffany than it is to go to parties and talk about the Avon line of jewelry. It was more fun. It's just like in advertising. You don't ever see ugly people in the ads. They're all beautiful. That's not life. Life's not all fun."

☐ ☐ ☐

PEOPLE AT MALLINCKRODT have not been having the time of their lives. In 1982, when the company was bought, the beauty business had not yet headed to the deep south, and everyone's expectations were that wads of money coming in from beauty would be handed over to Mallinckrodt to make it grow. Once the bad times started to roll, things began to change. Mallinckrodt has found itself squeezed for money to try to prop up beauty. Ray Bentele could be excused for feeling like a teenager who not only wasn't getting his two-dollar allowance but was now being asked to give his parents three bucks a week.

In June, Bentele seeks an audience with Waldron. He comes right to the point. He and his management might like to buy the company back.

Waldron, who has begun to think about selling Mallinckrodt (even the critical-care slice that belongs to the lofty Magnificent Seven) in order to get cash to pour into the fast-growing health-care-services business, is amenable. But he doesn't want to dillydally. You can have twenty-four hours, he tells Bentele, to collect your team and decide if you're really serious. The next day, Bentele answers in the affirmative. Okay, Waldron says, you can have two weeks to come up with a price. If it's too low, he warns, then Avon will put Mallinckrodt up for sale to all comers.

□   □   □

"I HAVE NOT READ word one of your proposal," Waldron says. "In fact, I'm not sure where your proposal is."

He rummages through a pile of papers on his desk. He picks up the garbage can and pokes through it. No luck. His eyebrows contract irritably.

"I know I had it. Now I can't find the son of a bitch. Well, I'll use yours."

Two members of Avon's governmental affairs group are briefing Waldron for a forthcoming trip to Washington to lobby three senators on the Reagan administration's proposed tax bill. Tom Knight, the general counsel, is also in attendance.

Robert McMillan, a man with a quick smile who is vice-president of public affairs, starts off. "If Treasury One went into effect, because Avon has such a high effective tax rate—high forty percent—the effect would be anywhere from a savings to us of from six to thirteen million dollars. So you ask, why not walk away from it? The reason is there are so many complications in there that everyone is lobbying the hell out of the bill. We want to educate the senators on two issues so that once the final mix gets agreed on, we don't get screwed."

"Right," Waldron says.

Thomas Farrell, whose imposing title is international counsel, director of legal and government affairs, takes the floor and spells out the two issues. The first has to do with the tax break American companies get in Puerto Rico. "If Treasury One gets passed, there could be a tax to Avon there of between nine and twelve million. A lot of companies like Avon are in Puerto Rico for one reason and one reason only—that's because of Section Nine-Three-Six. To offset the tax consequences of their own government."

"The argument is it works," Waldron says.

"It does work," Farrell says. "We're there providing twelve hundred jobs that wouldn't otherwise be there. We're paying above the minimum wage. If Section Nine-Three-Six is repealed, then the arrangement under which we went into Puerto Rico will be changed."

"So the government is reneging on its deal," Waldron says.

"In a sense," McMillan says.

Waldron says, "I think if Preston looks at this and sees there are no tax breaks and we're paying these people fifteen thousand dollars a year, then he'll say, let's get the hell out of there."

"Correct," Knight says. "There are other places to go."

"Like Ireland," Waldron says.

"Or Haiti," McMillan says. "Other places in the Caribbean."

"The other major issue we're concerned about is the government is thinking of changing the method under which the maximum foreign tax credit is calculated," Farrell says. He then explains the change, a lot of mumbo jumbo that is almost impossible to follow.

"Say it again," Waldron says.

"Okay," Farrell says, and he says it again.

"Okay," Waldron says.

"We unfortunately do business in a lot of high-rate countries," Farrell says. "Japan. Germany. Up till now, we could average those down with countries like Ireland, where there's no tax rate. We wouldn't be able to do that under this one provision. We stand to lose something like sixteen million dollars."

"Ugh," Waldron says.

"Our position," Farrell says, "is that no company's decision to move into a country is based on taxes."

"Except for Puerto Rico, which we just got done talking about," Waldron says.

"That's different," Farrell says. "That's not in this average."

There's a bit more rationalization and hairsplitting about why Puerto Rico is different. Then Farrell says, "The bill if enacted as is would benefit Avon, let's say, somewhere around eight to ten million a year. But Treasury One will not be enacted as is. The administration already said it is backing down on some things."

"We're not trying to be greedy, Hicks," McMillan says. "If the final thing comes out and we run the numbers through and it comes out even or a little ahead for Avon, we're not going to continue to extensively lobby on these things, or that would be interpreted as being greedy. But we think we should educate the senators."

"Okay," Waldron says. "I'll read this carefully."

□   □   □

REAMS HAVE BEEN WRITTEN about how the Japanese are strangling American business, and if the government doesn't do something then the Americans are finished. Talking to Waldron a few days later, I ask him about the Japanese threat.

"Being a complete fundamentally open market person, I don't think there is a big problem out there," he says. "I don't see how one can say fairly and honestly that, hey, I just built a plant in Japan or Germany or the UK and then on the other hand complain that we have to restrict that country from trading with this country. I've been in Japan with the chicken business, with the appliance business, and now I'm in there with the cosmetics business and I don't see it. I'm inclined to say that if we have a problem it's more a problem that business has developed without either government help or interference and the solution has to come without government help or interference."

Is a Japanese company more efficient than an American company? I ask Waldron.

"It would be a close call. I think what the Japanese lack in creativity they would make up in productivity. So it would be a tie."

Could the Japanese system work here?

"Can you imagine lining up every Avon employee out front on Fifty-seventh Street and having them do pushups? Can you imagine me telling everyone to wear a nice blue jacket with Avon across the back? Can you imagine if everyone had to go to me to get permission for their daughter to marry?"

American business, I point out, hasn't had much of a record lately. The major corporations have lost market share, they've created no new jobs, they've been slow to innovate. I remark that the combined

profits of the Fortune 500, adjusted for inflation,
have in fact shrunk over the last decade.

"Well, you may be looking at the deindustriali-
zation of the country from a smokestack economy to
a service economy," Waldron says. "There's the
cost of doing business in an inflationary economy. I
remember barely being able to keep pace with inflation and yet showing fifteen to twenty percent
gains. So I guess I would have to rack that up to
struggling to keep up with inflation and not being
able to raise prices in that environment and, more
importantly, the mix of the top five hundred companies. I don't know what effect the whole takeover
arena would have. Certainly, it would be negative.
The profitability is usually lower after the takeover.
The money is all going for the interest payments to
the banks."

"How do you innovate in a big corporation?" I
ask.

"Two words. 'Stay loose.' It's a very difficult
problem. Anyone who says he's conquered it—
that's a lot of bullshit. Whether we're doing it, I
can't say. One way to do it is by managing. Decentralization. Avon for many years operated under a
very centralized philosophy. We now call it cookie-
cutter conformity. If you operate a centralized
organization, then you have by definition a bureaucracy—and a big one."

Is the organization man still around?

"Well, you're getting a much more sophisticated
person," Waldron says. "But you're getting a
change in the sacrifice index. Before World War
Two, kids would enter the training program and
every six or nine months you'd move and after a
while you'd settle down. If the boss said, 'I think
you should go to Pittsburgh in three months,' the
worker would say, 'Yes, sir,' and go. Now you say it

and the guy says, 'Er, shit, Pittsburgh, my wife doesn't like Pittsburgh. And I'm still paying off the BMW.' So I think I'm seeing brighter faces, more talented people, but not ones willing to throw themselves on the spike for the company just for the sake of being loyal."

□ □ □

PAUL MARKOVITS IS ANXIOUS. Phyllis Davis is anxious. Four weeks have lapsed since they had been authorized to spend millions of dollars on their bold plan to rejuvenate the beauty business. They have worked feverishly and single-mindedly. Markovits has been talking about how Waldron has made him work "forty-eight-hour days." And now they have come to see Waldron and the other top management to update them on their progress. According to the chart they had shown, they should be seeing steady gains in the numbers of representatives.

Reality has played another cruel trick. The actual numbers are revealed. Waldron's gaze slides rapidly over the chart. Not only haven't the numbers shot upward, they have sunk a bit further. Markovits sheepishly explains that he and Davis had been too optimistic. They unfortunately underestimated how rotten morale was. They tell Waldron they can still deliver the results. Just one thing. Could they have another million dollars?

Phyllis Davis' later recollection of the mood of the meeting was: "It was heavy. It was very heavy." She added: "I think there was a little bit of, 'Well, I hope to hell you're right.' This language was not used. But there was some of that undertone. It was somber. Very somber."

Waldron is brusque this day. He okays the money. Then, like a teacher addressing a student who has spent most of class hurling erasers at his head, he asks Markovits if he could remain a moment after the others have left.

Markovits' later summation of that private exchange was: "He kicked my ass."

He elaborated: "He said he was tired of hearing promises and having us not deliver on them. He said that, by October first, if we are not on a clear path to recovery, then we are going to have to reexamine our strategy and find out if we really even know what is driving our business."

I asked Markovits if Waldron implied that his job was on the line. "No," he said. "He's not the threatening type. And if he had said that, I probably would have told him to kiss my ass."

21 □ DISTRACTIONS

SOMETIMES IT must be especially hard for Waldron. The uncertainties surrounding the beauty
business continue to engulf him, yet his workdays
remain thickened with all manner of peripheral demands. The corporate assumptions that an insistence on routine and regimentation is the only way
to go leave question marks in my mind. But not,
apparently, in Waldron's. One day when I drop in
on him, he is meeting with Glenn Clarke, the president of the Avon Foundation. Waldron sits in a
chair and Clarke sits on the sofa. They are talking
about various solicitations from charitable organizations and whether Avon should give or refrain, a
ritual that occurs every month. This is already late
in the afternoon and Waldron is a little bushed; he
says he hosted a dinner party last night and has another one to host at his apartment tonight. Clarke is
not in the pink of health, either. He had a Mexican
dinner last night that decidedly disagreed with him.

Clarke talks about an upcoming Salvation Army
dinner that Waldron has agreed to serve as chairman for: "We've got twenty-eight tables sold. Last
year, he had fifteen at this point. Sixteen co-chairmen. Last year, there were seven. Still, there'll be
seventy tables all together there."

"Are we going to make it?" Waldron asks.

Clarke strokes his chin and says, "Well, got a long

255

way to go. As you know, the dinner circuit is over-loaded. If you had Dionne Warwick there I don't know if you could draw all that."

Waldron shakes his head and grimaces. "How I got hooked into this goddamned thing I'll never know."

Clarke says, "Well, they're optimistic and we're having the co-chairmen follow up letters with phone calls."

Waldron says, "Make sure we leave enough time so that we can throw some more action into the pot if we have to—like put the arm on our suppliers."

"Okay, we will," Clarke says, making a note on a yellow pad.

It's quickly decided by Waldron to take a six-hundred-dollar ad in a Boys Club of New York journal and also to buy a table at their dinner. Then Clarke pushes ahead to the next subject.

"Marymount College wants a hundred and fifty thousand dollars," Clarke says. "I think we should write and say that a hundred and fifty thousand is really not in the ballpark unless you have a strong feeling about it."

Waldron says, "What did she want to do with the hundred and fifty thousand dollars?"

Clarke says, "It's very vague. I have to think it has something to do with endowment, where the money is put away and the interest used. I think we should say no."

"I think you're right," Waldron says. "It's pretty brassy to ask for it."

Clarke says, "And as you say in your eleven commandments, they can always try again."

"Send her a copy of the eleven commandments," Waldron says.

(The eleven commandments are Waldron's personally devised rules of how to successfully go begging for money at a corporation. He went public with them at a speech he gave some years ago, and has had them committed to a sheet of paper that is periodically passed out to uninitiated charitable organizations. They include such nuggets of wisdom as: "You shall not send a letter to the chief executive officer of a company because it won't be read"; "You shall not go far from home, where charity begins and usually ends"; "You shall not call today and expect shekels tomorrow"; "You shall remember that big companies like big projects, those with elements they can call their own"; "You shall say 'thank you.' The best form of thanks is a report on what's been accomplished with the gift. Business people, maybe more than most professionals, expect something to happen when they invest.")

Moving forward, Clarke shuffles through his sheaf of papers and pulls out a letter. He says, "NAACP has been writing three times a week, asking for thirty thousand dollars rather than the twenty thousand dollars we gave them. I didn't like the tone of the letters. It's like, 'We're owed it.' "

"Let's work this through Phil Davis," Waldron says.

Clarke says, "Okay, the National Museum of Women in the Arts."

Waldron arches his eyebrows and says, "Damn, I gave her a hundred dollars of my own money and it was the worst hundred bucks I ever invested. She keeps writing me."

Clarke says, "What they're talking about is one million dollars to have a hall named after us—the Avon Hall or something. That would be nice and all, but I don't think that fits in our strategy. So I think we should say, no, that it doesn't fit into our strategy and with budget cuts and all."

"Okay," Waldron says.

The final item on Clarke's agenda is the Fidelco Guide Dogs Foundation, a Connecticut charity that Waldron is fond of, one reason perhaps being that the founder lives next door to him in Connecticut. Fidelco trains dogs and donates them to the blind. Last year, at Waldron's urging, Avon wrote a check for eight thousand dollars, enough funding to train two guide dogs.

Clarke says that he is going next week to visit the foundation, which apparently is something of a novice in the fund-raising game, and so Clarke would like to suggest that a professional be hired to devise a fund-raising strategy for the organization.

"So we would fund the study?" Waldron says.

"Yeah," Clarke says. "Not only fund the study but implement it. That, I think, would be a better contribution to him than the dogs."

"Great idea," Waldron says.

As Clarke stands up to leave, Waldron offers him three suggestions of better choices for Mexican cuisine; he assures him the food at any one of them will have a more salutary effect on his stomach.

☐　☐　☐

TIME NOW TO FOCUS on human resources. Virtually every day, one of the heads of a division or staff responsibility is scheduled to report to Waldron's office to grade his management people, report on affirmative action, and identify succession plans. Waldron invited me to sit in on one of the sessions —he picked Direct Response as an appropriately typical one—with the proviso that I not identify by name any of the people being graded.

The ever dapper Bill Willett, the head of the division, arrives at Waldron's office with a stack of papers and a blue looseleaf notebook under his arm. He is the teacher who will be reporting the grades.

Willett spreads out the organization chart in front of him on the coffee table. Each manager is represented by a box with his name and the year or months in the position. Underneath, in little slots, are numbers that represent the ratings Willett gave the person. The range of numbers are from one to six, with one being the best someone can get and six being the worst. If someone is as low as five, however, it means he is probably going to be fired tomorrow. In elaborating on the numbers, Willett talks a bit about each of the managers:

"He's a great guy. He's really done a good job. His drawback is he's not a real P & L [profit and loss] guy. He's just starting to learn the importance of that bottom line. But we're making progress with him."

"You going to get him there?" Waldron asks.

"Yes, we sure are," Willett says.

Another manager is mentioned:

"Very bright. He's a solid P & L guy. I would like him to be a little more decisive. The jury is out."

The next name:

"Bright. Very well respected in the industry. Solid P & L guy. What we have to do is get him involved with more of our division. He has tunnel vision. And the planning and strategic planning process leaves him cold. We have to work harder with him on that."

Next man:

"His ability to interface with our managers is outstanding."

Waldron says, "He's probably a better man than ————," and he mentions the previously discussed men.

"Times four," Willett says.

The next man:

"He understands our business extremely well. He's an outstanding financial technician. He has two drawbacks, which is why I only gave him a four. He lacks an ability to effectively delegate. He does too much himself. And his communications skills leave something to be desired."

Next:

"He's good. Well organized. Hard working. What I have to do with him, Hicks, is instill a greater sense of urgency. The solution to every problem is not a task force. In fact, the solution to most problems is not a task force. We've had several conversations on this."

"Good," Waldron says. "Good."

Next:

Willett brings up a man who is the only internal candidate for the job of vice-president of marketing at Avon Fashions, a position that would entail relocating to New York.

"I can't imagine he's the leading candidate," Waldron says.

"He's not the leading," Willett says. "But if we can't find a heavy from outside, he's the only internal candidate with catalogue experience."

"Well," Waldron says, "you've got to find somebody from the outside."

"One problem is the personal consequences of a move," Willett says. "His wife loves where they live. And I sense that their marriage is tested right now. This could be the straw. And I don't want us to be the straw."

"Well," Waldron says, "let's make the decision right now. Let's find somebody else."

Willett runs quickly through a few more names, then he pauses to talk at some length about one particular manager.

"———— is very bright. Hard-working employee. Terrible general manager. No one knew that he was a one-way communicator. He didn't listen to anyone. He just told everyone what to do. We moved him to another position. Here we had hired him from another company. He was our mistake. So we said, 'Let's live with our mistake.' So we moved him into this other position. Works his ass off. But he goes and makes decisions in the distribution system without talking to anyone else. I talked to him again and again. Finally, I hired an industrial psychologist—this guy who works with Mobil and all and he met with him and he said, 'Boy, is he a one-way communicator.' I asked what we could do. And he said, 'I'm afraid it's a terminal case.' So I decided last Friday to let him go. He's extremely well paid for what he's doing. If you're paying someone top dollar and you can't live with him, it can't be."

"Plus it's bad for the organization," Waldron says.

"So we parted ways," Willett says. "This Friday will be his last day. And I must say he thought our severance package was entirely fair and we're going to do all we can to place him elsewhere."

"That's too bad," Waldron says. "That's your only five on the sheet."

"Right," Willett says. "My only five on the sheet."

Willet runs quickly through several other managers. Then he takes out a second sheet of paper. This is the replacement table. The same names appear here, but instead of numbers there are colored bars shaded in two slots under everyone's name. One slot is replacement timing and the other is replacement status. There are three color possibilities: red, green, and yellow. In the timing slot, red means a replacement is needed anywhere from immediately to six months from now. Green means seven to eighteen months. Yellow means nineteen or more months. In the status slot, red means no replacement has been identified, yellow means this is a weak slot, and green signifies a strong slot.

"Why are there no colors under Willett's name?" Waldron asks. "Do you consider yourself irreplaceable?"

Willett says that modesty prohibited him from coloring in the squares.

"Well, who can replace you?" Waldron asks.

"If I got hit by a truck tomorrow, I think there are two solid candidates," Willett says, and he mentions the two names.

"In that order?" Waldron asks.

"Hicks, I think you could almost flip a coin," Willett says.

Waldron says, "Bill, if you got hit by a truck, I don't want to have to visit you and say, 'Bill, before you die, which of these guys do you want to run Avon Fashions.' "

"Okay," Willett says, and he picks one of the two individuals.

Willett polishes off the replacement chart, then introduces a third chart that identifies "high-pots," extremely promising employees who are capable of advancing two levels up the corporate ladder, sort of like students who are smart enough to skip a grade. Willett quickly reviews the high-pots and briefly discusses a few of them.

Finally, Willett moves to yet another chart that deals with affirmative action.

"As you can see," Willett says, "it's only okay with females. With minorities, it's terrible."

"Well, this is the same issue we had last year, William," Waldron says. "Other than identifying it as an issue, you really haven't made any headway."

Willett is clearly a little ruffled by Waldron's suddenly censorious tone. He collects himself and says, "Well, I would take issue with not having made any headway." He mentions three new people. "We are clearly making headway. Are we making it fast enough? No way."

Waldron says that maybe he needs to help him by looking for high-pots in other divisions of Avon that can be transferred to Avon Fashions. "We'll see if we can help you out," he says.

Then, Willett having finished, Waldron winds things up with some backslapping.

"Bill," he says, "I would say on a scale of one to ten, a nine. Excellent job. I don't think I have any other questions."

□ □ □

WATCHING WALDRON sit through a parade of meetings, it becomes apparent that a CEO inevitably finds his field of vision narrowed to a small world. Waldron's mind is an encyclopedia of sales figures for campaign ten, margins for Avon skin-care products, print runs for the James River Traders catalogue, but there is never time to keep up with all else that goes on in the world which doesn't have a direct impact on Avon.

"To a certain extent, yes, you become one of those people who knows more and more about less and less until you know everything about nothing," he says a few afternoons later. "I've always been a big user of my staff to take care of some of the trivia. But you're right, there is a gap between what I should be tuned in to and what I am."

□ □ □

"LOOK AT THAT SHIRT!" Waldron exclaims. "We should have that in our catalogue. That is some shirt."

The shirt is pink. Bright pink. The wearer of the shirt is James Meyer, a securities analyst who follows the cosmetics industry for Janney Montgomery Scott, a Philadelphia brokerage house. He has stopped by, as he does approximately once a year, to interview Waldron in preparation for his latest research report on Avon. It is a confrontation that Waldon has a few dozen times a year with one analyst or another. This is the first week in July, when things are going far from well. Waldron has his work cut out for him if he is to convey suitable optimism at the same time that he avoids misleading Meyer. Being too positive can be as bad as being too negative. If Wall Street expects more than Waldron eventually delivers, then Waldron knows he will lose credibility and the stock price will take a drubbing.

Meyer, after some frivolity, asks Waldron a series of questions about a recently announced arrangement whereby Avon will manufacture cosmetics to be marketed by Liz Claiborne, a sizzling-hot clothing company.

Meyer: "Is there something in you as a marketing-driven person that makes it hard to go into a joint venture where they do all the marketing?"

Waldron: "No. I lose that ego when I look at the bottom right-hand corner."

Meyer: "What's been the reaction of your sales force?"

Waldron: "I don't know of any—plus or minus."

Meyer: "I can't imagine there's a plus."

Waldron: "I can't imagine a plus, so let's agree on that. We do see it as a risk. We've shaken that sales force up pretty hard."

Meyer: "Are you starting to see some evolution of direction that what you're trying to do in U.S. beauty is starting to take hold?"

Waldron: "Yes. Yes. I have to qualify that. Strategically thinking, we seem to be on track. I've said all along that we can't judge this really until after the third quarter. For the second quarter, we are starting to see some direction. Our strategy seems to be taking hold. What is keeping me awake—it's driving me batty—is what this means for 1985. All that shows in the bottom right-hand corner is expenses from all the things we're doing. We'll not be reflecting any results from operations for a while and it has to do with number of representatives. We budgeted for it to decline and it's declining further than we expected. We budgeted for it to come back and it's come back slower than I thought." (In actuality, it hadn't come back yet at all.)

Meyer: "You've seen the bottom?"

Waldron: "I feel we're sitting in the bottom of the sauce."

Meyer: "Are you saying, though, that we may still be a little disappointed in second and third quarter results?"

Waldron: "Yes. You could be. The hockey stick is more of a cereal bowl."

Meyer: "This may sound like a beating-your-wife question. You've been here two years and you still have a rep count problem. Why is it so difficult and why is it taking so long?"

Waldron: "That's not a beating-your-wife question. It's a question I ask myself every day. I even ask my wife—before I start beating her. There are four dimensions to it: recruiting, retention, endemic nature of the problem across the country, Avon execution of plan. We are suffering from recruitment and retention. The thing that's affecting us the most is our execution of the plan. We were being told that the execution was going well and it wasn't. If I had it to do over again, if I could have done something different in this office, I would have had my fingers in that broth up to my armpits to make sure what I was told was happening. What did it cost us? Probably a quarter."

Meyer: "You seem pretty confident in your answer that the worst is behind you. You're at the bottom of the sauce. What makes you think you are. It's tough to see the bottom of any business. How do you know?"

Waldron: "The answer is I can't be sure. But I don't see how we can fall off any more."

Meyer asks some questions about Avon beauty management and commitment to direct selling and about acquisitions, and then he says, "Avon itself as a takeover candidate. How much fear do you have?"

Waldron: "Well, fear isn't the word. Apprehension is there . . . I would think we're not a serious prospect, because of our problems and we have the one characteristic of being a direct seller and that scares a lot of people. You remember Princess House that Colgate bought? When I was at Heublein, I flew over to see it and the guy showed me the numbers and they looked terrific and I said what's your price. We started negotiating and I said I'd like to look at the rest of your company. He said that's it. Where's your sales force? There isn't any. I said you have no plant, you're reliant on your vendors, you have no sales force, and you want twenty million dollars or whatever it was, forget it, and I left."

After a few more things, Meyer says he's exhausted his questions.

Waldron says, "God, you're dynamite!"

□   □   □

NEARLY EVERY DAY Waldron thinks about success.
He thinks about it in particular on Thursdays when
he studies the latest representative count for the
domestic beauty business. In mid-July Markovits
and Davis had dutifully met with him and showed
him that, after a long stretch of leaden skies, some
sun had begun to poke through. The force was stabilizing and shyly sloping upward. As Markovits
later recounted the session: "He was content. He
didn't this time explain the facts of life to me."

Now in early August, there is more sun. During
one two-week stretch, some forty thousand new
representatives are added. Jim Preston himself has
been wearing out shoeleather motivating the
troops. During a twenty-day period in August, he
whirls through thirty-two cities in twenty-two
states, raising the flag before fifty-three thousand
Avon ladies. Phyllis Davis has gotten excited
enough that she has been delivering pep talks to
the field in which she has set "stretch" sales objectives for the rest of the year. They are highly ambitious, unlikely to be met, but she tells the force that
if they meet them she's going to rent a hall and call
in all the Wall Street securities analysts and there'll
be a ninety-piece string band and out will walk
Frank Sinatra singing, "They Did It Their Way."
She told Waldron that he'd have to pay for the band.
She'd pay for Frank Sinatra.

Something is stirring. But there is always a mur-
kiness about such things. Waldron had been duped
before. While I am visiting him one day in his office, we talk about how you can know when rock
bottom has been hit. What, after all, did something
as intangible as a turnaround look like? Waldron
hoists himself from the couch and goes to his cre-

denza and retrieves a Polaroid picture of a "turn-around." The picture was snapped in 1978, when Waldron was running Heublein. It shows him standing next to a giant chart with a jagged red line representing the average sales at Kentucky Fried Chicken outlets. The line shoots straight downward, until there is a blip and it starts to bob briefly upward. "We thought this was the bottom of the sauce. I took this picture and showed it to the board. I said, 'Boys, here's a picture of a turnaround for you.' Well, for the next four weeks, that line went back downward. Those were the worst four weeks in my life. Then, thank God, it went up and stayed up."

So, as he looks at the Avon numbers and sees what he hopes is a definite trend of them going the other way, he tells himself, "Let's give it time. I can't be sure this isn't a false pregnancy."

22 □ BANKERS, THE DUKE, AND DIVESTITURE

WALDRON TAKES his place at the head of the private luncheon table in Dining Room 4. The bank CEO flops into a chair to his immediate left. This is a Tuesday in August, and Waldron is lunching with the top officers of one of the major New York banks that Avon borrows money from. The bankers are circumspect. They don't want their names or the bank's name mentioned. Avon transacts business with a dozen or so big banks in New York, and it is business protocol that Waldron and the chief executive of each bank have lunch together at least once a year, whether they have something to talk about or not. There are four bankers: the chairman, two presidents, and a vice-president. Fortifying Waldron are Jack Chamberlin, Jules Zimmerman, and John Donaldson, the treasurer.

Drinks are ordered: Perrier, tonic, iced tea, a Fresca. The banker who orders the Fresca says it's funny but he hardly ever sees Fresca anymore, he wonders if it's doing all right. Waldron tells a story about how Dr Pepper got its name. The man who invented it, he says, named it after the pharmacist father of a woman he hoped to marry. The drink took off. She didn't marry him anyway.

Chamberlin says, "The father probably figured, if

he was crazy enough to do that, what else would he do."

The luncheon order is taken. The bank CEO, who has broad jaws and broad shoulders, says, "Now, Hicks, you've been here, what, about two years?"

"Yes."

"Where are you then in your plans?"

Waldron says, "I'd say we're about three months behind where we'd like to be, but directionally right where we want to be." He goes on to say that all the businesses are doing just great, except for the domestic beauty business. He recites the familiar ills of recruiting representatives.

The bank CEO chews on a roll and nods, resting his chin in his left fist.

Waldron says, "One of the things we've managed to do is increase productivity of our reps by fifteen percent. We've been trying to increase productivity for a hundred years and made absolutely no progress. So we're happy about that. One thing we're doing is, instead of knocking harder and harder on that door hoping the person who isn't there will answer, we're going to where she is. We're selling right in your office."

"What?" the bank CEO says. "What?"

One of the presidents says, "That fifteen percent increase in productivity is matched by a fifteen percent decline on our side."

"So the world passed us by, and we've turned around and are trying to catch the world," Waldron says. "If we had to do it over again today, though, we'd still do it the same way and sell direct. Any time we have a bad day and see bad numbers, we just walk through Bloomingdale's Black Hole of Calcutta, and they spray you with this and spray you with that . . ."

"Can't get through it," one of the bankers says.

"And to have a brand called Avon in that incredible zoo, who'd want that?" Waldron says.

One of the bankers asks, "What's your market in men's products?"

The bank chairman looks hard at the man and says, "You have a problem you want to discuss?"

"I can see it from here," Waldron says.

"I'll tell you this," the banker says. "Every time my wife goes to Georgette Klinger for a facial, she says, when are you going?"

"I had a facial," Waldron says. "Terrific experience."

"I tried one of those seaweed products or whatever they are that you put on yourself," the bank CEO says. "But I don't have the nerve to go to one of those places where they do it."

"I came out of there feeling like a million bucks," Waldron says.

There's a brief lull, then Waldron says, "We have a great new product that's going to come out called BioAdvance that we can't claim it does but that reverses the aging process."

"Stops it or reverses it?" the bank CEO asks.

"Reverses it," Waldron says.

"Incredible!"

"For a month," Waldron says, "I put some of it on the back of my left hand and nothing on the back of my right hand and within a week anyone could have walked up blindfolded and told the difference. So that's going to be a great product."

Waldron then glides into a PR talk about Foster Medical and how it's going gangbusters in the home-health-care marketplace, renting hospital beds and wheelchairs and canes to the infirm.

"I rented a hospital bed once," the bank CEO says. "I didn't need to be in a hospital, but I had to be off my back."

"Where'd you rent it from?" Waldron asks.

The bank CEO mentions a pharmacy in Summit, New Jersey.

"We probably own them," Waldron says.

"It's amazing all the things you can rent today," the bank CEO says. "Orgy equipment."

"Well, we don't rent any orgy equipment," Waldron says.

Waldron asks the bankers about the situation with Mexican loans, and then the discussion turns to the tax bill, which everyone at the table is dubious about.

"I think Reagan has created an issue where there was no issue," Waldron says.

The bank CEO says, "I was down in Washington the other day making the rounds, talking to people, and the consensus was that it was dead. The tax bill as it now stands is dead."

Waldron says, "You visit these politicians and so little seems to happen."

"I do very little of it anymore," the bank CEO says. "It's such a waste of time."

"These people work so hard," Waldron says. "Physically, they work so hard. Harder than I ever worked. And to not get anywhere must be so frustrating."

Everyone is done filling their stomachs, so Waldron, addressing the bank CEO, says, "Well, is there anything we should be doing with you, or without you? Are we doing all right?"

The bank vice-president says, "We do a little bit with you. A couple of years we did nothing with Avon. We're in two of your revolving credits now, which is delightful. It's a beginning. We're still not there."

"We think there's a lot of upward potential," the bank CEO says.

"We're long-term oriented in our relationships," one of the bank presidents says. "If we can move up in your credit, I'll start selling those beauty-care products in my office."

The bank CEO laughs and says, "The heck with your secretary, huh, you'll do it?"

"Right."

"Well, that's terrific," Waldron says. "Your slip is showing, as it were. So we're open. There's no reason our relationship can't get better and better."

□   □   □

IN EARLY SEPTEMBER, Avon delivers a statement to the press containing the information that management has decided to put up for sale the big Mallinckrodt division. The Bentele bid that had come in for the company was at once rejected by Waldron as being too low. Something on the order of seven hundred million dollars would do it, and Bentele and his people didn't quite have the wherewithal.

A few days after the announcement, I sit in Waldron's office as he explains what will happen next. He leans back on his couch and puts on a tight smile. Once it extricates itself from Mallinckrodt, Waldron says, Avon intends to buy back up to twenty million Avon shares and use the balance of the money to diversify into health-care services.

After the final decision was made, Waldron prepared a missive to all Mallinckrodt employees, telling them how splendid the company was and how Avon would do its best to find it a more proper owner. Bentele asked one favor of Waldron. Could he postpone the announcement a few days? In two days, he was appearing at a baseball game at Busch Stadium to kick off the United Way drive in the Saint Louis area. Hundreds of Mallinckrodt employees would be in the stands. He didn't want to get stoned. Waldron acceded.

(Unfortunately, word somehow leaked out, as it usually does, and Waldron decided that he had to release the news at once.)

Waldron is filled with enthusiasm that Wall Street will react with favor to the decision. He's right. Avon, long a dog with the Wall Street community, begins attracting some compliments. A few days later, he gets a memo from Margro Long of investor relations reporting that analysts at both Merrill Lynch and Salomon Brothers had upgraded their investment opinions and that Wall Street now had the most positive investment stance on the company since the late 1970's. One of the most influential followers of the cosmetics business is Deepak Raj at Merrill Lynch, and all year he had been complaining that Waldron and his team "were not able or realistic in forecasting the prospects in the direct selling business." He felt Waldron had been caught by surprise. Now, though, he is feeling better, and he tells me that Waldron's plan is "sound" and he is impressed with the "strong people he's brought in and the marketing discipline he's added. He's leading the company in a new direction." There were still doubters, of course. Jeffrey Ashenberg at the investment house of L. F. Rothschild issued a report that, while reacting favorably to the Mallinckrodt move, said "Our confidence in [management's] quarterly estimates is low . . . There remains considerable risk that management will not succeed in reversing the fortunes of its domestic door-to-door business over the longer term." The stock price, in any event, climbs immediately. Before long it is hovering near twenty-eight dollars a share.

□   □   □

AND NOW WALDRON, in shirt-sleeves, has his feet up
on the coffee table. Jack Chamberlin is across from
him, sitting on the sofa. With or without Mallinckrodt, the rhythms of Avon go on. It is their pattern
to meet alone once a week to inform each other
about sensitive issues. Chamberlin professes to
have a faulty memory, so he always composes an
agenda.

Chamberlin: "Hicks, you were asking about how
we were doing with key people taking courses.
Paul Markovits was scheduled to go to Harvard
Business School. And he's not going. It was decided that the pressures on the Avon division are
such that he will defer going."

Waldron: "Did we make our excuses properly?
Because I used some chits to get him in there."

Chamberlin: "Yes, but I'll check that again."

Chamberlin mentions that a presentation before
the CMC on infusion care is going to be postponed.
Then he tells about the whereabouts of an executive that Avon might be interested in hiring.

So it goes, with little over-the-table discussion.
In general, the subjects are familiar, the viewpoints
similar.

Waldron, looking at the agenda, says, "Canada?
You went salmon fishing?" Chamberlin has just returned from a business trip to Canada.

Chamberlin: "No. I said I'd visit Mallinckrodt on
business as usual. And it all went smoothly. I talked
to Henry, asked if he wanted me to say anything
about the sale and he said no. Everyone was very
positive."

Waldron: "Good."

Chamberlin: "We even had a mixed dinner with

the Avon people and the Mallinckrodt people. You run a risk there, because you worry that some people will come in with a sour-grapes attitude. But there was none of that."

Waldron: "Terrific. That's great."

Chamberlin reports that an exploration has begun about simplifying the organizational structure of the Avon division.

Then he says: "I guess, Hicks, you're familiar with the situation at Revlon [Pantry Pride has made a hostile tender offer for Revlon]. Do we want to look at anything there that might be for sale?"

Waldron: "Well, we looked at Revlon back when the first pass was taken. Then we took another peek last week. And frankly I don't think there's anything we want. I think the antitrust considerations would be bad . . . Why, do you think we should do anything?"

Chamberlin: "No. No. It's just that it's felt that it's still in play."

Chamberlin has exhausted his list. Waldron says, "I had two items." He spreads out a sheet that shows the weekly rep count and sales figures for the beauty business and points to an aberrational trend in one of the columns. "That doesn't make sense," he says.

"Okay, I'll look at that," Chamberlin says.

Item number two, Waldron says, is that Phil Davis, the vice-president of affirmative action, was in today and reported that morale is low among black male employees. Waldron says that when he was at Heublein, where a similar problem persisted, he used to invite some of the black employees to his house for drinks and they would talk out problems. "So Phil wonders if you and I could do the same thing with six or seven of the top black males in the company. We'd just find a place, not here, maybe the private dining room, and just sit there and rap."

"Fine with me," Chamberlin says.

☐   ☐   ☐

WALDRON COMPLAINS that he's really stiff. He says he spent three hours the previous day traipsing around the Bronx Zoo with his wife. When he awoke this morning, he found he could barely move. The day before that, he had been out in Los Angeles, doing some Avon business, and had spent an evening at a charitable affair at which he hobnobbed with Eddie Albert and Eva Gabor. "Not so bad, huh," he says.

This is related as he strolls across town to make a brief appearance at a Junior Achievement class at the Martin Luther King, Jr., High School at Sixty-sixth Street and Amsterdam Avenue.

Waldron's deep interest in Junior Achievement springs from his desire to polish the image of business, which he thinks is "terrible" among teachers. "I can give you anecdote after anecdote," he told me once. "I was invited to speak at a small seminar of teachers one time when I was at Heublein. It was a very small town. Almost a hundred people showed up. I spent a lot of time on my speech. I prepared a checkbook and wrote out our sales and then wrote out checks for different things and talked about the quality control and suppliers and maintenance men. I went through the overhead of transportation and at the end I spent seventy-four million dollars. But I only had thirty-two million dollars. So I had another book called the loan book. So I wound up the year borrowing forty-two million bucks. This was Heublein's actual year. And it was a good year. And so I showed how we weren't rip-ping off the public. I had two questions. 'Why is it necessary for all of you fat cats to make all of your decisions on a golf course?' And, 'I went on a tour of Heublein and I want to know why all of you have a leather portfolio at your chair and I have trouble getting a blotter for my desk.' I hope that these were the dumbest teachers in the system. They may have been the only two jerks in the room, for all I know. But this drove me to further involvement in Junior Achievement."

We take the elevator up to the fourth floor and enter a classroom where a handful of students are hunkered around a computer. Once Waldron walks in, one of the students shyly comes up and asks him for his autograph for herself and another one for a friend. He obliges.

The idea of the class, known as Applied Economics, is to pretend that the students are running a company. This particular enterprise sells candy.

"What's your role in the company?" Waldron asks a young man seated before the computer.

"I'm the president."

"El presidente, eh?"

One of the female students tells Waldron that, in her spare time, she's been working as an Avon representative.

Waldron hugs her and says, "Bless you. Bless you."

The students are listing their expenses on the screen. There are only a few at the moment.

"Right now, we don't have any other expenses," the teacher says.

"That'll change, unfortunately," Waldron says.

"Now, we're selling the candy at three dollars," the teacher says.

"I thought we said we'd sell it at two-fifty," one of the students says.

"No, three dollars. We found out that we wouldn't make any money at two-fifty."

Waldron says, "That, I'm afraid, is the way you find out sometimes."

After a few more minutes of observation, Waldron leaves the classroom. No one seems sure where the elevator is. Waldron meanders in several different directions hunting for it. "Jesus," he says, "here's one of the leaders in the business community and I can't find the damn elevator in a high school."

□   □   □

WALDRON ORDERS A RED WINE and then goes off to mingle. Now he finds himself in royal company. One of the beneficiaries of Avon money is a business and clergy organization called the Forum for Corporate Responsibility, and it has arranged to have the Duke and Duchess of Kent attend a luncheon with New York business leaders, educators, and members of the clergy. The duke, it is said, is keenly interested in promoting dialogue between the leaders of industry and arts, cultural and religious institutions. Waldron has been asked to host the affair.

This is being held in the "Living Room" of Saint Peter's Church, on Fifty-fourth Street and Lexington Avenue. The protocol is the guests will mingle for a half hour. Then the duke and duchess will arrive and mingle for a half hour. Then everyone will sit down and eat.

Waldron comes over to me when I arrive and says, "I have to remember not to say duck and duchess. That wouldn't be good."

Then he drifts off to drink and mingle. He talks to Leonard Goldenson, the founder of ABC. He talks to Nathan Pusey, the former head of Harvard.

I drift into a conversation with a businessman from England. He tells me, "You know, these things can be awfully embarrassing at times in England. The royalty come along and everyone stands around in a circle and just gapes. They don't say anything. So the guy hosting the thing—in this case Hicks Waldron—has to go and collar people and tell them, for Christ's sake, come over and meet the royalty and say something, will you. Open your mouth."

I look up and notice that the duke and duchess have arrived, and Waldron is indeed buttonholing people to come by and say something.

After the eating, Waldron is called on for some remarks. He says, "When I was asked to get involved in this, I leaped at the opportunity. For I felt business people and clergy and academia would all benefit from more gatherings like this. For too long there has been a communications gap. Communications gaps breed antagonism . . ."

Bishop Michael Mann makes some remarks. There is a toast to the Queen of England. There is a toast to President Reagan.

Shortly afterward, the duke and duchess take their leave. Waldron is close behind. The duke and duchess bend and get into their long black limousine. Waldron bends and gets into his long black limousine. The royal couple, I had been told, were in a rush. They had to get to New Jersey for a store opening.

□　　□　　□

WAITING FOR THE OTHERS TO ARRIVE, Jim Preston paces around, killing time. His hands are dug deep into his pants pockets. He grins while he waits. He is as giddy as a boy who just got a new Schwinn fifteen-speed bike. He has finished studying the latest week's numbers for the representative count and average sales order. They are the best in a year. This is the first week in October.

The rest of the invitees troop in: Tom Knight, John Cox, Jack Chamberlin, Jules Zimmerman, Hicks Waldron. Waldron has agreed to sit for an interview next week with a reporter from *The Wall Street Journal*, which will be tied to third-quarter earnings, scheduled to be reported then. Profits will be off by 15 percent, largely because of the poor showing of the domestic beauty business. But Waldron is pleased about doing an interview now. He has seen nine consecutive weeks of upward numbers in the rep count. He is feeling that the odds of a false pregnancy are shrinking.

Press interviews are never taken lightly, especially with the heavyweights of the media world. Preparations for them seem to take on the mood of what battle planning must be like in a Pentagon war room. John Cox has worked up a four-page, single-spaced briefing paper for Waldron, and now the top minds in the organization have gathered to review what he plans to say.

Cox says, "I've said how the divestiture may put us behind plans, and that may not be what you want to say."

"Well, let's stop right there," Waldron says. "I'd like to start more positively. Rather than say we're off strategy, I'd like to say that we are essentially tracking our long-term strategy. Essentially is enough of a qualifier."

Chamberlin wears a worried look on his face. He interrupts to say that he's not sure that would be an honest appraisal. He points out that the signs are out there that the home direct selling problem has been stabilized. "But we don't know for sure," he says. "And is business selling going to work? Is direct mail going to work?"

"But that's not part of our strategy," Waldron replies. "I'd like to say our strategy is working."

Preston clears his throat and argues that he agrees with Waldron, things are more or less on plan. "We're seeing improvements in average order and in service."

"Part of our strategy was to decentralize," Waldron says. "And we've done that. That's where we discuss the destabilization and we dipped a little—perhaps a bit further than we wanted to. So maybe 'essentially' is too strong a word. Maybe it's 'almost essentially.' "

Chamberlin wags his head. He is still not content.

"Would it help," Cox says, "if we say we are essentially tracking our long-term corporate strategy?"

"No," Waldron says. "We don't want to duck the issue."

Chamberlin says, "I'm just worried that if we say we are on plan, we are telling the world that definitely everything has turned."

"Well, why don't we say what we mean," Waldron says. "We are essentially tracking phase one of our strategy."

"I'll agree with that," Chamberlin says.

"And also phases two and three," Waldron says.

Everyone laughs.

The problem is that Waldron is not entirely sure what is in phase 1 of the strategic plan. He swivels to look at Preston and asks him to fetch a copy of the plan. Preston scoots out of the room and returns in a few minutes with a thick book.

He also has a sheet of numbers. "I thought you might also want to hear the latest numbers on appointments of reps," he says. The numbers are up.

"Nice work," Waldron says and slaps Preston on the back. Everyone else gives him a hearty round of applause.

"Okay, take out the word 'essentially,' " Waldron chortles.

Waldron flips through the strategic plan until he gets to the list of what is to be accomplished in phase 1, which was to cover the 1984–85 period. He reads aloud the items. They have to do with decentralizing. Stabilizing the force.

As each item is read, Waldron looks up at Preston.

"Done."

"Done."

"Sort of done."

"Done."

Waldron gets to the final item: "Formalize city strategy."

"We haven't done that yet," Preston says.

"That's essentially," Waldron says.

Waldron then reads from the phase 2 list, which embraces things to happen in 1985–86. "We should have done some of these, too."

Preston says some have been done and some haven't.

"Well, 'essentially' is the word," Waldron says.

"Yes," Preston says, " 'essentially' says it."

Now that a half hour has been consumed by the debate on the word "essentially," the meeting moves more quickly through the rest of the briefing paper. Occasionally, a word is altered here, a figure there.

Zimmerman, at one point, says, "Purging the line of nonbeauty products. I wouldn't say 'purging.' "

"Reducing the number of nonbeauty products," Preston says.

"Particularly the low margin," Waldron puts in.

"Now, we need some kind of conclusion for the Avon division part," Waldron says.

"Yeah," Preston says. "Needs a wrap. Needs a wrap."

Waldron says, "The news on the Avon division front is positive and seems to be strengthening. Positive."

Hums of approval.

Cox says, "Jim wanted me to change this part, 'We moved too fast and expected too much too soon.' He wanted, 'We underestimated the learning curve line and expected too much too soon.' "

"Okay," Waldron says, "that's better."

Preston then says, "John, you say the business had been trending down for more than forty-eight months. It's probably closer to sixty."

"You could go back to 1979," Waldron says.

"It actually started in the last quarter of 1979," Preston says.

Waldron starts ticking off months on his fingers. "Seventy-five months!"

"Jesus," Tom Knight says.

The meeting speeds through other subjects that may be addressed in the interview, including a new acquisition, a retirement chain called Retirement Inns of America, which Avon has agreed to buy for $30 million. Not a lot of money for Avon, but it marks the company's entrance into a new area from which Avon plans to fashion a senior citizens' health-care system.

The business of the meeting completed, the group once again looks at the Avon beauty numbers.

"Well, this puts us over four hundred thousand reps for the first time in I don't know when," Waldron says.

"That's got to be since last year," Cox says.

There is more congratulating, more smiling.

"Okay," Waldron says, "back to the trenches."

A week later, a story based on the Waldron interview is published in *The Wall Street Journal.* Nowhere in it does the word "essentially" appear.

23 □ SUMMIT AT SCANTICON

E ACH OCTOBER, in order for the important execu- tives in the company to hear about how the company is doing and where it intends to go, Avon puts on a Corporate Officers Conference. This year it is being held at the Scanticon Executive Confer- ence Center, a low-slung barrackslike affair buried on the perimeter of Princeton, New Jersey. Every- one who has at least scaled the vice-presidential level has been invited, some seventy individuals. The conference is to run for two days, and there has been time set aside for some levity and fun as well as for the serious stuff.

At five on a Wednesday evening, the executives drive in one by one. The sun is still up, and the day is warm. Most of the people are dressed for the office, but out of trunks they unload golf clubs and tennis rackets. There is no waiting around. The valet parking has already been paid for. The guests have been preregistered; all one has to do is retrieve the room key from the Avon Welcome Desk, where a beaming young woman awaits. Security has reached a new level here. For that extra little protection, the numbers on the room key don't match the actual room numbers. Thus someone could get hold of Hicks Waldron's key and wind up trying to get Phyllis Davis's door to unlock.

There is time to wash up and comb and splash on some Avon after-shave. Ties and suits are to be put aside. There is an injunction that attendees dress casually. Down at the cocktail reception in the Treehouse Lounge, Waldron appears in sport slacks and a puffy sweater, looking like an aging country club golf pro. He has a touch of a cold, but it doesn't slow him down. He shuffles through the throng, slapping people on the back, bestowing hospitality on his managers, seeing that everyone plies himself with liquor. There are more broad smiles than I have seen in a while.

Had this meeting been held a few months ago, it would have been like attending a funeral. Now, however, it has the feeling of a welcome-home party for a relative who had a kidney removed while also undergoing some open-heart surgery— despite everything, he is recovering.

Waldron and Avon have reached an approximate end to the first phase of the intended turnaround. The false pregnancy he feared no longer seems false. The representative count keeps climbing. Waldron is confident now that Avon beauty is stabilized and can begin to grow again. The October deadline has come and the decision has been made to stay the course. At the same time, Waldron knows that much toil remains. For all the relatives at the party, there is a certain uneasiness over whether the sick one's heart will really be sound now. Next year, new channels of distribution must be implemented, and no one is sure how well they will work. Waldron wants to make more acquisitions in the health-care area. A buyer has not yet been identified for Mallinckrodt.* At all events, as Waldron

* Subsequently, in December, an agreement was struck to sell it to the International Numeral and Chemical Corporation for $675 million, $40 million less than Avon had paid.

now says, "Everyone is now worshipping at the growth altar rather than the fix altar."

Waldron has learned some things during the past wrenching year. He believes people in the beauty division were more optimistic than they had a right to be. "They were too optimistic," he told me. "I did discount them a lot. Should I have discounted them more? I don't know." He thinks perhaps he should have made management changes sooner. The Avon task was a more difficult one than he ever thought, and he has often remarked lately how glad he is that he has Jack Chamberlin now to shoulder some of the load. I can't help wondering if so many of the banal activities that involve him—the dinner dances, the outside boards, the decisions on what to serve at the annual meeting—sapped too much of his time. At the same time, at any huge corporation it's hard to determine how much credit is due who for what, and I'm not entirely sure precisely what Waldron has done. Many of the moves he made were patently simple. It seems that Waldron has brought Avon back to a position where, properly managed, it should have been years ago. A lot of people lost their jobs in the interim. He performed ably in the role of company cheerleader, but I wonder if more should be demanded of CEOs. Where were the inspired visions? Where was the bold risk taking?

Dinner is served in the Tivoli Gardens. People gravitate randomly to tables of eight. There is lots of shop talk, not all of it sensible. At my table, somebody from Foster wants Phyllis Davis to have the Avon ladies sell crutches and wheelchairs.

Mark Russell, a political comedian, is the after-dinner entertainment. He had wondered if Avon wanted him to do an Avon routine. He was told to definitely not do an Avon routine. "Oh God," one of the Avon executives had said. "We've been on the spit enough this year. We don't need any more." Russell gives an uproarious routine. Waldron's booming laugh is heard often. Russell wraps up by telling the audience that they can now proceed to their bingo match. What they actually do is make a beeline for the hospitality suite to do some serious drinking and to catch the World Series on a big-screen TV. The Avon people steadily unbend, and a few of them start to unbuckle. "That's what we do at Avon," Phil Davis, the affirmative action chief, tells me. "Just hang out and drink." Waldron continues to spread the cheer until, at ten-thirty, he excuses himself, professing fatigue, and files off to bed.

The next morning, at eight o'clock sharp, Waldron is up at the podium in Conference Room B, back in business suit and tie, perspiring a little, delivering the welcoming speech. Last year, the officers' conference was held in Palm Springs, and Waldron warned the group then that if the numbers in the coming year were lousy the next meeting would be conducted on Riker's Island. "Our performance isn't Riker's Island bad," he says. "But it sure isn't Palm Springs good."

He reviews the fits and starts and says, "On every front, things are looking up, but we're nowhere home free. We still have a full plate of problems and opportunities. Many of our employees are still concerned about the future."

But the eternal optimist in him can't stay bottled up for long, and soon he is saying, "The promise is so great. So many departments and divisions are on the brink of blasting off into higher orbits that I have to take a cold shower before meeting with securities analysts."

Meetings plod on through the early afternoon,

then everyone is released to engage in sporting events or sightseeing. The sports-minded are guests at the Bedens Brook Country Club, where Jack Chamberlin is a regular member. Waldron heads for the golf course. Chamberlin plays tennis. Some volleyball games were scheduled, but the weather gets drizzly, so they're canceled.

That evening, everyone dines together at the club. Various awards are handed out for performance on the field. Waldron gets called up for hitting the longest drive. He gets a golf umbrella. "Hey, some gift," he says. "Really nice."

☐   ☐   ☐

SIX-FIFTEEN. Meetings have ceased. Waldron says goodnight to Maureen Ivory, after consulting tomorrow's schedule and learning that the stock price had closed unchanged in a down market. He packs some unfinished work into his briefcase, shrugs on his jacket. The phone trills. It's Mrs. Waldron; she reminds him to bring home the two bags of Avon products that he bought for his daughter, Jan, at the company store.

"Okay, honey," he says. "Will do."

Strolling easily down Fifty-seventh Street toward his apartment, Waldron says, "If the light is against us, we head the other way. The trick is to get to Lexington as soon as possible. You don't want to wait at Park. That's a horror."

Waldron has made it clear that he will retire when he turns sixty-five, in October 1988. There is a letter in Maureen Ivory's upper right-hand drawer that says who should be put in charge if, as Waldron puts it, "someone calls and said Waldron just got hit by a truck or he ran off with a great woman."

The letter identifies his successor. It is generally presumed that the name is Jack Chamberlin.

Waldron, when he once spoke to me about life after Avon, said, "I don't know what the hell I'll do in retirement. I'll still sit on boards, so it will be part-time retirement. I could never retire full time. I have to get up in the morning and have something to do. I'll become more active in Junior Achievement and Salvation Army and my other favorite charities. And Evelyn and I love to scuba and golf and ski. I have no yen to travel. I've spent my business life on an airplane and in a hotel room."

Will you miss all this?

"I suppose I will. All too often, you get to the last mile and you look around and you say, 'Jesus Christ, the planes and limos are gone. I have to make my own phone calls.'"

We walk down Sixtieth Street. A snaggletoothed man at the curb steps forward and asks Waldron if he's interested in buying any steaks or filet mignon. He remarks that he has some good buys and motions toward a blue van parked nearby.

"No, don't need any," Waldron says.

"Real fine meat," the man persists. "Never tasted stuff like this."

"I think I have," Waldron says, speeding up his pace.

"What a beautiful day," he says a few blocks later. "I took the helicopter this morning to Philadelphia. It was a perfect day for a helicopter ride. The sky was gorgeous."

He keeps walking. He is to have dinner later on with Bob Frederick, the RCA CEO, and his wife, and then he will be up at six-thirty, eat his cereal, watch the news, go to the office and have his shoes shined, and then go to a meeting and then to the next meeting and then to the next meeting. He is showing a bit of fatigue. His eyes are mildly glazed.

He reaches his apartment building. The doorman already has the door open. "Good evening, Mr. Waldron, how was your day?"

"Just fine," Waldron says. "Just fine."

INDEX